A SHORT HISTORY
OF FANTASY

A SHORT HISTORY
OF FANTASY

Farah Mendlesohn
and Edward James

Middlesex
University
PRESS

First published in 2009 by Middlesex University Press

Copyright © Farah Mendlesohn and Edward James

ISBN 978 1 904750 68 0

A CIP catalogue record for this book is available from The British Library

Cover design by Helen Taylor

Typesetting by Carnegie Publishing Ltd

Printed in the UK by Ashford Colour Press

Middlesex University Press
The Burroughs
London NW4 4BT
Tel: +44 (0)20 8411 4162
Fax: +44 (0)20 8411 4167

www.mupress.co.uk

Cover image: *A Dream of Apples* © 2009 Charles Vess

Dedicated to the many independent scholars whose scholarship in fanzines, in reviews, in books, on the web, and in emails, has made this work possible.

Acknowledgements

Wᴇ are very grateful to our "beta readers": Tanya Brown, N.M. Browne, Andrew M. Butler, Anthony Keen, Kari Maund, Maureen Kincaid Speller and Mark Yon. The expertise of David Langford and Celia Cozens saved us from a number of errors. Additional editorial assistance came from Jessica Nash. All remaining mistakes are of course our own.

There are far too many people to list individually who have helped in other ways with this book, answering queries and helping us to generate lists, so instead, below are named the communities and networks to which they belong and where we placed requests.

We would like to thank all those LiveJournal members, members of the mailing list Child_Lit, the mailing lists of the International Association for the Fantastic in the Arts (IAFA) and the Science Fiction Research Association (SFRA), the officers of the Science Fiction Foundation, as well as many editors and agents who specialize in publishing and promoting fantasy literature who have responded to queries and assisted us in tracking information.

Contents

CHAPTER ONE

Introduction

*A*T the time of writing, thirty-nine out of the forty top-grossing movies worldwide are fantasy or science fiction. J.K. Rowling is one of the world's best-selling authors. Terry Pratchett's books go straight into the hardback best-seller lists. *Star Wars* tie-ins dominate the *New York Times* paperback lists. A show about a cheerleader who kills vampires proved the cult TV hit of the 1990s and sparked a revival of TV fantasy. J.R.R. Tolkien's *Lord of the Rings*, which has never been out of print, topped almost every poll of favourite books taken in the UK at the end of the twentieth century. On the literary shelves, younger writers seem to be perfectly comfortable sliding from realist fiction to the fantastic. Yet there is a problem. Susanna Clarke and David Mitchell, who won critical and commercial acclaim in the early twenty-first century with *Jonathan Strange and Mr Norrell* and *Cloud Atlas*, books which any fan of fantasy would recognize, were presented to the world as literary writers, while Tolkien's pre-eminence and the popularity of both Rowling and Philip Pullman were dismissed as evidence of an adolescent society, an argument which tends to force defenders of fantasy into arguing for its adult qualities. (As the amount of children's fantasy discussed here indicates, we would prefer to challenge the notion that only one mode of adulthood is acceptable.) When Rowling and Pullman received nominations for the Whitbread there was a collective cry of outrage from the literary establishment. Even as fantasy seems to be increasing in popularity, critics try to separate out "the good stuff" and claim that it is "not fantasy", as happened with books by both Jonathan Lethem and Jeanette Winterson. Yet, as Margaret Doody has said, "when novels by admired novelists [Elias Canetti and Isabel Allende] deal with barons living in trees and girls with green hair, it is time to give up the pretense that the primary demand of a long work of prose fiction is that it should be 'realistic'".[1]

This all seems very strange. Fantasy, surely, is dragons, elves, broomsticks, fairies, ghosts, vampires, and anything which goes bump in the night? The problem, as we shall see in this book, is that even while we are explaining this to the latest author who denies that their work is fantasy there are plenty of fantasies which contain none of the above, but which have something about them that means we *know* they are fantasy (try Mervyn Peake's *Gormenghast* trilogy or the TV series *Lost*).

We (and we are using 'we' to indicate that there are two authors of this book, with interests in very different kinds of fantasy) are not going to get involved here with the cultural arguments which continue to sideline fantasy, although we will outline their origin. This book is quite happy to focus predominantly on writers proud to be fantasy writers, and books which have come to form the canon of fantasy literature. The book will cover many different kinds of fantasy, including horror, and ghost stories, and fantasy written for children. Although we are primarily concerned with the written form, we will also draw in works of the fantastic produced in other media, from painting, through comics, movies and TV, although for reasons of space we have been very selective and, perhaps ironically, the greater the interest in fantasy in a particular media, the less we have been able to represent that. So, for example, there is more about art in the early chapters when many of the artists and writers were the same people, than there is in the later, when fantasy art has developed an independent path. We hope, however, that our list of important artists at the end of the book will serve to compensate to some degree.

---

1   M. Doody, *The True History of the Novel*, New Brunswick: Rutgers University Press, 1997, 470.

The most obvious construction of fantasy in literature and art is the presence of the impossible and the unexplainable. This helps to cut out most science fiction (sf) which, while it may deal with the impossible, regards everything as explicable, but as an explanation it leaves in large swathes of horror, which fulfil both these criteria. Furthermore, this is a culturally specific explanation. There are many texts that read as fantasy if published for an audience that expects to be reading about something that is "not real"; these texts may, however, have originated from the minds of people whose ideas about the location of the boundary between "real" and "fantastical" were different. John Clute, who is by far the most important critic, coined the term "taproot" for an originating text that continues to serve as a reference point, thus *The Pilgrim's Progress*, can be understood as a "taproot" text for modern fantasy but was for its author the relaying of a divinely inspired vision and not in the least bit fantastical. Many magic realist texts from Latin America and the American South read as fantasy to fantasy readers, but were written with a firm sense of a supernatural world that exists in conjunction with the natural.

A second approach to defining fantasy is historical. Critics such as Brian Stableford and Adam Roberts have argued that in the middle of the eighteenth century the fantastic becomes material for self-conscious art. The rise of fantasy literature and art from the later eighteenth century is therefore a response to the Enlightenment, and to the contemporaneous rise of literary and artistic mimesis. We cannot have the artistic expression of the impossible until we have a clear idea of the limits of scientific possibility. But we may be misunderstanding the response of earlier times to the fantastic. A rather fine recent performance of the early-seventeenth-century play *Macbeth* drew our attention to the degree to which nothing supernatural is *ever proven to have happened* within the play. Does the script (and also the script of *The Winter's Tale*) reflect the credulity of the author and audience? Or is it a sceptical author inviting his rationalist audience to mock a king (James VI of Scotland and I of England) known to believe in witchcraft and the supernatural? If the latter, we must push the self-conscious use of the fantastic back in time by at least two centuries.

A third approach to fantasy is via the theories of the academics who have interested themselves in the field. Despite its popularity, fantasy has been relatively neglected by scholars, and there are just over a handful of important theorists in the field. Kathryn Hume understands fantasy in terms of its psychological and aesthetic response to mimesis. Tzvetan Todorov's ideas about fantasy narrow the field to a very tiny sliver, in which only those texts that maintain "hesitation" are fantastic. Of these, the most famous is Henry James's *The Turn of the Screw* (1898), in which the reader has to decide whether the fantasy is "real" or not. Rosemary Jackson understands fantasy to be a "literature of desire", a term picked up by those interested in the psychology of the fantastic. Jackson also argues that fantasy is innately subversive, in that it offers alternatives to and an escape from the "real world". Colin Manlove regards fantasy as a form of allegory, and his selection of texts is highly coloured by this. Our book will assume that if you are interested in literary criticism and defining fantasy, you will go and read these authors (and there is a recommended reading list at the end). The four theorists who will inform this book are Michael Moorcock, whose *Wizardry and Wild Romance* locates fantasy in the language in which it is written; Brian Attebery, whose *Strategies of Fantasy* understands fantasy as a "fuzzy set" with a core and an ever hazier corona of texts; John Clute, whose grammar of fantasy in *The Encyclopedia of Fantasy* is made up of four movements, wrongness, thinning, recognition, healing (although more recently he has substituted "return" for "healing");[2] and finally Farah Mendlesohn, one of the authors of this book, whose *Rhetorics of Fantasy* sees fantasy as a number of fuzzy sets determined by the mode in which the fantastic enters the text. What all four of these critics have in common is that they understand fantasy as a conversation that is happening, as we write, between the authors of the

---

2   In "Fantastika in the World Storm" (2007), http://www.johnclute.co.uk/word/?p=15.

texts and the readers. Much of the best criticism of fantasy literature has been written by fantasy writers, both in a formal critical context (the essays of C.S. Lewis, J.R.R. Tolkien, M. John Harrison and Diana Wynne Jones are some of the best known) and in the pages of their fiction. Many works of fantasy are direct critical responses to the field and we will try to reflect that.

Finally, there is what publishers and booksellers package and sell as fantasy. For many people fantasy can be identified by its cover art. A dragon or a wizard is usually a clue; but so is a half-naked barbarian (male or female) wielding a sword. This style of art was made notorious when original artworks by Rowena A. Morrill were found in one of Saddam Hussein's palaces. However, fantasy art has its origins in the work of the visionary artist William Blake, in the work of Gothic painters such as Henry Fuseli and those of the Pre-Raphaelite Brotherhood such as Edward Burne-Jones, and many covers are identifiable less by the actual icons than by the shades of light and dark and the lush use of colour that the artists have inherited. Most bookshops have sections called "fantasy and science fiction" and one would expect all the books to look much the same. But fantasy leaks, and can be found under "literature", in the separate section labelled "horror", and, with the rise of romantic supernatural fiction, even under "romance". Each of these sub-categories has its own genre-specific packaging.

Fantasy, now the most popular of the fantastical genres, was once the neglected cousin to both sf and horror. Some time in the 1980s the balance shifted, and approximately two-thirds of all books currently sold in "fantasy and science fiction" are now fantasy (see the annual surveys published in *Locus*). In a recent readership survey of almost 1,000 self-defined science fiction fans, the two youngest cohorts read more fantasy than science fiction.[3] Meanwhile, a cursory consideration of the horror shelves and the figures published in *Locus* in the 1990s revealed a market currently in decline: while this trend was reversed at the beginning of

---

3   See Mendlesohn, *The Inter-Galactic Playground*, Jefferson, North Carolina: McFarland Press, 2009.

the century, horror fiction is often shelved under "fantasy" suggesting that this is the more marketable label.

This book intends to fill a gap. While plenty of people have worked on defining fantasy, and John Clute and John Grant and their collaborators have catalogued it, there is no short history of fantasy. This book is going to start with a discussion of the emergence of the "fantastic" as a literary form in the eighteenth century, and with a glance backwards to its various progenitors: the epic, the romance, the fairytale. We will then move on to consider the rapid development of different "branches" of fantasy. While chapters two and three will cover around 150 years and 50 years respectively, and chapter five will deal with the immense (if delayed) influence of two writers from the mid-twentieth century (Tolkien and Lewis), the rest of the book will proceed roughly decade by decade, from the 1950s through to the first decade of the twenty-first century, pointing both to the dominant trends and the conversation at the margins. There will, however, be a pause for chapter ten, which considers the influence of another three writers, Rowling, Pullman and Pratchett, who have made as much of an impact in the 1990s and 2000s as Tolkien and Lewis did in the 1950s and through the 1970s. Although some non-English works will be discussed, the emphasis here is on English language fantasy. We realize that this will give the curious sense that English fantasy dominates the world but in sheer numbers this is probably true. For various cultural and economic reasons, very little translated fantasy enters the Anglo-American market, while not only is there a great deal of translation from English into other languages, in Europe, at least, English-language material is widely read by fantasy fans. Where such works have come through to the Anglo-American market, however, whether by E.T.A. Hoffmann, Jorge Luis Borges, Isabel Allende, Astrid Lindgren or Michael Ende, they will be discussed.

The purpose of the book is to track the conversation of fantasy writers as they develop and extend the genre. The book will make very little reference to critics, but should provide readers with a very long reading list.

CHAPTER TWO

From Myth to Magic

ANTASY and not realism has been a normal mode for much of the history of Western fiction (and art). Arguably however, fantasy *as a genre* only emerges in response (and contemporaneous to) the emergence of mimesis (or realism) *as a genre*: only once there is a notion of intentional realism, so the argument goes, can there be a notion of intentional fantasy. Yet the ancient Greek and Roman novel, the medieval romance, and early modern verse and prose texts all commonly use what we consider to be the tropes of fantasy: magical transformations, strange monsters, sorcerers and dragons, and the existence of a supernatural world.

The earliest forms of written fiction that we have from the ancient world are works that we might understand as fantasy and which have influenced many modern fantasy writers: stories about gods and heroes, such as the *Epic of Gilgamesh* and the works of Homer. His *Odyssey*, about the travels of a hero through a world inhabited by giants, sorcerers and monsters and prey to the vagaries of interested supernatural parties, is a precursor for much later fantasy fiction. The Greek stories about the gods and goddesses were, of course, for most ancient Greeks part of the structure of their religious belief, but they could be elaborated by poets or playwrights, and some contemporaries even referred to them as "the lies of poets". Epics about gods and heroes were sometimes used for obvious political purposes, like Virgil's *Aeneid*. The Greek and Roman heroic tradition remained well known to Western romancers throughout the Middle Ages, and beyond; but the Egyptian tales of gods and the underworld had little impact on Western tradition until the nineteenth century; after that they offered a rich seam of unnerving notions about death, ritual and a cyclical world.

At the beginning of the first millennium the various "barbarian" peoples (that is, non-Romans) had their own traditions of gods and heroes, and presumably had their tales and poems about them. However, they were not recorded until very much later, or if they were then the manuscripts have not survived. Almost all that remains of the heroic tradition from pre-Norman England is the epic poem *Beowulf*, with its three-fold story of the hero fighting the monster, the monster's mother, and the dragon, while what little we can know about the Old English gods has to be reconstructed from a reading of Snorri Sturluson's *Prose Edda*, written in Iceland in the thirteenth century. Snorri Sturluson may also have been the author of one of the many surviving Icelandic sagas, telling mostly of the doings of farmers in the newly settled land of Iceland, and dealing with ghosts and visions in the same matter-of-fact way in which they discussed feuds and family politics. The Icelandic sagas became known to a wider audience in the nineteenth century, through translations by William Morris and others, and provided an important new thread in the development of English-language fantasy: they influenced many of the writers of fantasy we will be discussing here, most notably Morris himself, J.R.R. Tolkien, Diana Wynne Jones, Alan Garner and Neil Gaiman.

Much more was written down in the Celtic-speaking world, including the many stories of ancient Irish heroes such as Cúchulainn and the collection of Welsh legends called *The Mabinogion*. However, these traditions were largely marginalized and unknown to the wider European tradition until the beginnings of the nationalist revivalist movements of the nineteenth century. The Celtic material was so little known that when in the eighteenth century the Scottish poet James McPherson claimed to have translated the ancient Irish myths of the poet Ossian, his fraud was accepted and incorporated into the contemporary Gothic and medievalist enthusiasms. In the later nineteenth century medieval

Welsh and Irish literature was published and studied, and right across Europe, and well into the twentieth century, elites would continue to 'collect' folklore and to reconstruct (sometimes rather naively) the supernatural thought-world of the European peasant. "Celtic" fantasy loosely based on these traditions continues to form a strong thread in modern North American fantasy with authors such as Evangeline Walton, Charles de Lint, Lloyd Alexander, Katherine Kerr, and Emma Bull developing the tradition further.

While myth, legend and saga provide many of the components of modern fantasy, the influence of ancient novels has only recently been recognized. These are mostly melodramatic stories of shipwreck and adventure, but some of them have strong fantasy elements. Probably the most widely read throughout the Middle Ages was the *Alexander Romance*, the earliest version of which can be traced to the third century BC: eighty medieval versions survive, in twenty-four languages. The *Alexander Romance* tells many of the stories of Alexander the Great we are otherwise familiar with from near-contemporary biographies, but also narrates fabulous travellers' tales of impossible encounters with talking trees and five-eyed animals. There is even a moment of science fiction, in which Alexander explores the bottom of the sea in a glass diving bell. The most famous Roman imitation of the Greek novel was Apuleius's *The Golden Ass*, which has been in translation since the sixteenth century and relates the adventures of a man who has been transformed into an ass.

The ancient tradition of tales of marvels and wonders continued in the Middle Ages in the form of the romance. The most familiar of these concern themselves with the "Matter of Britain": stories about King Arthur and his knights. The earliest references to Arthur occur in a Welsh context, but the first complete narratives about Arthur were written in Norman England and France, and in the course of the thirteenth century became popular right across Europe. Many of the "French romances" were indeed written in England, whose aristocracy spoke French after 1066 and whose political and economic fortunes were entwined with France. The earlier Arthurian stories can be seen as part of the wider tradition of chivalric literature and revolve around love and adultery: later, under the influence of the Church, the stories bring in more Christian themes, codified as the quest for the Holy Grail. Some of the Arthurian traditions, such as the figure of Merlin, seem to have been invented wholesale by Geoffrey of Monmouth, whose fictional *History of the Kings of Britain* (1136) was by the end of the twelfth century regarded as genuine history, and not questioned until the sixteenth century. The medieval Arthurian tradition in England reached its full form in the fifteenth century in Sir Thomas Malory's *Le Morte d'Arthur*.

Medieval romances also concerned themselves with the Matter of France, stories about Charlemagne and his Paladins, which followed the same generic rules as the Arthur stories. However, the Arthurian cycle was periodically revived to support the English monarchy and this may have ensured the Arthurian revival in the mid-nineteenth century when Alfred Tennyson and the Pre-Raphaelites were looking for material. The best-known authors in this field in the twentieth century are perhaps Rosemary Sutcliff, Mary Stewart, Marion Zimmer Bradley, Peter David, and Stephen Lawhead.

One way to understand the survival of the Arthurian cycle is to see it as the folklore of the elite, reinforcing Christian claims to temporal power and also a chivalric code of ethics, which gave a moral authority to the aristocracy. Running alongside it, however, were alternative traditions belonging to the middling sort, the poor and the dispossessed. One of the strongest traditions has been that of Robin Hood. This has had relatively little place in the history of fantasy as it has mostly been constructed in mimetic terms although it has accounted for a number of fantasised middle ages, most famously the Errol Flynn and Richard Greene versions. In the 1980s, when the United Kingdom was at its most socially divided for fifty years, ITV showed a series called *Robin of Sherwood* (1984–6) which linked the Robin Hood legend to the resistance of the working poor, and to Herne the Hunter. The series was overlaid with Celtic mythology and a soundtrack from Clannad, a popular folk ensemble of the period (sealing an already strong association between Celtic music and fantasy literature, constructed during the folklore revival movements of the 1880s, 1920s and 1960s).

Arguably, the fairy tradition is Celtic in origin, although it has mutated greatly over the centuries. Morgan Le Fay, drawn from the Arthurian cycle, is part of the fairy tradition that emphasized the fey as wild and unpredictable. In this conception, fairy is a separate world that lives alongside ours. Mortals can be kidnapped for the mere caprice of fairies, changelings left behind and souls sacrificed to hell. The ballads of "Tam Lin" and "Thomas the Rhymer" (in several versions) encapsulate this vision of fairy, as does Shakespeare's *A Midsummer Night's Dream*. Alongside this runs also an Irish tradition in which fairies were a much more physical range of creatures with their own courts and their own customs, interacting with humans only when forced. Both of these forms of fairy are current in contemporary fantasy among writers such as Charles de Lint and Emma Bull and more recent authors such as Marie Brennan, Susanna Clarke, Elizabeth Hand and Hal Duncan. However, the tradition of fairy*tale* as it descends from Charles Perrault is something else entirely.

At the end of the seventeenth century Charles Perrault and Madame d'Aulnoy popularized courtly fairytales. These polished-up versions of the folk tales, which we see also in the later collections of the Brothers Grimm, are both more formulaic (three wishes, three tasks, three brothers) but also more random in their construction of fairy. In these tales fairies are intimately concerned with humans, and their powers often arbitrary, yet also moral. Perrault and Grimm were collectors and revisers, who domesticated the tales for their (respectively) aristocratic and bourgeois readers, but in the nineteenth century we begin to see original fairytales for the modern reader and for modern manners. The Baron de la Motte Fouqué's *Undine* (1811), about a water sprite raised as a changeling, became a classic in Germany, and was soon translated into English. In 1814 it became an opera, composed by E.T.A.

Hoffmann, who himself wrote numerous adult fairytales, sometimes with a macabre element. They too became known throughout Europe, and "The Sandman" (1816–17) was later staged as part of Jacques Offenbach's opera *The Tales of Hoffmann* and as Leo Delibes's ballet *Coppelia*, while "The Nutcracker" was transformed by Tchaikovsky into one of the most enduring of ballets. In America, Nathaniel Hawthorne wrote self-consciously American fairytales such as "Feathertop", a tale of a wooden puppet infused by life (published in two parts, in February and March 1852), which still had a very strong Irish feel. But the most successful nineteenth-century writer of fairytales by far was Hans Christian Andersen (1805–75). Andersen's tales were written with the courtly polish of Perrault, but with the dark morality of the Brothers Grimm: "The Little Mermaid" (1837), "The Snow Queen" (1844), "The Little Match Girl" (1845) and "The Red Shoes" (1845) are all bitter tales in which right and wrong, good and evil are obscured and the world does not end happily or well. "The Ugly Duckling" (1844) perhaps best displays also the rigid and defensive destinarianism of Andersen's stories in which the only route to true happiness is finding or accepting your place in society: perhaps a legacy of his own displacement and bad experiences as a fostered child, and later as a parvenu in Danish society. However subversive fantasy was to become, Andersen's political legacy lingered on in the structures of many tales.

At the same time that Perrault was bringing his stories of Cinderella and Puss-in-Boots to a wider audience, the Arabic scholar Antoine Galland was translating *The Thousand and One Nights* (or *The Arabian Nights*) into French. It is only very recently that accurate translations into Western languages of these late medieval Arabian fairytales have appeared. However, the versions by Galland and other early translators were extremely popular and by the end of the nineteenth century tales of Sinbad and Aladdin were part of the Western tradition, most popularly in pantomime. The stories have continued to inspire fantasy writers, most notably the academic Robert Irwin, whose *The Arabian Nightmare* (1983) is an impressive revisioning. The first unexpurgated version of *The*

Arabian Nights was produced by Richard Burton in 1885 and, although scandalous, was part of a general enthusiasm for all things oriental. It was in the nineteenth century too that Europeans became aware of the fantasy traditions of China and Japan: the Japanese ghost stories of Lafcadio Hearn and the Chinese fantasy stories of Ernest Bramah (at the turn of the century), purporting to be tales told by a professional storyteller, Kai Lung, are the obvious examples.

Another thread in this story of the ever-widening foundation of Western fantasy were the anthropologists James Frazer and Andrew Lang. Frazer's *The Golden Bough: A Study in Comparative Religion* (1890) argued among other things that myth and legend were the survival of structures of primitive belief, embedding agricultural seasons into the narrative tradition, an idea taken up with enthusiasm by a range of groups including new pagans and left-wing folklorists. For Frazer, myth was fundamental to the psyche of humanity. Andrew Lang was a more pragmatic man than Frazer; although he argued that fairytales were the remnants of legend, he was not convinced about their mythopoeic significance. He is best known for publishing eleven folk and fairytale collections named after colours, beginning with *The Blue Fairy Book* in 1889 and ending with *The Lilac Fairy Book* in 1910. Lang's books, in which he which he collected together tales from all over the world, were instrumental in cementing some of the forms of the classic fairytale, as readers noted structural and thematic similarities between different traditions. In the 1890s and 1900s, Rudyard Kipling's *The Jungle Book* (1894) and his *Just So Stories* (1902) brought Indian fables and animal stories into common currency, while in the United States Joel Chandler Harris, like Andrew Lang understanding himself as an anthropologist (or folklorist) rather than a writer, published *Uncle Remus: His Songs and His Stories* (1881). The work of Harris and Kipling created a tradition of animal and trickster stories that would be hugely influential at the beginning of the twentieth century, and create an entire separate-but-related strand, linked to, but never quite of, fantasy.

Fairytale was originally intended for adults, but although much of Grimm, Andersen and other early writers is horrific and brutal, fairytale came increasingly to be seen as a genre aimed primarily at children. Today the classic fairytale for adults is somewhat scarce, although fairytale still is a major taproot for modern fantasy. In the 1980s there was a surge in feminist subversion of the form – Angela Carter is the best known of these writers – but the classic fairytale that the nineteenth-century authors would have recognized is rare. Robin McKinley, Gregory Maguire and Gail Carson Levine are perhaps the most modern examples. Their novels take traditional fairytales and render them realistic, while conforming rigidly to the structural demands of the form.

By the end of the nineteenth century, the "traditional" forms of the fantastic were being pulled in towards a common centre, combining with new forms that had rather more modern origins. The rise of modern fantasy is partially dependent on the changes wrought by the Enlightenment on the intellectual climate of modern Europe. Until the clampdowns of the late eighteenth century in response to the revolutions in Europe, the nations of France, Britain and Germany in particular saw an unprecedented rise in free-thinking, manifested in the growth of deism, and progress in the pure and applied sciences. The world became something one could both understand and control. Sometimes the manifestations of this are near invisible to modern eyes. It is something of a shock to realize how many landscape paintings of the late eighteenth century are as much formal compositions as any still life. Increasingly there was a sense that something existed below the world as it was delineated by those in power. The very idea of a world that could be controlled and understood was subverted into a mode of literature, the Gothic, in which this surface world is a delusion. These ideas can be seen in two of the early classics of Gothic literature, Horace Walpole's *The Castle of Otranto* (1764), republished in the following year with the subtitle *A Gothic Story*, and Ann Radcliffe's *The Mysteries of Udolpho* (1794).

The Castle of Otranto was originally published as a "found manuscript".

Only after it aroused widespread acclaim was it revealed to be a fantasy, yet this did not diminish its appeal. By the late eighteenth century, the move away from an imminent understanding of religion and increasing scepticism about the possibility of supernatural influence in the world (as what was understood as supernatural fell to scientific explanation) opened a space for a playful approach to the fantastic. For the Gothic, however, much of the pleasure was in the tension between these two positions. Even from the beginning, readers detected a difference between the fantasy of *The Castle of Otranto* and the rationality of the other most famous "Gothic", *The Mysteries of Udolpho*.

It has been estimated that by 1825 around 5,000 novels or pamphlets of Gothic fiction had been published in English. The earliest of these tend to be set in a vaguely realized medieval world. The "discovery" of the Gothic (a word which in the mid-eighteenth century meant barbarous or primitive) was in part a search for a period in which to set social critique, in order to escape the scrutiny of the sedition acts. The construction of the Gothic was a commentary on the barbarity of the modern age. It was no accident that Horace Walpole was the first eighteenth-century gentleman to build in neo-Gothic style. William Beckford, a young MP whose Gothic novel *Vathek, An Arabian Tale* (1786) featured sinister jinns and ifreet, squandered his fortune by building Fonthill Abbey for himself, on a larger scale than most medieval monasteries. The Gothic, along with the historical novels of Sir Walter Scott, ushered in the nineteenth-century cult of the medieval. By the early nineteenth century, Gothic stories were tending to be given contemporary settings: the place of horror was no longer the castle or the monastery, but was domesticized into the attic, the cellar, and the dark urban streets. But medievalism fuelled the early Gothic, and remains highly influential in fantasy writing even today. The early nineteenth century saw the study and republication of "real" medieval fantasy, such as *Beowulf* and Arthurian romance, and much of these was seen through the Gothic sensibility: Shakespeare, an embarrassment to the Enlightenment, was now valued for its "medieval" qualities, its ghosts and fairies were given a new lease of life, and Macbeth and Hamlet valued as "Gothic" heroes.

The hallmarks of the Gothic fantasy include a surface story which will be proved wrong, such as the monarch's delusion of rightful rule in *The Castle of Otranto*, the scientist's belief in his own righteousness, the created man's monstrosity in Mary Shelley's *Frankenstein* (1818), or the notion of aristocratic virtue in John William Polidori's *The Vampyre: A Tale* (1819). Gothic fantasies are frequently claustrophobic. The claustrophobia can be created through the *mise-en-scène* of landscape. In Gothic art, such as Caspar David Friedrich's *Chalk Cliffs on Rügen* (1818), landscape is constructed in terms of Edmund Burke's Sublime – mountains loom and trees crowd in, but we stand, rendered small and insignificant, at the bottom of the picture. In Gothic fiction, these landscapes are constructed through words, most memorably, perhaps, in the final ride to the castle of Dracula at the end of Bram Stoker's novel (1897), or in the killing whiteness of ice and icebergs at the beginning and end of *Frankenstein*. Claustrophobia in the Gothic can also be constructed of family secrets: Edgar Allan Poe's "The Fall of the House of Usher" (1839), Nathaniel Hawthorne's "Rappaccini's Daughter" (1844), and Oscar Wilde's *The Picture of Dorian Gray* (1891) depend for their tension on the growing sense of horror of the secret to be revealed. (One of the problems with the Gothic is that the moment of revelation is often an anticlimax in comparison to the stress induced in the reader from the period of apprehension.) Finally, the claustrophobia can be constructed by a sense of imprisonment. In the written form, the most famous example is perhaps Poe's "The Pit and the Pendulum" (1843), but Henry Fuseli's painting *The Nightmare*, in which a monster sits on the chest of a sleeper, both bringing bad dreams and preventing escape, well represents visually this aspect of the Gothic.

The content of the Gothic picks up on the theme of subverting the visible world. Gothic fantasies constantly flirt with the unspeakable and share with the sensation fiction of the nineteenth century the desire to shock. In Gothic fiction fathers desire their daughters, nuns are just there to be raped, promiscuous women contemplate multiple lovers and prey on children, and these are merely the tropes that the authors felt would escape censorship. *The Monk* (1796), published by Matthew Lewis, like William Beckford a young MP, detailed the fall into depravity of a Spanish cleric. It was initially withdrawn because of its obscenity and blasphemy, but immediately reissued, with enormous success. Robert Louis Stevenson's *Strange Case of Dr Jekyll and Mr Hyde* (1886) and Wilde's *The Picture of Dorian Gray* both speak in such vague terms of the iniquities practised by their protagonists that there is a century of academic speculation on the specifics. The Marquis de Sade was *so* specific that *The One Hundred and Twenty Days of Sodom* (1784) remained unpublishable until the twentieth century.

The literature that is known as "The Gothic" is understood by specialists as that published between the 1760s and the 1820s. In the wider field of fantasy, however, the Gothic and "Gothic fantasy" is a form which, as some of the dates above make clear, remains active very much longer. In the next chapter we shall be discussing the work of writers such as H.P. Lovecraft and M.R. James, who understood themselves as writing in this tradition, and in later chapters the works of authors such as Stephen King, Anne Rice and China Miéville.

Before we move on, one strand that needs to be mentioned, even though it produced relatively little fantasy, is Romanticism. Poets such as Keats, Byron, Wordsworth, Coleridge and Shelley took the sublime landscapes of the Gothic and gave them a lighter and more inspiring colour. What they gave to fantasy was glowing imagery. Three examples which continue to influence the writing and art of fantasy to this day were Percy Bysshe Shelley's "Ozymandias", with its barren grandeur and appeal to a mysterious past, Samuel Taylor Coleridge's "Kubla Khan", with its exoticism and epic language, and John Keats's "La Belle Dame Sans Merci", which offered compelling imagery of palely loitering knights to both artists and writers of high fantasy. One writer and artist whose work drew new attention in the late twentieth century, is William Blake (1757–1827): his visionary art (an accepted term for art influenced by mental illness) and eschatological poetry has probably been more influential in the late twentieth century than ever before, particularly on folk and rock singers, and on writers as diverse as Thomas Harris, Salman Rushdie and Philip Pullman. Alan Moore (the graphic novelist) cites William Blake as a major influence, and Blake appears as a character in his *From Hell* (1991–8).

The mid-nineteenth century saw the emergence of distinct strands of a new kind of fantasy, self-conscious in its homage to Arthurian romance and fairytale, but which was moving beyond the matter of retelling. We can identify these strands with specific artists and authors. Richard Dadd's fairy paintings, in particular *The Fairy Feller's Masterstroke* (1855–64), influenced the *look* of fairies for most of the century. His work was so convincing that Conan Doyle's acceptance of the authenticity of the fraudulent Cottingley fairies in the 1920s was influenced by their resemblance to Richard Dadd's paintings. William Makepeace Thackeray's most notable contribution to fantasy is *The Rose and the Ring, or The History of Prince Giglio and Prince Bulbo: A Fireside Pantomime for Great and Small Children* (1855), a subversive mockery of the morality of fairy gifts, which questioned the assumption that such gifts go to the deserving. Thackeray made the fairytale vulnerable to both expansion and subversion. He also combined comedy with fantasy in a way which rendered fairytales more palatable for adults at a time when the court fairytales of Perrault, and to an extent even those of Hans Christian Andersen, were being sidelined into the new "children's literature". Thackeray helped to create an interest in the writing of new tales, a challenge taken up by Oscar Wilde in his 1888 collection *The Happy Prince, and Other Stories* and, in the twentieth century, by Walter de la Mare in collections such as *Broomsticks and Other Tales* (1925).

Thackeray's story was clearly a fairytale: other writers had begun to use fairy tropes to write something different. Charles Kingsley's *The Water Babies: a Fairy Tale for a Land Baby* (1863) contains three fairies, Mrs. Doasyouwouldbedoneby and Mrs. Bedonebyasyoudid and, at the end, Mother Carey, whom he uses to impart a moral message very different to that the destinarian structures of traditional fairytales or the works of Hans Christian Andersen. Kingsley's work is remembered (and avoided) for its Christian didacticism, but Kingsley was also using fairytale to argue for a different, scientific way of seeing the world; bizarrely, the book was written partially to promote Darwinian ideas. Also writing in the Christian tradition was George MacDonald. His early work *Phantastes: A Faerie Romance for Men and Women* (1858) is a portal fantasy in which the main character strays into faerie (by going through a doorway, the 'portal' into the fantastic world), and observes the doings of the fairy world; almost forty years later, he wrote a second Christian fantasy, *Lilith* (1895). *Lilith* tells of a man's encounter with Adam and Eve in a fantasy world. In between these two philosophical fantasies however, George MacDonald produced three very popular children's novels heavily influenced by fairytales. *At the Back of the North Wind* (1871), in which a boy is befriended by the North Wind, owes something to the Eastern fairytales which were becoming available. In *The Princess and the Goblin* (1872) and *The Princess and Curdie* (1883) a young lad, Curdie, twice rescues a princess, expanding the fairy quest with character and character development. The most memorable things about the book are the fairy great-great-grandmother, intended to be inspiring but frankly terrifying to many young readers (she gets Curdie to place his hands in a fire and he receives from it the gift of sensing people's character by feeling their hand as that of the animal they most resemble), and the equally terrifying goblins, fully realized as characters and the direct ancestors of Tolkien's orcs.

It was George MacDonald who, after the success of Kingsley's *The Water Babies*, suggested the publication of Lewis Carroll's *Alice's Adventures in Wonderland* (1865). Lewis Carroll's work takes us into the realms of something we might call whimsy, although that suggests something light-hearted, and whimsy in genre fantasy has often contained a not-so-hidden threat. Whimsy is fancy, and the slightly surreal, with a sense of randomness that can be both delightful but also unnerving. Whimsy delights in puns, in word play and in the double or triple meaning and is frequently very visual. *Alice's Adventures in Wonderland*

and *Through the Looking-Glass, and What Alice Found There* (1871) are both complex fantasies run through with riddles, mathematical puzzles and subversions of social norms. There are many critical studies of these books, but the things worth noting here are the space Carroll created for nonsense and surrealism, the very realistic portrayal of a child suffering the whim of crazy adults, and the creation of a protagonist who was very firmly a child with no didactic responsibilities to the reader. Carroll's influence on the mode of telling children's tales was as great as – perhaps greater than – his role in fantasy. Another author experimenting with whimsy as a mode was F. Anstey. *Vice Versâ, or A Lesson to Fathers* (1882) is a body-swap story that has been reproduced in many different contexts since, including the book *Freaky Friday* by Mary Rogers which was filmed twice (in 1976 and 2003). In *The Brass Bottle* (1900) a genie showers its benefactor with increasingly embarrassing gifts. Both of these stories laid the ground for modern urban fantasies in which faerie and the modern world collide.

The writers discussed above provided emergent genre fantasy with many of its core concepts and tropes. However, the movement which most contributed to the look and feel of the kind of fantasy that would dominate in the bookshops in the later twentieth century, was the Pre-Raphaelite Brotherhood. As its name suggests, the Brotherhood was devoted to "restoring" the supposed ideals of medieval craftsmanship (before Raphael), and in the process provide a visual response to the much broader cult of the medieval which flowered in northern Europe in the nineteenth century. This manifested above all in architecture: across Europe, churches, public buildings and even factories were designed in mock medieval style (see either the Houses of Parliament, or the much later Anglican Cathedral in Liverpool, which we both, independently, christened "Gormenghast" and which was designed by Giles Gilbert Scott, whose grandfather, George Gilbert Scott, designed the fantasia that is St. Pancras railway station). Pre-Raphaelite landscape painting was rich, saturated in colour and detailed far beyond the possibility of perspective. The work of William Holman Hunt (see *Our English*

Coasts, 1852) or Ford Madox Brown (*Carrying Corn*, 1854–5) renders in paint the lush descriptions of the three-volume quest fantasies of the later twentieth century. In the nineteenth century the most vivid literary vision of the fantastic was Christina Rossetti's "Goblin Market", a poem that provided both the language and the plot for many later fantasy writers. Pre-Raphaelite illustrations with faux medieval costume, flowing hair and an emphasis on drapery and line similarly influenced the costuming of the fantastic for the next hundred years.

Alongside the visual arts, nineteenth-century medievalism also developed the study of medieval documents and medieval national histories. Often these histories were used for obvious nationalist purposes: the Finnish national epic, the *Kalevala*, was produced in the nineteenth century from folk traditions, while in Britain the cult of Arthur could be seen everywhere. Among the Pre-Raphaelites, none contributed more to this visual fantasy than Edward Burne-Jones, who became noted for his Arthurian tableaux, oddly staged pictures in which form and movement were captured in silk and velvet tents, drooping maidens and pale loitering knights. Later, the photographer Julia Margaret Cameron (1815–79) staged "fancy" pictures that conjured both allegory and Arthuriana. Yet the folklore that the Pre-Raphaelites constructed also embraced the world of work. Ford Madox Brown's luxuriant and glowing paintings of working people contributed as much to the imagery of fantasyland (as we'll see in the work of Hope Mirrlees in the next chapter) as Richard Dadd's work did. Brown's influence extends even to the popular "Renaissance Fairs" – creations of faux medieval markets which host independent craft work and which are as vital a part of the current United States "fantasy tradition" as any fantasy novel.

The Pre-Raphaelite who encompasses the whole movement in his career is William Morris, craftsman, scholar, writer of fantasies and revolutionary socialist. His *News From Nowhere* (1890) imagines an ideal *medieval* future from which the horrors of the machine age have been expunged, and fine craftwork celebrated. Morris was the first person to translate the Icelandic sagas into English, and he incorporated their material into his medievalist fantasies. Previous fantasy writers had donned a cloak of belief that the fantastic could occur in our world, or had provided a shell structure (such as a dream) to allow the reader to travel. In such books as *The Wood Beyond the World* (1894), *The Well at the World's End* (1896) and *The Water of the Wondrous Isles* (1897), William Morris constructs a world as if *it is the only world that exists*. This is sometimes called a "full fantasy" world, a term invented by John Clute. David Langford has suggested that Morris's "principal fantasy heritage is the indefinitely extensible QUEST in which the LANDSCAPE itself plays a major part."[4] Morris's heroes, presaging Tolkien and his imitators, spend the narrative journeying through the landscape in search of a metaphorical Grail. Morris's other contribution, which has fallen by the wayside in most fantasy writing, was to create a pseudo-medieval diction for his characters. As he did so, writers of vernacular fantasy were already beginning work (see the next chapter) but the quest fantasy Morris created, and which Lewis and Tolkien would revise, continues to make creative (and sometimes humorous) use of Morris's elevated language. The one writer still working to refine Morris's ideas of proper fantasy language is Greer Gilman, whose novel *Cloud and Ashes* (2009) is written entirely in iambic pentameter.

In the same year that Morris published *The Water of the Wondrous Isles*, another book appeared, perhaps still more widely read than any other book of nineteenth-century fantasy, Bram Stoker's *Dracula*. The two books stand at opposite poles in the construction of fantasy. In the next century, the poles would part even further, as horror emerged as a separate genre (although as we shall see, by the end of the twentieth century horror and fantasy began once again to merge). What they have in common, however, and what all of the fantasy writers, artists, and craftsmen of this period had in common, is an intense focus on detail. In the late nineteenth century, Impressionist art would take over

---

4   Clute and Grant, eds., *The Encyclopedia of Fantasy*, London: Orbit, 1997, 665.

as the dominant visual form, while mimetic literature would move to concentrate on intense concern with the inner self. Literary and artistic fantasy would continue with an intensity of observation, and an attempt to create a fantastic world through the accretion of detail that we can see in the earliest Gothic works by Walpole and "Monk" Lewis, in the mid-nineteenth-century paintings of Dadd and the writings of Thackeray, and in the late-nineteenth-century Pre-Raphaelite painters and writers. At the start of the twentieth century, however, the "voice" with which this detail was written shifted dramatically.

CHAPTER THREE
1900–1950

*A*T the end of the nineteenth century, important authors were writing fantasy for adults. So it is perhaps a shock to realize that the two figures from the beginning of the twentieth century who arguably had the greatest influence on the development of fantasy were writing very specifically for children: L. Frank Baum and E. [Edith] Nesbit. Baum and Nesbit between them created what Brian Attebery has termed "the indigenous fantasy". We know more about Baum's ideas for this. Baum wrote that he wished to create for American children a fantastic world that owed nothing to the fantasy traditions of Europe. Nesbit was less forthcoming. A professional writer who wrote to support a growing family, Nesbit wrote in a number of different genres for both adults and children. *The Story of the Treasure Seekers* (1899), a non-fantastical book, seems to be written as much to present children to adults as for children, in the tradition of Richard Jeffries's *Bevis* (1882). In her first fantasy for children, *Five Children and It* (1902), that tone disappears, and instead we get one of the first examples in children's literature where the reader is asked to ally with (rather than be amused by) the child. In this and her subsequent fantasies (including *The Phoenix and the Carpet* (1904), *The Story of the Amulet* (1906), *The Magic City* (1910), Nesbit also introduced the idea that the fantastic could burst through into *our* world at any moment, without necessarily being scary. These tales are told in a matter-of-fact voice: London, or your back garden in bright daylight, become venues for fantastical occurrences. A fairy can be found in a sandpit at the bottom of the garden; but as fairies with gossamer wings would not survive long, evolution (and Nesbit was a very scientific person) has produced something hairy, that hibernates, and has a terrible temper before breakfast.

Edith Nesbit created what we now think of as the urban fantasy (or sometimes "low fantasy") which, while the definition keeps changing (currently it seems to require werewolves), can be understood as magic entering into and disrupting the urban environment. L. Frank Baum Americanized the other-world fantasy. The portal fantasy was still quite new when Baum wrote *The Wonderful Wizard of Oz* (1900), the first in a long series. Previous fantasies in this mode from the English tended to be rather vague about modes of transport to the fantasy world, the location of that fantasy world, and its politics. Baum's Oz appears on maps (indeed, his are arguably the ancestors of all the maps which introduce so many modern fantasy trilogies). In later books there is a suggestion that Oz exists very close to Kansas. It can be reached in a house picked up by a whirlwind, or by sailing down a river. It has different countries, each with different polities, and there is a suggestion of an economic system. None of this accounts for the popularity of this book and its sequels. In 1900, when *The Wonderful Wizard of Oz* was published, there was a debate in progress about the nature of the American child. Concern about large numbers of apparently abandoned children in American cities had led to the growth of a number of children's aid societies and to the orphan train movement, which took children and placed them as workers on farms. The idea was that the values of independence and self-sufficiency that these children had learned on the city streets would benefit these rural areas. Baum's Dorothy is a construction of one such child: smart, cocky, and thoroughly self-centred. In the book the three main characters, the Lion, Scarecrow and Tin Man, join with Dorothy solely because their mutual purposes intertwine; the notion of friendship and cooperation run second to a philosophy in which each achieves the best for all by serving their individual goal (in the film, friendship and helping Dorothy is much more to the fore). This, as much as the fantasy element, is one reason why many Christian Americans were repulsed by the book, while others adored it. A second reason for its popularity was its apparent allegorical element. The drought in the book's Kansas, the silver shoes,[5] and the fraudulent wizard, all appeared to speak to the state of contemporary America. The third element in its popularity is that Baum was a highly professional publicist who moved rapidly into the movies. Before 1939 there had been six silent Oz movies. The 1939 MGM version hugely boosted the book's popularity but it was its recycling on television from the 1950s onwards that sealed its classic status throughout the world, among many people who have never actually read the book (and for whom the book can come as a shock).

Whether Baum or Nesbit were the trigger, the first years of the twentieth century produced highly inventive fantasy for children. In 1911 J.M. Barrie published *Peter Pan and Wendy*, a novelization of his 1904 stage play. In 1906 Rudyard Kipling, already well known for his Indian stories, including a number of ghost stories and the celebrated animal fantasies, *The Jungle Book* (1894) published *Puck of Pook's Hill*, an innovative collection in which Puck tells a story and magically plucks other people from different periods of British history to tell their tales. In 1908 Kenneth Grahame's *The Wind in the Willows* began its progress to become one of the most established classics of children's literature. A gentle satire on the English gentry, this animal fable also contains an astonishingly elegiac strand of pagan revival which stands out from an otherwise hyper-conventional novel of Englishness and which later formed a core in P.L. Travers's Mary Poppins books (the first is *Mary Poppins*, 1934) as well as influencing – among others – the band Pink Floyd. The Mary Poppins books were nostalgic, looking back to a perhaps nonexistent Edwardian England, but radical in the

---

5   Shortage of coin was leading to inflation, and the populists, a
     predominantly rural movement, were campaigning for a switch from
     the gold to a silver standard in order to increase the amount of money in
     circulation.

degree to which they incorporated the ideas of the occultists, including practitioners such as Madame Blavatsky and the Theosophists. They were also rather sinister, without being particularly moral.

After the initial pre-war flourish, there is rather a gap in the provision of fantasy for children. From Australia, Norman Lindsay wrote and illustrated the children's classic, *The Magic Pudding: being the adventures of Bunyip Bluegum and his friends Bill Barnacle and Sam Sawnoff*, which tells of a walking, talking pudding who loves to be eaten and is never wholly consumed. The characters are a sailor, a koala and a penguin. It was written to settle an argument: a friend argued that children liked fairy stories, while Lindsay argued that they would much prefer to read about food. Eleanor Farjeon's Martin Pippin series (*Martin Pippin in the Apple Orchard*, 1921) and John Masefield's *The Midnight Folk* (1927) appeared, but it is in the 1930s that a revival really occurs, with the work of P.L. Travers (see above), Masefield's *The Box of Delights* (1935), the work of Hilda Lewis (*The Ship That Flew*, 1936, and others), and perhaps the best-known children's writer of this period, Elizabeth Goudge (*The Little White Horse*, 1940), who continued producing excellent fantasies into the 1960s. Enid Blyton, the writer who would dominate children's adventure fiction across the British Commonwealth after the Second World War, produced three important fantasies in this period: *The Adventures of the Wishing-Chair* (1936), *The Enchanted Wood* (1939) and *The Magic Faraway Tree* (1943).

Not strictly fantasy, but always included in the rollcall of the fantastic, are works of animal fable. The most famous of course are those of Beatrix Potter. Potter published her first fable, *The Tale of Peter Rabbit*, in 1902 and followed it by a series of similar fables. The illustrations are a strange combination of the extremely realistic and the fabulous. Geese look like geese even with a bonnet on; a small kitten looks as if a little girl has stuffed him into a jacket. Yet the tales are surprisingly bitter. Squirrel Nutkin (1903) loses his tail to the owl. *The Tale of Pigling Bland* (1913) is either a story of two pigs sold off to become bacon, or alternatively a metaphor for the abuse of child labour. In *The*

Tale of Jemima Puddle-Duck (1908) are we learning about a careless duck, or a seduced maidservant? Read metaphorically or metonymically, these are frightening tales for a small child and a lesson to adults in just how much children can thrive on fear fiction. Kenneth Grahame's *The Wind in the Willows* also fits this category, as does Hugh Lofting's *Dr Dolittle* adventures (1920–52) and, while not for children, George Orwell's powerful satire, *Animal Farm* (1948).

The toy story had been a staple since Hoffmann and has retained its appeal for very young children. A.A. Milne's *Winnie-the-Pooh* (1926) is a tale of a child's imagination, although as much later re-imagined by Disney it has become clearly fantasy. Across the Atlantic, Margery Williams's *The Velveteen Rabbit* (1922) offered a combination of animal fantasy and toy story. Joel Chandler Harris had popularized and Americanized animal fables with the publication of *Uncle Remus* in 1881 and these were filmed in 1946 by Disney as *Song of the South* – the book, it should be noted, lacks the racial stereotyping of the movie and is an excellent piece of anthropology. Walter Brooks's *Freddy the Pig* (1927–52) placed a pig in the role of a curious young boy and E.B. White charmed readers with both *Stuart Little* (1945) and the slightly later *Charlotte's Web* (1952). *Stuart Little* is a novel of "fancy", one of those tales that makes no sense whatsoever, in this case of a mouse born into a human family. *Charlotte's Web* is about a pig rescued from his fate by a spider. However, there seems to be relatively little children's fantasy, in the sense of *full* fantasy, in the United States in this period. There is Carl Grabo's, *The Cat in Grandfather's House* (1929), and Rachel Field's *Hetty, Her First Hundred Years* (1929), but the only truly fantastical books aside from *Oz* seem to be Ruth Gannett's *My Father's Dragon* (1948) and its sequels, and the two short stories from James Thurber, *The Thirteen Clocks* (1949) and *The Wonderful O* (1955) which are whimsy-verging-on-nonsense fairytales. In hindsight the two key books for children in this period are Tolkien's *The Hobbit* (1937) and C.S. Lewis's *The Lion, The Witch and the Wardrobe* (1950) but their impact was so enormous that we will discuss them separately in chapter four.

The emergence of something clearly marketed for children may have supported the growth of fantasy that had a very adult feel. In Britain and Ireland we can identify something that we could call "weird fancy". This material was highly experimental, and if you approach it with the kinds of expectations imposed on post-1960s fantasy it can too easily read as failure. It is this period, however, which has provided the taproot texts for the fantasy writers of the late 1990s and 2000s. Arthur Machen's first success was "The Great God Pan" (1894), in which the pagan god sires a charismatic young woman who causes a stir on the London social scene; but he achieved more popularity in the early years of the new century with stories inspired by his love of the occult. His short story "The Bowmen" (1914), about ghostly soldiers from the Battle of Agincourt coming to help the British troops in the First World War, allegedly inspired the belief in the Angels of Mons. William Hope Hodgson, who himself died in the War, had similarly produced a number of fantasies of supernatural horror: *The Boats of the "Glen Carrig"* (1907); *The House on the Borderland* (1908); and the astonishing prolonged vision of an eerie far future landscape, *The Night Land* (1912). Algernon Blackwood's *John Silence, Physician Extraordinary* (1908) and Hodgson's *Carnacki the Ghost-Finder* (1910) invent the magical or supernatural detective story. Lord Dunsany, an Irish peer, developed the full fantastic world in such novels as *The King of Elfland's Daughter* (1924) and in numerous short stories in which powerful gods and demons play with mankind. Even more extraordinary was the fiction of E.R. Eddison: *The Worm Ourobouros* (1922) tells of the war between Witchland and Demonland in a world strongly influenced by Norse myths, that Eddison called Middle Earth; the trilogy which began with *Mistress of Mistresses* (1935) was about three kingdoms ruled by King Mezentius, in a kind of afterlife of the fantasy world of the previous novel. These novels still have the power to shock through their hedonism and amorality. In the 1930s, however, we have a revival of Christian fantasy, by Charles Williams (starting with *War in Heaven*, 1930) and, most memorably, by C.S. Lewis, with his pre-Narnian "space trilogy" (*Out of the Silent Planet*, 1938; *Perelandra*, 1943 and *That Hideous Strength*, 1945). Lewis's most striking book of this period was *The Screwtape Letters* (1942) in which a devil offers advice to his nephew. These books will be discussed in the next chapter.

The two British authors who arguably merit most attention are both known for just one of their books: David Lindsay and Hope Mirrlees. Lindsay's *A Voyage to Arcturus* (1920) tells of a traveller who arrives at a séance where a stranger persuades him to join him on a rocket trip to another world. This is about as straightforward as the book gets. From here on in, a tale of planetary exploration is combined with a version of Norse mythology and Christian mysticism to produce a blinding headache of a book in which the tone shifts constantly from 1920s colloquialisms to William Morris high fantasy excess. The book is completely amoral, totally unpredictable, and constantly fascinating. In contrast, Mirrlees's tale of a middle-class, stuffy faux-English village, corrupted by the importation of fairy fruit (probably a reference to the heroin problem of the 1920s) seems quite sweet. *Lud-in-the-Mist* (1926) is an unusual book, in that the first two-thirds of the story are about keeping fairy at bay and pretending that it does not exist. Clearly influenced by Christina Rossetti's poem "Goblin Market" (1862), Mirrlees uses all the techniques so far devised to create the air of the fantastic to describe the small town in which the story is set. Faerie when it intrudes, and when we eventually cross over into faerie, is often described in quite mundane terms. The protagonist of the tale is a simple burgher, neither young nor handsome, an unremarkable man: in a way he is a precursor of Bilbo or Frodo Baggins. Although recognized at the time, neither of these books stayed in print, and were largely forgotten until reprinted in the Ballantine Adult Fantasy series in the 1970s. David Lindsay's *A Voyage to Arcturus* has inspired writers as diverse as Gene Wolfe and M. John Harrison, while traces of Hope Mirrlees's *Lud-in-the-Mist* can be seen in the work of John Crowley, Elizabeth Hand, Robin McKinley, Michael Swanwick and Neil Gaiman.

A third British author to begin writing in this period, whose major book has rarely been out of print and has been much more widely read than Lindsay and Mirrlees, was T.H. White. His masterpiece was *The Sword in the Stone* (1938), the story of the education of the young Arthur by his tutor Merlyn. Much of the humour comes from the anachronisms: knights like Sir Grummore Grummursum and King Pellinore presented as old-fashioned English gentry who treat questing much like fox-hunting, but above all Merlyn, who is living backwards and has thus already experienced Arthur's future. The most memorable sequences are when Merlyn transforms the Wart (Arthur) into various birds and animals as part of his education (and ours). The story was continued with *The Witch in the Wood* (1939), in which King Arthur starts his reign, and *The Ill-Made Knight* (1940), which deals with Lancelot and the Grail quest, and is much closer to Sir Thomas Malory than the first two volumes. In 1958 White published *The Once and Future King*, in which these three novels are rewritten – *The Witch in the Wood* is halved in length and becomes *The Queen of Air and Darkness* – and a fourth is added, *The Candle in the Wind*, dealing with the last weeks of Arthur's life. The tone of the whole is much darker, and what began in *The Sword in the Stone* as a light-hearted parody of the Arthurian tradition, eminently suitable for young readers, became a depressing lament for a past age, very much reflecting Britain's experiences in the 1940s. Luckily, the original version of *The Sword in the Stone* has often been reprinted, and is much recommended. Another much-loved fantasy by T.H. White was also published in this period, this time very clearly intended for children. *Mistress Masham's Repose* (1946) imagined that the descendants of the Lilliputians whom Gulliver brought back home with him are still living on an island in the grounds of Malplaquet (that is, Blenheim Palace).

Alongside the rise of the fantasy novel, the growing magazine market provided a venue for a number of short-story writers. Publications such as *Blackwood's Magazine* (1817–1980) and towards the end of the nineteenth century, *Strand Magazine* (1891–1950), *The Idler* (1892–

1911) and *The Pall Mall Magazine* (1893–1937) all carried ghost stories. At the end of the nineteenth century *The Pall Mall Magazine* carried stories of the fantastic in almost every issue. In this period, tales of the fantastic were still very much part of the mainstream of the British publishing scene. It is in these magazines that we see the continuing tradition of the "English" ghost story, extending out from the mid-nineteenth-century custom of telling ghost stories as Christmas stories (as in Charles Dickens's *A Christmas Carol*, 1843). By the 1900s, ghost stories were staple and highly popular magazine fare, attracting contributions from writers as prominent as Rudyard Kipling and Conan Doyle. The English ghost story of this period is strongly associated with the popularity of spiritualism and the occult generally, particularly in the period of widespread grief and melancholy that affected Britain in the years immediately after the First World War. Conan Doyle was himself an advocate of spiritualism; however, most of the major ghost story writers were sceptics.

The best remembered writer of ghost stories of this period is M.R. James, a distinguished academic and medieval scholar whose ghosts frequently erupt into the quiet world of the cathedral or university college. James started writing in the 1890s when Conan Doyle's detective fiction led the short-story field, and James brought into the ghost story a similar "domestic" setting. James's main collection, *Ghost Stories of an Antiquary* (1904), was followed by other collections including one of medieval Latin ghost stories. James and his emulators (including a group of Oxbridge academics and clerics now known as the "James Gang", such as A.C. Benson, R.H. Malden, and A.N.L. Munby) created a distinctive form of ghost story, often quiet, with a ghost that threatens through social disturbance and the revelation of secrets. These are stories of unease and tense fear, rather than of horror and terror. The mode of ghost story championed by James is predominantly a short-story form, and as a consequence one of the best-known names in the history of the English ghost story is Lady Cynthia Asquith, a ghost story writer herself, but best known for editing superb collections: *The Ghost Book*

(1926) and its numbered sequels, such as *Shudders* (1929) and *When Churchyards Yawn* (1931). Another significant anthologist was Christine Campbell Thompson who edited an annual series starting in 1925 with *Not at Night* and ending in 1937 with *The Not at Night Omnibus*. In 1951, Robert Aickman and Elizabeth Jane Howard collaborated on *We Are For the Dark* (1951). The English ghost story is very much of its time although it was revived briefly in the 1970s when Pan began a series of anthologies which reprinted many of these stories, and also through the work of Robert Aickman ("The Trains", 1951 and "Compulsory Games", 1976,) and Joan Aiken who brought to the ghost story a touch of affectionate whimsy (as in "Humblepuppy", 1972, and "A Foot in the Grave", 1989).

On the other side of the Atlantic, the publishing context for fantasy was rather different. Until the late nineteenth century a combination of paper shortage and poor transport networks limited the emergence of a national magazine industry. There were some small elite magazines, for example *The Clack Book* (1896–7), but the first fiction magazine really to achieve anything like national circulation was *The Argosy*, running under various names from 1892 to 1988. This was converted from a children's magazine in 1896, and regularly ran stories of the weird and the fantastic. As wood-pulp paper became available the economics of printing shifted, creating a demand for material to fill new magazines. The first specialist fantasy magazine was *The Thrill Book*, which lasted for six months in 1919. Far more important was *Weird Tales*, which was established in 1923 and ran to 1954. *Weird Tales* provided a platform for authors including H.P. Lovecraft, Robert E. Howard, and Ray Bradbury. After *Weird Tales* the most significant was the short-lived *Unknown* (1939–43), a spin-off from the great science fiction editor John W. Campbell's *Astounding Science Fiction*. Because most of the American writers of this period were professionals aiming to earn a living, they wrote across genres and in many different modes, but we can still identify some differences between *Weird Tales* and *Unknown*.

Weird Tales is most identified with the work of H.P. Lovecraft: indeed, his stories proved so popular that his presence arguably guaranteed the magazine's financial soundness, and the universe he created attracted other writers to work within it. His most famous short stories include "The Call of Cthulhu" (1928), "The Rats in the Walls" (1924) and "The Color Out of Space" (1927). Lovecraft's stories were typified by a morbid belief in something terrifying beyond, but it is his language that continues to identify the Lovecraftian sub-genre. As Colin Wilson and David Langford wrote, "HPL was always inclined to hurl around words like 'eldritch', 'monstrous', 'miasmic' and 'gibbous' with the abandon of a tachist artist, flinging paint at the canvas."[6] Lovecraft's long-term influence among writers of fantasy seems to be mostly as an entry text, and enthusiasm is frequently followed by cringing embarrassment. His influence is nevertheless evident, among the writers fostered by August Derleth, Lovecraft's publisher and publicist, and much more recently among the highly intellectual writers of the New Weird (see chapter eleven). Lovecraft's work has lived on beyond the written page. In 1981 Sandy Petersen and Chaosium released *Call of Cthulhu*, the role-playing game, complete with Cthulhu, the Malign Sleeper, and a pantheon of terrifying Great Old Ones such as Yog-Sothoth and Shub-Niggurath; the game has been enormously successful and produced a range of merchandise. The one most commonly seen is the green stuffed Cthulhu monster, which has been photographed eating the brains of many a famous science fiction writer.

Other writers of weird fiction in *Weird Tales* included Clark Ashton Smith, who wrote short stories set within several imaginary worlds, based very loosely on traditional mythological places, including Hyperborea (stories from 1931 to 1958) and Atlantis. The best-known female writer of this loose grouping was C.L. Moore. Her "Shambleau" (1933), a story of a soldier seduced by a Medusa, is strictly speaking science fiction, but it is painted in the dark colours and enduring sense of threat we associate with the weird. Her other well-known story, "The

---

6   Clute and Grant, eds., *The Encyclopedia of Fantasy*, 596.

Black God's Kiss" (1934), was the first of a series of stories featuring a female warrior in fantasy medieval France, Jirel of Joiry. This short story, with its similarly florid language, and dark overtones, is also strongly associated with the emergent sub-genre of sword-and-sorcery, which is initially understood as adventures of sword-wielding non-magical heroes up against various forms of magic.

The first name in sword-and-sorcery is Robert E. Howard. He began writing for *Weird Tales* in 1925 when he was nineteen and published most of his stories featuring King Kull and Conan the Barbarian, in that magazine, up to his suicide at the age of thirty. Howard's reputation has been badly damaged by the posthumous editing and rewriting of his work by L. Sprague de Camp and Lin Carter starting in the late 1960s, and more recently by the movie starring Arnold Schwarzenegger (1981). The version of Conan handed down to us is of a not terribly bright, muscle-bound, over-sexed adolescent fantasy hero. The original stories are quite different: John Clute has written that "In REH's hands... the barbarian's shrugging contempt for effete civilisation is married to a wintry fatalism clearly reminiscent of the doom-laden worldview expressed by heroes of Nordic saga."[7]

Robert E. Howard's Conan set the model for a new kind of hero, but also for a new kind of tale, one frequently episodic and set beyond the kind of fey civilization that the late-nineteenth-century British fantasy writers had constructed. It is not stretching a point to argue that Howard (along with authors we have not discussed because their work is not strictly fantasy, such as Edgar Rice Burroughs), constructed both an "American" hero, and a frontier landscape in the historical settings they chose. Almost all sword-and-sorcery tales take place in worlds reminiscent of the Roman, Greek or early medieval worlds. There are decadent empires and violent barbarians, and conflict is often over conflicting ideas of morality and honour. The stories are told in a context in which gods, demons and the supernatural are an ever-present and assumed reality. Unlike the quest fantasies to which they sometimes

---

7   Clute and Grant, eds., *The Encyclopedia of Fantasy*, 481.

seem allied, they are almost always episodic. Frequently, the hero breaks up other people's grand narratives.

Sword-and-sorcery is a term apparently invented by Fritz Leiber, who himself began one of the best known sword-and-sorcery series with a story called "Two Sought Adventure", published in *Unknown* in 1939. Leiber approached the mode with wit and humour, and his stories featuring Fafhrd and Gray Mouser, which appeared at intervals right up to his death in 1992, are much loved favourites in the field. Sword-and-sorcery continued in popularity throughout the next few decades even when the field is superficially dominated by quest fantasy; perhaps surprisingly (as we will see) it was picked up by feminist writers such as Joanna Russ, Samuel R. Delany and Marion Zimmer Bradley to very great effect.

The principal rival to *Weird Tales* was *Unknown*. Its short life reflected not a lack of success but the paper shortages of World War II (it was in the end reabsorbed by its progenitor, *Astounding*). *Unknown's* editor, John W. Campbell, was himself a science fiction writer, and his approach to fantasy was coloured by this: Campbell wanted fantasy that was susceptible to the same rules of consistency and logic he applied to science fiction. For this purpose Campbell recruited a number of his favourite science fiction writers. Robert A. Heinlein, the most influential of all, contributed stories such as "The Unpleasant Profession of Jonathan Hoag" (1942), a Lovecraftian tale of a permeable world told in hard-boiled detective style. Campbell was quite an interventionist editor, and this resulted in *Unknown* becoming a home for what then was termed science fantasy and we now call "rationalized fantasy". Rationalized fantasy is fantasy in which laws of magic are explained pseudo-scientifically. These stories are frequently set in other worlds in which magic is as fundamental as physics and treated in much the same way. Heinlein's 1940 novella "The Devil Makes the Law!" (invariably re-published as "Magic, Inc.") is one example. In this story magicians establish a monopoly that is then broken through a combination of magic and legal practice. Two other notable practitioners were Fletcher

Pratt and L. Sprague de Camp, who together wrote the *Incomplete Enchanter* sequence of short stories, in which Harold Shea and his accomplices visit various fantasy worlds such as the world of Norse mythology or the world of Ariosto's *Orlando Furioso*. Many of these worlds have different physical laws. Some of the stories in *Unknown* (like these) are part of the developing tradition of genre-referential metatexts in which characters move in and out of earlier fictional works which genre readers are expected to know. These will crop up more and more in succeeding decades as the genre develops the conversation.

Also characteristic of *Unknown* are "slick" fantasies (so called because they were considered acceptable in the "slick" magazines that were increasingly distancing themselves from fantastic fiction, such as *The Saturday Evening Post*). Slick fantasies are a form of modern fairytale in which a wise-cracking urbanite is confronted with the kinds of three wishes which faced the fisherman who caught the king of the fish (or other equivalent), or is accidentally cursed by creatures from fairy, or makes pacts with the devil. The endings of these stories almost always assert the cleverness of modernity. The most famous of these stories within the genre, is probably Horace L. Gold's "Trouble With Water" (1939), which has been extensively anthologized. In this story a man offends a water gnome, and is cursed to do without water in any form. After a few days the man is filthy and dehydrated. He is advised by a barman to appease the gnome by offering him sugar, and the "trick" is to work out how to give sugar to a creature that lives in water. The solution is the newfangled cellophane used to wrap candy.

In the midst of rationalized fantasies, and neat slicks, *Unknown* also published the Arabian fantasies of L. Ron Hubbard. These consisted of fully built faux-Arabian worlds, with plots drawn mostly from nineteenth-century adventure fiction. They are full of flashing swords, swarthy turbaned villains, and vulnerable maidens. They sit oddly with the other contents of *Unknown*, however. The best of Hubbard's stories, "Typewriter in the Sky" (1940), is better seen as a rationalized fantasy: in this story the protagonist is caught inside a book, and as the author alters the text, the protagonist's world changes around him. The influence of orientalist ideas in fantasy, however, continued to provide one alternative to the medieval European settings that would dominate full fantasy in the later twentieth century.

The magazines were the location of *genre* fantasy in America, but fantastical material was being published straight into book form, and displayed a very different sensibility. Abraham Merritt, who also published in the magazines, was probably the most popular American fantasy writer in the first decades of the twentieth century (Lovecraft's popularity grew posthumously). Merritt published in many of the magazines at the beginning of the century and some of his novels received their first readings there, but Merritt also developed one of the first independent novel careers in American fantastic fiction. His best-known works are the science-fictional *The Moon Pool* (1919) and his full fantasy, *The Ship of Ishtar* (1926). *The Ship of Ishtar* has many of the characteristics of full fantasy, including a climactic struggle between good and evil.

At a more elevated, self-consciously literary level was the Southern writer James Branch Cabell who during the 1920s and 1930s was weaving together a series of novels known as the "Biography of the Life of Manuel". Many of these books are set in the pseudo-medieval world of Poictesme, whose motto is "The World Wishes to Be Deceived". Cabell's mixture of irony and allusion often makes his work difficult to understand, but the New York Society for the Suppression of Vice was in no doubt that *Jurgen: A Comedy of Justice* (1919) was rife with playful double-entendre references to Jurgen's "sword" and "sceptre" and the like, and the resultant scandal brought Cabell much publicity. *Jurgen*, like some of his later novels, forms an anarchic and anachronistic picaresque. In his travels, Jurgen meets Guinevere, the Lady of the Lake and Helen of Troy, and finally, which perhaps caused most contemporary upset, Jurgen visits heaven and discovers God to be an illusion.

Three other authors of this period worth noting are Charles G. Finney, Evangeline Walton and Robert Nathan. Finney's *The Circus of Dr.*

Lao (1935) tells of the arrival in Arizona of a circus whose freaks include mythical and legendary creatures such as unicorns and werewolves. The book is heavily inflected with the promise of liberation through the abandonment of Christianity and the embracing of paganism – which the movie version (*Seven Faces of Dr. Lao*, 1964) left out. Evangeline Walton was for a long time one of the hidden secrets of this period. Her one novel, *The Virgin and the Swine* (1936) received little recognition at the time, but was reprinted in the fantasy boom of the early 1970s as *The Island of the Mighty* (1970). This was received well enough to support three more volumes, completing her reworking of the four branches of the medieval Welsh legend, *The Mabinogion* in 1974. Robert Nathan was the best known of the mainstream authors of the period to produce well-received fantasy. Some of his works are anti-Christian fantasy such as *The Bishop's Wife* (1928) where the archangel Michael falls for the eponymous character (filmed in 1947), or *There is Another Heaven* (1929) in which the protagonist discovers heaven to operate an alternative morality. The novel which had the widest readership (and was later filmed) is *Portrait of Jennie* (1940) in which a painter meets a small girl whom he paints at regular intervals but who is very much older each time he meets her.

Finally in this chapter we should take a quick look at the role of fantasy in the developing movie industry. Before the 1930s there had been a number of fantasy shorts including the work of Georges Méliès, Baum's own shorts of *The Wizard of Oz*, Cecil Hepworth's version of *Alice in Wonderland* (1903) at twelve minutes the longest movie yet shot in England; and versions of *Peter Pan*, various Shakespeares, and some silent *Frankensteins*. The most famous are *The Thief of Baghdad* (1924, featuring Douglas Fairbanks) and *The Sorrows of Satan* (1926). During the silent era, European films were also available, and directors such as Friedrich Wilhem Murnau (*Nosferatu*, 1919 and *Faust*, 1926) and Fritz Lang (*Metropolis*, 1927 and *M*, 1931) have a clear impact on the horror cinema of America, particularly as many European directors were forced to migrate in the 1930s.

There are a number of interesting movies in the 1930s: a version of *Alice in Wonderland* (1933) and of *A Connecticut Yankee* (1931), and a second version with Bing Crosby, *A Connecticut Yankee in King Arthur's Court* (1949), helped to keep both of these texts in the popular eye. From Britain came *The Man Who Could Work Miracles* (1936) based on a story by H.G. Wells: a man is given the power of gods to change the world but discovers that this creates problems rather than solutions. The two most memorable movies of the 1930s however, were Disney's groundbreaking *Snow White and the Seven Dwarfs* (1937) and MGM's *The Wizard of Oz*, which used Technicolor to realise the fantastical images painted by words. In the 1940s Disney again struck gold with *Fantasia* (1940), a very mixed movie but one sequence of which, to the music of Dukas's *The Sorcerer's Apprentice*, experienced an afterlife beyond the movie as a whole. A movie of Oscar Wilde's ghost story "The Canterville Ghost" was released in 1944, and David Lean's *Blithe Spirit* (1945) revived Noel Coward's ghost play. But perhaps the most interesting fantasy movie of the 1940s and the one which has had most influence in the work of modern writers, is Frank Capra's *It's a Wonderful Life* (1946). In this movie George Bailey, on the verge of suicide, gets offered a chance to see what the world would have been like without him. The movie was a flop financially, but like *The Wizard of Oz* it achieved an afterlife as a Christmas TV movie, which is rather strange because the movie records the slow death of all George Bailey's hopes and ambitions. Whether one regards the movie as uplifting (as the American Film Institute does) or depressing depends on whether one believes that George's family life is ample compensation for the college education, travel and writing career for which he had hoped. *It's A Wonderful Life* has become the model for a range of personalized parallel world stories and has been reworked in some notable movies, the best of which may be *Groundhog Day* (1993) and *Sliding Doors* (1998).

CHAPTER FOUR
Tolkien and Lewis

*I*n the middle of the century two English fantasy writers produced works whose significance would overwhelm the simple chronological structure of this book. This chapter is going to consider *only* the works of J.R.R. Tolkien and C.S. Lewis. It is also going to discuss only their life and work, and not their influence, which in Tolkien's case was quite belated. In later chapters we shall discuss their influence, on those authors inspired by them, on self-conscious imitators, and also on writers whose rejection of their influence can be seen in their work.

Tolkien and Lewis were both born in the 1890s, received a traditional classical education at school, fought in the Great War (1914–18) and were invalided out. Both lost many of their friends in that war, and in the 1920s became Oxford academics specializing in medieval language and literature. Perhaps more important is what they shared in their reading experience: both adored Greek, Roman and Norse mythology and both were interested in the fantasies of the medieval world at a time when such were considered inferior to the works of the ancients. Perhaps even more significant, both read the fantasies of the nineteenth century, above all the works of George MacDonald and William Morris. And yet, when Tolkien and Lewis became friends in Oxford in the late 1920s, what impressed Lewis at first were their differences: "At my first coming into the world I had been (implicitly) warned never to trust a Papist, and at my first coming into the English Faculty (explicitly) never to trust a philologist. Tolkien was both." (*Surprised by Joy*, p.173).

The English Faculty in Oxford in the 1920s was bitterly divided between literature and philology and Tolkien and Lewis were on different sides of the divide. Philology, the study of languages, is what had attracted Tolkien to the early Middle Ages in the first place. As a schoolboy, while Lewis was writing stories about his imaginary fantasy world, Boxen, Tolkien was inventing languages. This is not as unusual as it sounds – in this era Zionists were modernizing Hebrew, and Esperanto was available from 1887. Much later Tolkien wrote "A Secret Vice", an essay on the joy of inventing languages, where he talked about how he met a man at an army training course similarly passing the time by inventing a language. Tolkien always said that he wrote his fantasy in order to explain the world in which his languages would have existed. Tolkien's fantasy world was something in which he had been living since he was a teenager (a pattern not uncommon among his emulators). For many readers the main attraction of *The Lord of the Rings* was precisely the feeling that Middle-earth has depth. If you turn a corner in Middle-earth, you know that there will be more world there. Tolkien spent almost twenty years writing the history, and creating the culture and economics of Middle-earth before the first taste of it was given to a broader public, in the children's book *The Hobbit* (1937).

We know a lot about the writing of *The Hobbit* because Tolkien was writing in the context of a small, supportive reading group. The Inklings met weekly, usually beginning in an Oxford pub, but retiring to Lewis's rooms in Magdalen College for the serious business of reading out chapters of the ongoing works of members, of whom the most regular, apart from Lewis and Tolkien, were Hugo Dyson, Owen Barfield, Lewis's own brother Warren, and, later on, Roger Lancelyn Green and Charles Williams. For Tolkien the major benefit was receiving the enormous enthusiasm Lewis in particular had for his work. Lewis later said that the only real influence he had on Tolkien was to persuade him to finish his work: he regarded Tolkien as congenitally lazy.

In the mid 1930s, Lewis and Tolkien agreed that they would both write some science fiction: Tolkien was to write on time travel, and Lewis on space travel. Lewis's book was eventually published, as we shall discuss in a moment; Tolkien's barely got beyond a single chapter. Instead, Tolkien decided to finish a story set in the world he had devised for his Middle-earth mythology. His master-stroke was to invent a new species for Middle-earth, the hobbits. This allowed him to shift the perspective of fantasy; instead of writing about great wizards and warriors whose motives are hard to understand, he introduced us into Middle-earth through the eyes of a very ordinary "little man" from a kind of England still recognizable to most of his readers. Bilbo Baggins is not a mere conceit: he is a representative of the "little men" whom Tolkien greatly admired, the ordinary workers and middling classes who became the soldiers of the Great War, who had served stoically and shown enormous courage in appalling circumstances. Bilbo, like them, is ripped unwillingly from his familiar world and sent out to deal with consequences of decisions made by great men. The stoicism of the English Tommy is also the context for Sam Gamgee, who is modelled on the canny and loyal English batman, and is in many ways the real hero of *The Lord of the Rings* and of the restoration of the Shire/England at the end of the novel. Those who mock *The Lord of the Rings* frequently miss the point that it is as much a novel of the Great War as Erich Maria Remarque's *All Quiet on the Western Front*.

At the beginning of *The Hobbit, or There and Back Again*, Bilbo Baggins – a very respectable hobbit of the local gentry – is "recruited" by Gandalf to join a band of dwarves who are on a mission to rescue treasure from a dragon. Bilbo, to his horror, is hired as the party's burglar. Tom Shippey suggests that this is a little philological joke, as the respectable "burgher" and the disreputable "burglar" both draw their names from the same Anglo-Saxon root word. In the course of his adventures, Bilbo discovers himself to be both cleverer and braver than he had imagined. He tricks the repellent Gollum, a creature encountered underground, and acquires a magic ring that grants him invisibility. He uses this both to rob a dragon, and to survive a battle (although as Tolkien wrote, "a magic ring of that sort is not a complete protection in a goblin charge, nor does it stop flying arrows and wild spears, but it does help in getting out the way, and it does prevent your head being specially chosen for a sweeping stroke by a goblin swordsman", 2nd ed. p.293). But Bilbo's bravest moment is negotiating the peace: at the end of the novel, Bilbo risks his share of the treasure to strike a bargain between the dwarves who have disturbed the dragon and the men whose town the dragon has destroyed. This moment, in which Bilbo's stature is signified by his rejection of power and wealth, foreshadows the trajectory of *The Lord of the Rings*.

When *The Hobbit* was submitted to the publisher Allen and Unwin, it was given to Unwin's son, Rayner, then aged ten, to read. Rayner's report was overwhelmingly positive, and the book was published. It was an immediate success, and has remained consistently in print (apart from a short period during the Second World War, when paper shortages reduced printing). It was almost entirely ignored by Tolkien's colleagues in the English Faculty at Oxford – somewhat to his relief – but won the *New York Herald Tribune*'s prize for best children's book of the year. Allen and Unwin were keen to publish some kind of successor to the book but were distinctly unhappy at Tolkien's suggestion that they publish *The Silmarillion*, Tolkien's collection of mythology and legend. They wanted something with hobbits in it. Tolkien very soon had the idea that the ring that Bilbo had acquired in *The Hobbit* should be the key to his new book, but it took him a long time to work out precisely how he was to use it. The writing of *The Fellowship of the Ring*, the first volume of his sequel to *The Hobbit*, took him twelve years. In the end, *The Fellowship of the Ring* and *The Two Towers* were both published in 1954 and the final volume, *The Return of the King* in 1955. Different imprints vary but the entire book is in the region of 1,000 pages.

The current popularity of *The Lord of the Rings* has been fuelled by the fantasy genre's recursive plundering of its own material, by "mentorship" (people handing the book to their children and to other people's children), the long historical memory of fandom and of course by the impact of Peter Jackson's three spectacular movies. When the book was first published, however, it had to stand alone. For readers "groomed" by William Morris, George MacDonald and (as we will see in a moment) C.S. Lewis, *The Lord of the Rings* seemed a perfection of a particular type of fantasy. The book is rich in cultural resonance: Tolkien described it as a Catholic epic, but it also draws heavily on Norse and Old English traditions and has similarities in structure with Wagner's Ring cycle. The sheer consistency of the world was a first: there is a sense of a pre-history, there is a map (setting a precedent for all subsequent quest fantasies), there are poems in Elvish. The plot too, is incredibly tightly woven: when the original companions go their separate ways at the end of volume one (*The Fellowship of the Ring*), the subsequent two volumes follow two (and later three) sets of protagonists, each of whom has a very clearly marked path. The result is a world in which no one protagonist really knows what is going on with the quest as a whole, deepening the mimetic qualities of the adventure. Only the reader has a full grasp of the ways in which one set of adventures influences another; the protagonists can only hope and agonize.

Furthermore, Tolkien expanded on his "little man among great men" theme in his construction of Frodo as the tragic hero, sidelining the more obvious fantasy figure of Aragorn (a classic "missing prince" of fantasy/Ruritanian tradition), and developing in Sam Gamgee a figure of the rising yeoman. Alongside these characters are others, Merry and Pippin, who represent a new, younger, and more ardent generation whom we see move from the cheery bright young things (i.e. infuriating adolescents) of the Great War generation to become the young officers who served in the Second World War. There are, as is often noted, few women, but in the one really interesting female character, Éowyn, Tolkien expressed the bitterness and mourning of the women left behind in wartime Britain and who served, unrecognized, in the First and Second World Wars.

Although Tolkien was very keen to deny it, part of the popularity of the books is almost certainly down to many contemporary readers' assumptions that *The Lord of the Rings* was an allegory of the *Second World War*. A superficial reading of the work reveals a book with very clear lines drawn between good and evil. The presence of slave races and industrial tyranny does little to dispel this impression. However, the reality is more complex: the books are about power and the temptations of power (again, a very Catholic theme). When Bilbo's ring is revealed as the Great Ring of Power, an adventure starts which is not about claiming a thing of power, but about destroying and *rejecting* it. Everyone in the book is tested, and almost no one remains completely pure; even Frodo is not immune. Even when a character (such as Frodo or Sam) successfully resists the blandishments of the ring, they are damaged by that resistance. Furthermore, other characters who stay distant from the ring besmirch their souls in order to support the quest: it is a shock when one realises that Gandalf, the mighty and moral wizard, has threatened little Gollum with torture to secure the information he needs.

The most important innovations which Tolkien introduced were structural. First of all, previous quest fantasies tended to be episodic or, if they contained a goal, it rarely had great import. Tolkien married the adventure fantasy with epic: suddenly, the journey on which the participants embarked had world-shattering consequences. We not only care, we more or less have to care. Second, Tolkien took the companion structure of traditional folk tales (in which a poor peasant acquires companions with power who do everything for him/her: see *The Wonderful Wizard of Oz*) and reinvigorated it by marrying it with what Joseph Campbell in 1949 argued was the archetypal hero's journey, and then, as we have already mentioned, complicating it by having more than one hero, each of whom (Aragorn, Frodo, Sam, Faramir, Merry, Pippin, and Éowyn) follow the path Campbell outlined in very distinct ways. Third, there is a very distinct musical trajectory in the construction of *The Lord of the Rings*. Diana Wynne Jones argued that

> *The Lord of the Rings* is organized in movements, just like a symphony, but with this difference: each movement has an extension, or coda,

which reflects partly back on the movement just completed, and partly forwards to what is to come.[8]

Jones takes note of another innovation, the rapid switch from a demotic voice to a heroic one, from the domestic to the epic, and argues that each of these can be understood as a musical theme, one of which takes the top line or "tune" of the narrative at any given time. Fourth, and for this book finally, Tolkien took the moral landscapes of Gothic fantasy and turned them into character within his world: the association of a vibrant landscape with moral stature and moral governance would be worn to death by later emulators, but in *The Lord of the Rings* the sheer power of the writing, the intense attention to detail and in particular the role of Aragorn as a king linked in both body and soul to his land, was hugely powerful, and in gloomy post-war Britain may have chimed with the kind of promise that came with the coronation of a new Queen in 1953, widely heralded as a new Elizabethan age. The mirror image to Aragorn is Sauron, whose Mordor represents the degradation of landscape, above all by industry. This is why the penultimate chapter, "The Scouring of the Shire", is such a vital part of the book (although Peter Jackson was clearly not of this opinion). "The Scouring of the Shire" does three things: it emphasizes that the devastation of war and moral responsibility cannot be kept at a distance, it draws attention to the bitterness of post-war recovery, but most of all, it draws attention to what Tolkien felt a moral landscape to *be*. The first thing the returning hobbits do is to destroy the new industry and try to recreate the rural beauty – and moral essence – of the Shire.

Initial critical reactions to *The Lord of the Rings* were favourable from those in Britain who read fantasy. C.S. Lewis reviewed it for both *The Times* and *The Times Literary Supplement* in ecstatic terms; Naomi Mitchison declared it super science fiction: "It's odd you know,

---

8   Jones, "The Shape of the Narrative in *The Lord of the Rings*", in Robert Giddings (ed.) *J.R.R. Tolkien: This Far Land* (Vision and Barnes and Noble, 1990), 88.

one takes it as seriously as Malory." Not everyone agreed. *The New York Times* disliked the pedantry of the books; *The New Republic* thought them shallow. Some of Tolkien's friends, such as Hugo Dyson, simply disliked the high fantasy. However, the book sold out quickly and had to be reprinted six weeks after initial publication. One factor here is simply generational: a ten-year-old in 1934 was thirty in 1954, more than able to go out and buy the long-desired sequel to a much-loved book. But for ten years *The Lord of the Rings* was only available as three quite expensive hardback volumes and its really big sales did not come until the American paperback editions of 1965. An unauthorized version was published by Ace books, whose editor Donald A. Wollheim decided the book was unprotected by American copyright laws, and one – in response – authorized. The unauthorized edition sold around 100,000 within a few months, but the authorized edition rapidly passed a million sales. Tolkien made one more set of revisions in the 1960s, printed as the Second Edition. Sales have remained consistently high, with boosts given both by Peter Jackson's movies, and by the much contested appearance of the book at the top of almost every "favourite" and "best" list commissioned at the end of the twentieth century.

Four years before the publication of *The Fellowship of the Ring*, C.S. Lewis published *The Lion, the Witch and the Wardrobe*, the first of a sequence of seven books about the world of Narnia, which have proved to be his enduring legacy to fantasy. In other circles, Lewis is best remembered as one of the most prolific and inspiring popularizers of Christianity. Lewis himself recognized that his conversion to Christianity (his own expression) in September 1931 was a watershed in his life. It was the result of a late night conversation between himself and his two friends Hugo Dyson and J.R.R. Tolkien. On that night Tolkien persuaded Lewis that the pagan myths he found so entrancing were God-inspired precursors of Christianity. This meant that Lewis could convert without abandoning the joy and inspiration he found in pagan mythology: later in life, when in Greece, he would pray to Apollo for the health of his dying wife, arguing that Apollo was one manifestation of the Christian God. This understanding had already shaped the way he had argued for Christianity in his fiction.

Lewis's contributions to the fantastic include novels such as *The Great Divorce* (1947), set in heaven. However, he is best remembered by fantasy readers and writers for three major achievements. The first is the marvellous (and already mentioned) *The Screwtape Letters* (1942), which brought to the fantastic a wicked sense of humour. Thackeray had been funny, but the targets were distanced: Lewis picked up where Jonathan Swift had left off with *Gulliver's Travels*, to use fantasy to attack the reader on his moral hindquarters. In his letters to his nephew, the devil Screwtape unpicks contemporary ideas about courage and moral behaviour, demonstrating the degree to which bravado and public demeanour frequently mask secret sins. The book ends, however, when Screwtape's nephew makes the mistake of encouraging his target to join the army, and to lay down his life, not for his country but his friends. The satire dissolves into a very moving account of death in the trenches.

Lewis's "space trilogy" began, as we have seen, with an agreement with Tolkien that they would both write some science fiction. Lewis, a very much more fluent writer than Tolkien (by this time Lewis had a second career writing religious essays) produced *Out of the Silent Planet* in 1938, *Perelandra* (a.k.a. *Voyage to Venus*) in 1943 and *That Hideous Strength* in 1945. Anyone familiar with 1930s science fiction would be astonished if not astounded by Lewis's fiction: although there is evidence that Lewis was very well read in astronomy (the death of Charn in *The Magician's Nephew* follows the theories of Sir Arthur Eddington), the Perelandra sequence takes no account whatsoever of contemporary astronomy or physics. Lewis's planets have individual personalities, and his outer space is filled with an infinite number of spiritual beings. But it makes sense if one recognizes that the scientific world that Lewis is recreating in these novels is that of the medieval world. Its nearest literary precursor is probably David Lindsay's *A Voyage to Arcturus*, which Lewis greatly admired. The first volume takes the reader from the silent planet (Earth) to Mars, inhabited by various alien races, including the eldils, who resemble the angels of Christian mythology. Perelandra is Venus and there the protagonist (Ransom) finds himself involved in a re-run of Eden, complete with satanic tempter. The third book, which was heavily influenced by Lewis's new friend, the Christian fantasy writer Charles Williams, takes place entirely on Earth, and contrasts the wicked scientists of N.I.C.E. (National Institute for Co-ordinated Experimentation) with Ransom, who defeats them with the aid of Merlin and the planetary spirits of Mercury, Mars, Venus, Jupiter and Saturn. Many of the tropes Lewis devised for this trilogy recur in his Narnia sequence but here, they resulted in a rather heavy-handed, and for the non-Christian unpleasantly antagonist, narrative. If they have a modern-day descendant it is the sequence of *Left Behind* novels (1985–2007) by the Christian science fiction writers Tim LaHaye and Jerry B. Jenkins.

Lewis is now best remembered for the hugely successful sequence of seven Narnia books, published between 1950 and 1956. *The Lion, the Witch and the Wardrobe* has proved second only to *Pilgrim's Progress* as the most popular Christian fantasy novel ever, and the 2006 Hollywood film version will probably secure it for some years to come, even as the book begins to feel a little old-fashioned. The seven books have a chronological sequence and a publication sequence. As a chronological sequence they begin with the creation of Narnia in *The Magician's Nephew* (1955) and end with its destruction in *The Last Battle* (1956); the first published, however, is *The Lion, The Witch and the Wardrobe*.

C.S. Lewis was once asked by a young reader what the Narnia books were about, and he replied that they were all about Christ. The Lion, Aslan, who functions as the Christ figure, is the only character who appears in all seven books, but it is the three books mentioned above that are most obviously re-tellings of Christian narrative. *The Magician's Nephew* tells of the creation of Narnia by Aslan; in *The Lion, the Witch and the Wardrobe*, he is martyred to redeem a traitor, and resurrected; while in *The Last Battle*, we see the end of Narnia, the final judgement, and a curiously Platonic idea of heaven.

All of the above makes the books sound very dull, but they are anything but. In *The Magician's Nephew*, Diggory and Polly explore the internal spaces in an old house, and are tricked by a magician into testing magic rings which take them first to a wood between worlds (possibly a reference to William Morris) and then to the old, dying world of Charn, from which they accidentally release the enchantress Queen Jadis: the scene in which Jadis causes chaos in a London street, Lewis acknowledged he had drawn from the work of E. Nesbit; its mundane rambunctiousness contrasts well with the much more lyrical language heard later as Aslan sings the world into being. Lewis is one of the few writers of fantasy who has successfully conjured the moment of marvellous creation, and these scenes in Narnia in which animals push themselves to the surface of the world are genuinely joyous. Similarly, while Diggory is asked to make choices no eleven-year-old should make – to worship God or to try to save his mother – Lewis (who lost his own mother at about the same age) handles this bitter element of Christian humility with tenderness and warmth.

The Lion, the Witch and the Wardrobe is the best known of the books. When the four Pevensie children are sent to an old house in the countryside to escape the war, one of them finds a magical wardrobe that leads into another world. Lucy, the youngest, enters a world of winter, and is taken home by the faun she meets there, to have tea. When she returns, no time has passed, and none of the others believe her. A few days later, Edmund, the younger of the two boys, also finds his way through the wardrobe, and he meets the White Witch, who is responsible for the hundred years of winter which Narnia is enduring (later this witch will be retrofitted as Jadis, but here is referred to as a daughter of Lilith). When all four children finally come to Narnia, they find that Tumnus the faun has been taken away by the witch; they are hailed as "sons of Adam and daughters of Eve", and their presence is taken as an indication that Aslan will come again. As their new friends the talking beavers take them on a trek to Cair Paravel to be crowned, the winter begins to thaw. But Edmund has betrayed them. There are some unexpected domestic moments at this point in the book: helping Mr Beaver to fish, eating trout in the house under the dam, Mrs Beaver's sewing machine, and on their trek an encounter with Father Christmas. While most of the rest of the book is written as high fantasy, these scenes seem to owe their origin to *The Wind in the Willows*, and they seem incongruous. But moments like these, repeated in later books, help to punctuate texts which could become unbearably moralistic. In the second half of *The Lion, the Witch and the Wardrobe*, Aslan offers his life to save Edmund's, and is sacrificed on the Stone Table. One of the most moving moments is just before dawn when Lucy and Susan attempt to undo his bonds, and mice arrive and begin gnawing at the rope. In contrast to those cosy domestic scenes, this is dark and damp and unpleasant, and you can feel the two children's fear and misery. When the Stone Table breaks and Aslan returns to life, it is a genuine ecstatic moment. Which is why an awful lot of adults remember the shock they felt when they discovered they were reading Christian allegory. However, if we ignore the Christianity for the moment, the greatest significance of this book is that it sets a pattern for future portal fantasies, in which the travellers from Earth are uniquely equipped to rescue another land from its travails. We will discuss some of the critique of this in a moment.

The Last Battle is the third of the clearly Christian books, telling as it does of the end-times of Narnia and the winnowing and salvation of the faithful. Two children from previous adventures (Eustace and Jill) return to Narnia to answer a cry for help from King Tirian; Narnia has been invaded by Calormenes, who have been invited in by a duplicitous ape, who has cloaked an ass in a lion's skin and pretended that the ass (a Holy Fool) is Aslan. Tirian organizes a resistance, but falls to the superior technology of the Calormenes, and the novel moves towards an ending when Tirian, Eustace, Jill and others, find themselves in a

Stable, which appears to be a portal to heaven, and in which Aslan manifests himself. This is the point at which this book becomes hugely controversial. As the world ends, we see creatures cast away from the potential paradise on the basis of their reaction to the face of Aslan, and we discover that a character for whom we felt great affection has been excluded from paradise. This is too important a point to include in this summary, and we will return to this.

Of the remaining books in the sequence, taken in order of publication, *Prince Caspian: The Return to Narnia* (1951), in which the four Pevensies find themselves in a Narnia many hundreds of years after their first visit, is rather confusing in Christian terms, because when Aslan returns the land of Narnia has an outbreak of Greek gods. *The Voyage of the Dawn Treader* (1952), in which only Edmund, Lucy and their obnoxious cousin Eustace enter Narnia, through a painting, may have been modelled on the *Odyssey* or the Grail stories. It is episodic, and each encounter with magic or with magical creatures contains some kind of moral lesson (such as Eustace's arrogance leading to his transformation into a dragon, and his repentance being rewarded by a very traumatic meeting with Aslan). In *The Silver Chair* (1953), Eustace returns to Narnia with a school-friend, Jill, both of them refugees from the horrors of progressive education. Here they are sent on a mission to find King Caspian's lost son, a journey across Narnia in the company of one of the best fantasy characters in Lewis's creation, Puddleglum the depressed Marsh-wiggle, who takes them to the land of the giants and, eventually, underground. There they find Prince Rilian ensnared by the glamour of a shapeshifting witch, who was once the serpent who killed his mother. This book is essentially a lesson about learning and following your catechism. Most of the adventures occur when Eustace or Jill ignore the warnings which Aslan gave Jill at the beginning of the adventure. The book contains some truly memorable scenes: the giants' kitchen, the writing in the snow, the underground cavern with the silver chair, and the glamour which the witch casts, and last and not least the land under the underground caves, which opens up when the witch is dead to allow her slaves to return to their lands of molten rubies. In the middle of the sequence Lewis produced *The Horse and His Boy* (1954), which is the book that has proved most vulnerable to the charge of racism. It is the story of Shasta, "a white-skinned northern boy", who escapes from his Calormene foster-father (a fisherman) and the Calormene lord to whom he is about to be sold, on that lord's horse. The horse turns out to be a talking horse from Narnia, stolen while a foal and trained as a war horse for the Calormene armies. As the title of the book implies, it is Bree who steals Shasta rather than the other way round. The world of Calormen is heavily orientalised, and depicted as rich, cruel and selfish. When Bree and Shasta are joined by Aravis, a runaway Calormene bride, and the horse Hwin, much of the conversation is about the differences between Aslan's Narnia and Tash's Calormen. There are two overtly religious moments, one where Shasta is kept company by a cat in the graveyard outside the city of Tashban, and the second when Aslan chases the children and horses, both to increase their speed (by this time they are carrying a warning that Narnia is going to be invaded) and to teach Aravis a lesson. Aravis receives ten claw wounds, one for each of the stripes her maid received when Aravis ran away.

We have gone into a great deal of detail on these books, because while the details of *The Lord of the Rings* are what fans argue over, it is the intent and meaning of the Narnian books that arouses the passions of fans and critics (many of whom are fantasy writers).

The first issue, which aroused contention from the beginning, is the inconsistency of world-building, which seemed to some a retrograde step. Tolkien, when asked his opinion of *The Lion, the Witch and the Wardrobe*, said that it was "as bad as it could possibly be". He didn't elaborate, but it is fairly clear that he was referring to the total mish-mash of mythological allusions in Narnia. "Narnia" itself is used interchangeably for the whole planet, and for the country of talking animals. The historical Narnia is a town in Tuscany, and the faun fits into that picture, and yet in the same world we have Father Christmas, while the Christ figure is named Aslan (the Turkish word for lion). In later books, particularly *Prince Caspian*, Greek myth disrupts the pseudo-Christian world. Michael Ward has recently suggested an encompassing explanation for the Narnia books: Lewis's space trilogy had demonstrated his interest in the different characteristics of the planets in the medieval world view, and Ward suggests that the seven books of the Narnia sequence correspond to the seven heavenly bodies of the medieval worldview. *The Lion, the Witch and the Wardrobe* is full of imagery relating to Jupiter and to joviality, as in the incongruous arrival of Father Christmas in his red costume, while Peter is forever swearing by Jove. Each of the other books in the sequence clearly relates to one or the heavenly bodies, so that *The Silver Chair* links to the Moon, while *The Voyage of the Dawn Treader* links to the Sun. While this may seem absurd at first sight, it is a theory that repays thought. Ward points out that Lewis was known for his secrecy and delight in burying hidden significances in his work.

As we have already mentioned, it is quite a shock for many child readers of non-Christian traditions to realize that their much-loved fantasy was an evangelical text. However, Lewis was not necessarily trying to convert non-Christians. Rather we should see these books arguing for a variety of Christianity that is both ecstatic and generous. Although *The Magician's Nephew* contains within it a doctrine of the elect (not all animals are given the grace of speech), in his dealings with the humans Aslan makes it clear that he will speak to anyone who will listen. In *The Lion, the Witch and the Wardrobe*, the Judas figure (Edmund) is granted both forgiveness and the chance to redeem himself. The crucial emphasis is always on hearing Aslan. All those who cannot hear him are condemned, such as the schoolchildren in *Prince Caspian* who are turned into little pigs (although their teacher is liberated). All of this is summed up in *The Last Battle*, in which the division reiterated over and over again is between those who hear and recognise Aslan and those who deny him. A party of dwarfs who have become so cynical that they cannot see the miracle of the world inside the barn, but insist on sitting in darkness, are almost all condemned to the Wastes when Narnia dies. Yet a young Calormene who has done his best all his life is told that when he gave honour to Tash, the devil-god of the Calormenes, he was in reality worshipping Aslan. What we have here is a mixture of religious absolutism and a form of ecumenicism. This is why our understanding of Lewis's intended audience is crucial. He was speaking to people who already accepted the idea that God is open to everybody – this is a standard theology of the Church of England – but in a Britain where some forms of Christianity, such as Catholicism, were still treated with deep mistrust, it was assumed by many people that most Asians worshipped different and false gods. To a reader from a Calvinist Christian family, Aslan's insistence that it was the nature of the worship and not the name of the god which counted would be a revelation.

While Lewis may have been arguing for ecumenicism, however (as he did also in his best-seller *Mere Christianity*), his attitude to the unfaithful appeared to harden with time. Edmund and Eustace may both have been given a second chance, but the unfaithful at the end of *The Last Battle* appear to be condemned forever. The destiny that has most disturbed readers is that of Susan, once High Queen of Narnia. When Tirian, Jill and Eustace go through the door of the barn they enter a marvellous world and are greeted by a party of kings and queens. These are the transformed (and adult) Diggory, Polly, Peter, Edmund and Lucy. Slowly we discover that they are in a Narnian heaven. They and the Pevensie parents have all died in a train crash. Only Susan has been left behind. Susan has denied the existence of Narnia and been entranced by the pleasures of the world, mentioned briefly as boys, lipstick and nylons.

The fate of Susan is deeply disturbing. What kind of God leaves a young woman entirely abandoned and excludes her from heaven? Different critics have focused on this in different ways. The two best-known literary responses have come from Philip Pullman and Neil Gaiman. Pullman, who focused on the second half of this, sees Susan as excluded from heaven because she has attained sexual maturity (none of the other kings and queens have married). On the basis of this reading Pullman structured the theology of the three books which form *His Dark Materials* around the issue of adolescent sexuality. Pullman ignores the issue of the denial of Narnia and hence of Aslan and also that Susan is, after all, still alive on Earth: things may change. He also underestimates the degree to which many young female readers heaved a huge sigh of relief that feminine accoutrements were not that crucial after all. Gaiman is much more concerned with Susan's apostasy and also with the consequence of the train crash. Gaiman's story "The Problem of Susan" begins with a young woman going to interview an elderly female professor who, it is alleged, is the model for Susan. Her life was turned upside down when her entire family was wiped out in a train crash when she was seventeen. The story moves between a straightforward interview, in which we hear how she survived both emotionally and financially, and a fever dream in which the professor both is and isn't Susan, and in which the White Witch and Aslan have sex. Its overriding point is to force readers to challenge Lewis's casual cruelty.

This brings us to the question of whether the treatment of Susan is sexist. We would argue that it is a particular model of female behaviour to which Lewis objects. Overall the books are extraordinarily supportive of female adventure. In *The Lion, the Witch and the Wardrobe* Susan is always portrayed as not terribly brave, but Lucy is shown struggling against the limitations imposed. Aslan's comment that women do not belong in war is irritating, but in *The Last Battle* we will see Jill every bit the equal of Eustace, and with far better scouting skills. In *The Magician's Nephew* Lewis explains to us that Diggory and Polly have different fears and different strengths. The only time that Polly is put down by Diggory *as* a girl he appears very clearly in the wrong, is shamed by the narrator, and is later forced to apologize by Aslan.

A final criticism raised by fantasy writers China Miéville and Rhiannon Lassiter is that the books are colonialist. As we indicated above, it is explicit in every single book that Narnia is only ever properly ruled when sons of Adam and daughters of Eve, people not born in Narnia, are on the throne. The pleasant power-fantasies of readers have happily elided the iniquity of this idea and only in the 1980s do we start to see portal fantasies which do not automatically adopt Lewis's assumptions.

CHAPTER FIVE

The 1950s

_T_H E two primary trends we are going to outline in this chapter are, first, the apparent dominance of whimsy among many of the fantasists writing in this period and second, a sort of anti-trend, in which this is the last period in which writers appear to write both science fiction and fantasy, without this being considered worthy of comment.

Mervyn Peake's _Titus Groan_ conjures one of the two main trends that we think we can perceive in the 1950s, a period which otherwise did not particularly present a strong move in the fantastic. Whimsy is a form of fantasy of the odd and the fanciful. Unlike "modern fantasy" there need be no coherence and no sense that the world has a moral order. In whimsy, the world and many of its inhabitants may act apparently out of caprice. Whimsy can be, but does not have to be, a fiction of sentiment. It tends to arouse pleasant emotions of amusement, delight, and sometimes sweet heartbreak. However, whimsy can also be sinister.

Mervyn Peake's _Titus Groan_ (1946) and its sequels _Gormenghast_ (1950) and _Titus Alone_ (1959) have long proved a challenge to critics of the fantastic (both professional and fan). They feel like fantasy: there is a castle (called Gormenghast), in which very strange things happen, populated by grotesques; and at least in the first two volumes Gormenghast appears quite unconnected to our own geography and history. However, there is no magic.

Mervyn Peake was born in China in 1911, the youngest son of medical missionaries. He spent most of his childhood in China, moving back to England in 1923. In 1929 he enrolled in the Royal Academy of Art. Throughout the 1930s Peake was known as an artist and illustrator, and in recent years his artwork for such texts as *The Hunting of the Snark* and *The Rime of the Ancient Mariner* has become better known, thanks to a recent exhibition and to reprints and discussions of Peake's work in the present century. Peake started writing *Titus Groan* in the early 1940s, but was conscripted into the army. His application to be a war artist was turned down, but after a nervous breakdown in 1942 he was taken on as a graphic artist by the Ministry of Information. His most productive period as an illustrator was between 1943 and 1948. His artistry has a whimsical air. However, that whimsy grew progressively darker and the pictures Peake produced for Gormenghast are positively unnerving. One must not place too much emphasis on any one incident, but in 1945 Peake was commissioned by a magazine to visit France and Germany, and was one of the first British civilians to enter Belsen. This may have influenced the comparatively more casual cruelty and horrors that are visited on the characters in the second book, *Gormenghast* (1950).

The Gormenghast trilogy can be understood as a Ruritanian romance, an opportunistic fiction developed in the late nineteenth century, in response to growing awareness of a number of small principalities in the Balkans which appeared to have the kind of romantic royal families and aristocracies no longer found in post-revolutionary Europe. It is linked both to the historical novel, but also to the lost race novels of the same period. The word itself first appears in Anthony Hope's extremely popular romance *The Prisoner of Zenda* (1894), but is now used very widely. Ruritanias are kingdoms which don't exist, and in which therefore anything can happen. Their connection to fantasy is frequently through their use of fairytale plots, the classic one being the Missing Prince. The Gormenghast trilogy takes most of these tropes, rendering them sinister. The kinds of ritual and pomp that marked typical nineteenth-century Ruritanias, in *Titus Groan* become absurd and threatening.

The first two books in the trilogy, *Titus Groan* and *Gormenghast*, recount the story of the Groan family, ostensibly through the life of the heir to the earldom, Titus. Titus, however, is not born until very late in the first novel, and he is invisible for much of the second. If there is a point-of-view protagonist it is the unpleasant young man Steerpike, who begins as a drudge and rises to control and eventually destroy the family. Nothing about the plot explains why people read this book and understood it as fantasy. John Clute points to the castle itself as the protagonist, adopting the term "edifice fantasy" to describe a text in which the building appears organic and to have a physical and moral relationship to its inhabitants.[9] This is one of our first clues to the taproots of Gormenghast, because in these terms one of its nearest cousins is Walpole's *The Castle of Otranto*. Like Otranto, Gormenghast is a world of portents and prophecy. That it is frequently Steerpike who "helps" these prophecies come to pass does not undermine their fantastical qualities. We therefore understand Gormenghast as fantasy because we *recognize* the fantastic from the correlations between this text and its precursors. This relates to the second contributing factor that constructs Gormenghast as fantasy, and that is its landscape, described in the language of the Gothic. The scale of Gormenghast dwarfs the human and it is against this daunting backdrop that the Groan family and their retainers have developed an all-consuming set of rituals to provide a delusion of control, which have come to dwarf the protagonists. The Gormenghast trilogy is also a picaresque, in which even the notion that the universe is moral and structured by fate and destiny is stretched until it breaks, clearly harking back to Laurence Sterne's *Tristram Shandy*, whose structure the Gormenghast sequence seems to emulate.

Mervyn Peake's mode of whimsy is unusually dark for the period. More typical are writers such as Ray Bradbury, Lucy M. Boston, Fredric Brown, Eleanor Cameron, Edward Eager, Paul Gallico, Mary Norton, Barbara Sleigh, James Thurber, P.L. Travers, and E.B. White,

---

9   In Clute and Grant, eds., *The Encyclopedia of Fantasy*, 749.

although each has a very different audience. At one extreme we have Paul Gallico's *Jennie* (1950) in which a small boy is transformed into a cat and learns from Jennie, also a cat, how to survive as a stray. The book is either charming or sickly sentimental, depending on your taste for sugar. Similarly E.B. White's *Charlotte's Web* (1952), about a pig whose life is saved by a spider, arouses astonishing loyalty and affection in its fans (see Scott Westerfield's recent story "Ass Hat Magic Spider", 2008). Yet not all whimsy is sentimental. Mary Norton's Borrowers books, beginning with *The Borrowers* (1952), present a world of tiny people, coping in a world made for humans far larger than themselves. The resulting humour is precisely whimsical in the absurdity of these juxtapositions, but the stories are often rather gritty. P.L. Travers's Mary Poppins, as she developed in the 1950s, is downright scary. The whimsicality of these books renders the nursery and the streets of London deeply unstable places, where what you see and what is then admitted publicly are very different things. In later books, such as *Mary Poppins in the Park* (1952), Travers introduced a great deal of pagan imagery, and adventures included a visit to cats on a different planet and a very strange scene in which children dance with their own shadows. Eleanor Cameron's *Voyage to the Mushroom Planet* (1954) and its sequels get cited as both science fiction and fantasy. Written at the request of her son, who asked for a book about space flight, it tells of two boys building a spaceship out of old tin and scrap wood. They take the ship to Mr Bass, an astronomer living in a secret observatory, who shows them a planet that can be seen only through a special filter, gives them special fuel for their spaceship, and sends them on a mission. In later books Mr Bass is revealed to be a magician.

What is clearly evident also is how very fine the writing for children is in this period. One of the most popular newcomers was Edward Eager. His novel *Half Magic* (1954), in which only half of any wish comes true, combined the pragmatism of Edith Nesbit with a form of whimsy. The American children in the story have to apply logic to the capriciousness of magic. Philippa Pearce's *Tom's Midnight Garden* (1958) is a time-slip novel in which Tom enters a garden each evening, and meets Hattie, a girl of the nineteenth century, at different periods of her life. The novel is permeated with bitter-sweet melancholy, culminating in Tom's realization that the elderly landlady is his childhood friend. Perhaps one of the best-known children's writers of this period is Lucy M. Boston, a British author who did not begin publishing until she was over 60. The first book in a series of six about the fictional manor house of Green Knowe is called *The Children of Green Knowe* (1954). The house is inhabited by the spirits of children who had lived in the house in the past, but these are not strictly ghosts because they are seen to grow up. Time passes in parallel rather than in sequence, and Tolly can slip between the leaves of time. The trajectory of the series is about the nature of belonging and emphasizes the house as protector and the children as its purpose. Two other children's authors worth mentioning are Elizabeth Marie Pope, whose historical ghost story *The Sherwood Ring* (1958) has stood the test of time, and Eleanor Farjeon, who is better known as a poet.

Whimsy is inextricably associated with a playful approach to language. James Thurber's *The Thirteen Clocks* (1950) and *The Wonderful O* (1955), demonstrate the possibilities inherent in this approach. In *The Thirteen Clocks*, a man becomes obsessed with the stopped clocks in his castle that become a symbol of his iniquity as time rejects him. The plot is nonsense, but the language captures us and it is not until one exits the book that the implausibilities register. In *The Wonderful O*, pirates ban the use of the letter O, again allowing Thurber joyful play with language. Finally, the king of anarchistic whimsy is probably Dr Seuss (Theodore Seuss Geisel). Dr Seuss already had a reputation in the 1940s for children's poems and stories, but *The Cat in the Hat* (1957), written to a predefined restricted vocabulary, sealed his reputation as one of the premier children's writers of the twentieth century.

In America, and within the fantasy magazines, the 1950s were the last period of the "hack" writer, who wrote across genres and was often identified with magazines and magazine editors rather than the community of a particular genre. The late 1950s and the 1960s is a period in which science fiction and fantasy, and their fans, begin to look like rather separate beasts, although there is plenty of evidence (in such areas as the Hugo Awards) that the language of the boundary is more rigid than the reality. One element in this is that although the 1950s is not a particularly vibrant period for the writing of fantasy, it is considered by many to be the Golden Age of science fiction, and in particular sees the emergence of "hard sf", which is far more ideologically antithetical to fantasy than was the "scientific romance" of the 1930s. The 1950s was also the last period in which the science fiction magazine was the dominant publishing platform for the genre. By 1955 the paperback was taking over, and would remain the primary publishing format until the price of hardbacks began to sink (relative to the paperback) in the 1990s.

For much of the 1950s there was no magazine that specialized in fantasy alone: *Weird Tales* ceased publication in 1954 (to be revived in 1988). However, an important event for the history of fantasy was the appearance of two new magazines: *The Magazine of Fantasy and Science Fiction* in the USA at the end of 1949, and *Science Fantasy* in the UK in 1950. Although both magazines did publish a great deal of science fiction, the absence of a specialist market for fantasy meant that they became the major market for writers wishing to sell fantasy. *Science Fantasy*, which saw 81 issues between 1950 and 1966, almost all under the editorship of John Carnell, was home for various types of fantasy, mostly by British writers. Brian Aldiss and J.G. Ballard both published their first stories there, John Brunner was a major contributor, and Michael Moorcock first developed his Elric series there, as we shall see in the next chapter.

Of the two magazines, *The Magazine of Fantasy and Science Fiction* (which has had an uninterrupted and regular publication history until the present day) was much more important. The editor of *F&SF* until 1958, Anthony Boucher, was determined to raise the literary level of stories and published writers who were not known as genre writers at all, including Robert Graves, P.G. Wodehouse, and Shirley Jackson.

To begin with, Boucher had banned "heroic" fantasy in the style of Robert E. Howard. Heroic fantasy is frequently episodic fantasy; the quest fantasies that came in during the late 1950s, as the works of Tolkien spread, were far less suitable to the part publishing of the magazines, and we see very little of this form here for the rest of the century, even while (as we shall see) it flourished in the paperback. Instead, Boucher encouraged supernatural horror and ghost stories, and even returned to reprints of old stories by writers such as Lord Dunsany. In the UK, Dennis Wheatley was publishing books such as *To the Devil – a Daughter* (1953) and by the early 1960s there is some justification for an argument that supernatural fiction had come to dominate fantasy.

Boucher inherited some of his authors from *Weird Tales*, including Ray Bradbury, but also began to publish new writers, of whom probably the most important was Richard Matheson. Richard Matheson wrote a great number of short stories most of which were science fiction. He did write *A Stir of Echoes* (1958), a novel about the psychic residue of a murder, but his best known novel is the thrice-filmed *I Am Legend* (1954).[10] *I Am Legend*, however, brings up an important point: it is a vampire novel with a science-fictional premise. In *I Am Legend*, vampirism is a contagious disease, utterly un-mysterious. "Rationalized Fantasy", or science fiction that felt like fantasy, may be one of the dominant "moods" of the period. A classic story that exemplifies this is Jerome Bixby's "It's a *Good* Life" (1953). This story was voted by the Science Fiction Writers of America (SFWA) as one of the twenty finest science fiction stories ever written, yet it is essentially a supernatural tale: the story is about three-year-old Anthony who is hugely powerful and can transform the world in any way he wishes. He has pulled his small town into a pocket universe where his infantile desires are inflicted upon the population. The title comes from the mantra the townsfolk recite in order to appease Anthony. If this sounds like a *Twilight Zone* episode, it is because it is this kind of fantasy-sf-horror crossover which formed the staple for the

---

10   As *The Last Man on Earth* (1964), as *The Omega Man* (1971) and as *I Am Legend* (2007).

show's scripts. Bixby's "It's a *Good* Life" was adapted for the show in the third season (1961–2) and again for the *Twilight Zone* movie where it formed a segment directed by Joe Dante (1983).

When we look at the big names in American fantasy in the 1950s, we are struck both by the degree to which we understand most of them now as science fiction writers, and the degree to which their "fantasy" is very often contextualized in science fiction codes. These include writers such as Poul Anderson, Ray Bradbury, Fredric Brown, Theodore Sturgeon and Jack Vance.

Fredric Brown and Theodore Sturgeon are best remembered today for their biting (and often very funny) short science fiction stories. Fredric Brown published probably his most memorable work in the 1940s but was still very active in the 1950s and some of his best stories from *Unknown* were reprinted in paperback in 1954 as *Angels and Spaceships*. The spread of the paperback into drugstores gave a writer such as Brown a new audience. As Brown said in his introduction to *Angels and Spaceships*, the fantasy can always be given a science-fictional rationale. He gives the instance of King Midas, which, if seen as the story of a Greek in New York to whom an alien gives the power to change the molecular structure of matter by touch, is clearly science fiction. In "Etaoin Shrdlu" a Linotype typesetter acquires intelligence, possibly through alien intervention, while in "The Angelic Angelworm" the typos that are bringing chaos to Charlie Wills's life (a teal duck appears in place of a Chinese tael in a coin cabinet) are the result of errors in the Head Compositor's office in heaven. One is science fiction and the other fantasy, but with ingenuity each story could have been rewritten in the other genre. Like Fredric Brown, Theodore Sturgeon was also reprinted in paperback, and his stories from the very end of the 1940s demonstrate the trajectory that was emerging. His "monster horror stories", such as "It" (1948) and "Professor Teddy Bear" (1948) could be interpreted as either sf or as supernatural fiction.

More significant, however, is the work of Anderson, Bradbury and Vance. Poul Anderson's *Three Hearts and Three Lions* (1953) was *F&SF*'s

first serialized novel. *Three Hearts and Three Lions* is a "science fantasy", written with the codes of sf but the settings and voice of fantasy. The Danish hero Holgar Carlsen is blown up in an explosion while in the Danish resistance during the Second World War. On waking he finds himself in a medieval fantasy world fighting dragons and werewolves, and even meeting Morgan le Fay. Anderson uses this novel as a way of offering twentieth-century comment upon a medieval fantasy world much in the tradition of Twain's *A Connecticut Yankee at King Arthur's Court* (1889) – a book that also sounds like fantasy, but is very clearly science fiction. In 1954, Anderson followed up with *The Broken Sword* in which he abandoned the science-fictional frame and offered a fantasy set wholly in the world of Dark Age England (now known as the early medieval period) but one inhabited by elves, trolls and fairies. Its success hinted at the popularity of full fantasy worlds that were to come.

Jack Vance was also dabbling in medievalist fantasy although his science-fictional rationale was quite different from Anderson's. The sequence of stories that was gathered together as *The Dying Earth* (1950) and in other collections from the 1960s and 1980s purports to take place millions of years in the future in a world which exemplifies Arthur C. Clarke's dictum: "Any sufficiently advanced technology is indistinguishable from magic."[11] It should be noted that non-fantastical, post-nuclear-holocaust, medievalist worlds were also popular in science fiction at this time, the best known being John Wyndham's *The Chrysalids* (1955), in which a future desolated world produces mutants with the pseudo-magical power of telepathy (one of the most popular themes in sf in the 1950s), and Walter M. Miller Jr.'s *A Canticle For Leibowitz* (1960). The division between "proper" sf and "proper" fantasy in terms of themes and settings was very cloudy. Vance's *Dying Earth* is populated by amoral sorcerers, monstrous beings (some of them probably produced by magic), and strange apparently supernatural forces like Chun the Unavoidable. There is very little plot but its picaresque encounters with magical or monstrous beings is strongly reminiscent of medieval

11   Clarke, *Profiles of the Future*, London: Macmillan, 1973, 21, fn 1.

Arthurian romance. Most of Vance's output between 1950 and the present day is technically science fiction in that the action takes place on alien planets but the atmosphere of many of these (such as *Big Planet*, 1952), is very similar to his Dying Earth sequence.

Ray Bradbury began his writing career in 1941 and during the 1940s much of his work was published in *Weird Tales* where his predominant tone was the macabre, with or without a supernatural element, and these were collected in 1947 as *Dark Carnival*. His favourite locale was the small mid-western town. In 1950 Bradbury published *The Martian Chronicles*, made up of a number of linked stories about the colonization and ultimate abandonment of Mars. Some of the stories were published earlier, but it was their linking together which created the text that people remember. The colonization of Mars is clearly a science-fictional theme but Bradbury ignores what was known at the time about space travel or about the planet; he transfers mid-western small town life, complete with its racism, to Percival Lowell's Mars (a nineteenth-century vision of Mars with canals and an atmosphere). Bradbury is not interested in technology, but in the day-to-day life of the settlers. Apart from his famous novel *Fahrenheit 451* (1953) Bradbury's output in the 1950s was almost entirely either weird fiction or science fiction with a fantasy element (all published as short stories). In the collection *The Illustrated Man*, while all the stories are science fiction, the framing device is fantastical: the tattoos on the body of a vagrant each animate and tell a story of the future. The best-rounded collection of Bradbury's stories is *The Golden Apples of the Sun*. In the first edition, published 1953, we can see the range of his fantasy work. Of the stories from the 1950s, "The Fog Horn" is a monster story, in which a monster is attracted by the sound of a fog horn on the remote east coast of America; "The April Witch" (1952) tells of a girl born into a magical family, who is told that she will lose her magical abilities if she marries a human. She takes over the body of a human girl in order to explore a human man's love. "The Golden Kite, The Silver Wind" (1953) is an allegory about human desires for hostility set in a fanciful China. For all that in the 1950s the sheer number of science-fictional elements link Bradbury to sf, he understands himself as a fantasy writer, writing the impossible. For the reader, it is the tone of his work, and of his later writing in the 1960s and 1970s, which link him retrospectively to the fantasy of the 1950s.

If Boucher did not publish heroic fantasy, and if the fantasy of the magazines more generally concentrated on supernatural fantasy, fantasy writers of the period had to adapt. Three writers whose careers continued into the 1950s but in a changed fashion were L. Sprague de Camp, Fletcher Pratt and Fritz Leiber.

In this period, L. Sprague de Camp, responsible in the 1940s for *The Incomplete Enchanter* (with Fletcher Pratt), began to write "planetary romances" very much in the style of Edgar Rice Burroughs's Mars/Barsoom books. Planetary romance is a sub-genre of science fiction which has a close relationship with fantasy in the sense that the planetary cultures that are described are very frequently pre-industrial: the pseudo-medieval warfare with bows and arrows and swords is frequently reminiscent of medievalist fantasy, but this is also a space in which some writers explored American notions of the primitive, mapping the mythology of the American West on to the plains of another planet. Alongside these, L. Sprague de Camp began the process of collecting and editing the stories of the by now deceased Robert E. Howard. In 1955 he published *Tales of Conan* and then in 1957 *The Return of Conan*, which he produced with Bjorn Nyberg. As we have already discussed in chapter two, de Camp did more than simply collect the stories. As well as reworking some of the stories, de Camp began the process of moulding them into the new form constructed by Tolkien, a fantasy with a "deep" back history and maps. These texts, however corrupt, helped prevent Howard's work from disappearing under the hostility of Boucher's editorial dominance, and as we shall see later, were available for the writers of the 1970s fantasy revival.

L. Sprague de Camp's collaborator on the Incomplete Enchanter series was Fletcher Pratt who also produced two significant sole-authored fantasy works: *The Well of the Unicorn* (1948) and *The Blue Star* (1952). For the first of these Pratt borrowed background from a short story by Lord Dunsany. *The Well of the Unicorn* is set in a medieval world with a strong resemblance to medieval Scandinavia but it has no connections to our own world and is a full fantasy world. The protagonist Alvar Alvarson is a warrior but has some magical powers. Drinking from the well of the title brings peace but this is not the promise of a solution. When enemies invade, Alvar's wife suggests bringing peace from the well but Alvar responds by summoning the troops and saying "There is no peace but that interior to us" and wonders why she weeps. This idea of what peace is, and when it is appropriate, seems to have been of major concern in American society at the time, and may be a comment on the cold war. A similar ending concludes the 1952 movie, *High Noon*, in which a Quaker wife fails to dissuade her husband from picking up a gun to conclude a vendetta. Pratt's novel was not widely known at the time but reprinted at the beginning of the fantasy boom in 1967 (two years after Tolkien was published in paperback), and had considerable influence. It was regarded as ahead of its time in both tone and content, and the peace theme resonated particularly strongly with a generation of Americans for whom American involvement overseas was becoming an ever greater issue. Pratt's second solo novel, *The Blue Star*, is likewise very impressive. It is set in a faux-eighteenth-century (magical) world, in which the hero endeavours to win control of the magical jewel known as the blue star on behalf of a revolutionary movement. This "alternate historical novel" was almost unknown at the time, but it has become one of the most popular forms of "alternate fantasy". Keith Roberts's *Pavane* (1968), a tale of England descended from a successful counter-reformation and one of the most important alternative fantastical histories, was clearly influenced by it, and in the 1980s and 1990s Mary Gentle, John Whitbourn and Delia Sherman specialized in this kind of fiction. The most successful author to follow Pratt today is Susanna Clarke, whose *Jonathan Strange and Mr. Norrell* used the form to great effect and broke out of the "fantasy" market to become a bestseller in 2004.

Fritz Leiber, previously a writer of heroic fantasy – a form he would revive in the fantasy boom of the late 1960s – turned in this period mostly to science fiction. However, he did produce a number of supernatural short stories and in 1953 his *Conjure Wife* appeared. This supernatural fantasy is set on the campus of a small university, one of whose exclusively male faculty discovers that the faculty wives are supporting their husbands' academic rivalries through witchcraft. By the end of the book the protagonist has concluded that all women are witches, controlling their men (and the world) through witchcraft. This was made into two movies, most recently as *Burn Witch Burn* (1961), but may have also had some influence on the TV series *Bewitched* which ran from 1964–72: for most of the 254 episodes Samantha works magic, against her husband Darrin's wishes, only to have to clear up the consequent mess. Leiber's book, the non-fantastical *I Love Lucy* (1951–57), *Bewitched*, and the inferior but very well known, *I Dream of Jeannie* (1965–70), a rival show about a genie's desire for her master, all show the same anxieties about women's right to work and to self-expression which were about to explode into Women's Liberation at the end of the decade and which would have a huge and contentious impact on genre fantasy.

Perhaps the most important new writer in the 1950s was one whose connection to fantasy is somewhat tenuous. Shirley Jackson, short-story writer and novelist, specialized in the *possible* supernatural. Jackson made an initial hit with the short story "The Lottery", published in *The New Yorker* in 1948, a frightening tale of a town which selects and collectively kills a scapegoat each year. The story struck a chord with an America already in the psychological grip of the House Un-American Activities Committee and both *The New Yorker* and Shirley Jackson received hate mail as well as plaudits.

Jackson's two most impressive novels are *The Haunting of Hill House* (1959 – filmed as *The Haunting* in 1963, and under its proper title in 1999), and *We Have Always Lived in the Castle* (1962). In *The Haunting of Hill House* a group of people are gathered together to investigate their own psychic abilities and the nature of a house: the house may be haunted, or the events that unfold may be the consequence of introducing a disturbed and unhappy young woman into a sexually charged atmosphere. This is one of the earliest mainstream novels to feature lesbian sexuality as no more threatening than heterosexuality. *We Have Always Lived in the Castle* tells of the survival of a family after most of it has been poisoned and the effect on that family of an intruder. The protagonist has a claim to the supernatural, but the trajectory of the book is towards the rational. In the earlier *The Sundial* (1958) we can see clearly the links to the eighteenth-century Gothic which haunt Jackson's later work. Twelve people gather in a fantastical house wait for the end of the world and are haunted by moving statues and other supernatural portents. Jack Sullivan wrote of it, "if these people are microcosms of the world, as several reviewers have suggested, the world is clearly in trouble – whether it ends or not."[12]

Despite the presence of really excellent writers, by the end of the 1950s fantasy appeared to be in trouble. Science fiction was booming, the supernatural was popular, but fantasy seemed to have lost its way. In the next decade, thanks to the impact of Tolkien, and of the Ballantine adult fantasy series, all of this was to change.

---

12   In Bleiler, *Supernatural Fiction Writers*, New York: Charles Scribner and Sons, 2002, 1034.

The 1960s

A T the beginning of the 1960s it was not obvious that there was a boom on the horizon. To a very great degree this is because fantasy contained two marketing divisions that split the field. The first was geographical. In the 1960s the cost of importing books into either the United States or the UK was sufficiently high that the two markets operated more or less independently (and this would continue until the reconfiguration and internationalization of many publishing houses and the Age of Amazon). Many of the books we are going to be discussing in this chapter are British and their impact in the United States was delayed by at least a decade. Far more American books were published in British editions than vice versa. For individual writers seeking to write for the magazines, the sheer cost of international postage, combined with the cost of sending copies that were inevitably unreturnable, similarly proved prohibitive. This helped to nurture British fantasy publishing, which was dependent on home-grown writers.

The second marketing division was between adult and children's fantasy. The 1960s was a genuine golden age for children's fantasy, but whether coincidentally or not it emerged at the very time when the notion of "a children's book" was becoming a much stronger category. Concomitant to this there would be a tendency to argue that fantasy *was* for children, which may have shaped the notion of adult fantasy (represented by Ballantine books and Michael Moorcock's time at *New Worlds*) that emerged later in the decade. Just to complicate matters the end of the 1960s saw the emergence of Young Adult fiction, a form that in this period was vehemently realist and rejected fantasy at the very moment that children's fantasy was making great strides.

Perhaps the most important publishing event in the 1960s in terms of the *long-term* development of the fantasy market was the paperback publication of *The Lord of the Rings*. In America, *The Lord of the Rings* was published first in an unauthorized edition by Ace in 1965, and then later in the same year the official edition was released by Ballantine Books of New York.

Ian and Betty Ballantine had long been publishers of science fiction but the success of the paperback Tolkien inspired them to move into paperback fantasy. From Tolkien they moved on to reprints of E.R. Eddison, Mervyn Peake and David Lindsay and then in 1969 they launched the "Ballantine Adult Fantasy" series which, by reprinting many of the classics of fantasy discussed in chapters one and two, helped to establish the idea of fantasy as a genre in the minds of the reading public. Between May 1969 and April 1974 they printed sixty-five fantasy titles. Of these sixty-five, sixty-three were reprints, and the remaining two were the first two volumes of a new medievalist fantasy series by Katherine Kurtz, *Deryni Rising* (1970) and *Deryni Checkmate* (1972), which we will discuss in the next chapter. The Ballantine series helped to claim serious critical attention for fantasy, and in addition helped to create a collective history for the genre. Fans of fantasy could now begin to argue about what fantasy was and to align new writers to older traditions. The most important of the books we discussed from the late nineteenth and early twentieth centuries were all reprinted in this series.

One of the most significant fantasy writers of the 1960s was Andre Norton, who crossed over from both science fiction and juvenile fiction into fantasy for adults. In this, Norton anticipated a more general trend which we will explore in the 1970s, in which a number of sf writers moved into fantasy. In the 1950s and early 1960s Andre Norton had been the most prolific writer of sf for juveniles, taking over from

Robert A. Heinlein as the most popular, and retaining much of that popularity to this day. In the 1950s Norton had written some fantasy, such as *Huon of the Horn* (1951), a retelling of a medieval romance, but in 1963 she published the first of what was to become a long-running and very popular series set on Witch World. The first, named *Witch World* (1963), is embedded within a science-fictional rationale: the protagonist is an Englishman called Simon Tregarth who is brought to the planet named Witch World through an ancient stone arch in Cornwall, and meets the witches of Estcarp, who use special jewels to enhance their powers. He defends the planet from an invasion by the alien Kolder whose superior technology allows them a kind of mind control. However, the alien Kolder disappears from the scene early in the series, Tregarth is assimilated and many of the stories are about his new family and the matriarchal society of Estcarp, ruled by the witches. From then on the series reads exactly like fantasy.

The popularity of the Witch World books was in part due to the desire of the new Tolkien fans for more full fantasy material in a somewhat barren publishing landscape. In the 1960s Andre Norton produced six of the Witch World novels; slim volumes of around one hundred and fifty pages each, together they run almost as long as *The Lord of the Rings*, and offer a world of breadth and depth. Norton's work remixed several forms: on the surface these are sword-and-sorcery books with little technology and your standard brawny warriors, but physical violence seldom solves anything and is not the focus of the descriptive language of the books. Resolution of conflict is almost invariably achieved through the careful application of magic, and women have a near monopoly of magical powers on Witch World. The appearance of strong female characters in fantasy was at this time rather unusual and the books – although sometimes wooden – are held in strong affection for this reason. Furthermore, the books are classic 1960s responses to contemporary political stresses. The issue of intolerance is explored in a number of ways, perhaps most memorably through the treatment meted out to werewolves and other shapeshifters. Norton continued to write the Witch World books into the 1990s, and began a pattern which Marion Zimmer Bradley continued, of hosting anthologies of fan stories written within the universe.

As we intimated at the beginning of the chapter, the development of fantasy in the UK and US were taking very different routes. Probably the most important development in the UK was the arrival of Michael Moorcock as fantasy author and leading light of what came to be called the British New Wave (although some of its participants were Americans and Canadians resident in London). Moorcock's first significant fantasy publication was a novella called "The Dreaming City" which he published in the magazine *Science Fantasy* in 1961. This story introduced the character Elric, 428th Emperor of Melniboné. Elric inhabits a fairly typical fantasy world furnished with demons and dragons, but although this sounds a great deal like Tolkien (particularly the damage wrought by association with a thing of power), Elric is a deliberate antithesis of earlier fantasy heroes. He is a neurasthenic albino who, left to his own devices, would never be a hero. His power – and the interest of the stories – comes from his relationship with his sword, Stormbringer. When Elric picks up his sword, energy courses through him but also a lust for blood: Stormbringer feeds on the souls of those it kills. Until late in his life, the better to feed his sword, Elric serves the demon Lords of Chaos. The Elric stories were not written to an internal chronology and infill stories were still being written thirty years later: Elric could also be found in comic books, role-playing games and on the albums of the rock band with which Moorcock was associated, Hawkwind.

Moorcock was very strongly influenced by Tolkien but understood this in a negative fashion: he despised what he termed the consolatory conservatism of Tolkien. The series to a great degree encodes many of the critiques of fantasy that Moorcock established in *Wizardry and Wild Romance* (1987). It is an irony, however, that while Moorcock set out to subvert both the sword-and-sorcery genres and the moral themes set by Tolkien, it is his work which served as the butt of much of Terry Pratchett's humour in the early Discworld novels of the 1980s.

Moorcock was hugely prolific throughout the 1960s and 1970s: much of his output was hackwork sold initially to *Science Fantasy* and then to the rapidly expanding paperback market. For this market Moorcock produced a series of subversive fantasy heroes including Dorian Hawkmoon, Corum, and name-variants of a hero known mostly as Jerry Cornelius. If Moorcock began as a hack writer, how did he emerge as one of the most significant writers in the field, with a reputation that has been sustained over forty years? Part of this is sheer quantity, but also the ways in which he linked his heroes together in the concept of the Eternal Champion, in which all his heroes become manifestations of the same figure, turning Campbell's notion of the hero with a thousand faces (from the book of the same name) into a fantastical mythos. One of the best-known books in this sequence is *A Nomad of the Time Streams* (1982), which pays homage to Edith Nesbit through the main character, a grown-up Oswald Bastable.

Moorcock's most impressive fiction was produced predominantly in the 1970s: the *Dancers at the End of Time* sequence (1972–78) is more associated with science fiction, but is set in a far future world that is an heir to Vance's Dying Earth and plays with the borderlands between science fiction and fantasy. Moorcock's best known stand-alone novels are *Gloriana, or The Unfulfill'd Queen: Being a Romance* (1978), which is set at a fantastical Elizabethan court and owes strong debts to Edmund Spenser and Peake, and *Mother London* (1988), a contemporary fantasy which sets its characters adrift in post-war London. The hallmark of all these works, as may be obvious, is their intense meta-critical approach, a sense of an author whose work unfolds to the degree that the reader shares a common immersion in the field. Moorcock's immersion in the field was a function of both his critical interest and his editorial role in the 1960s.

In 1964 Moorcock became editor of *New Worlds*, a position he held until 1971, although he did not edit every single issue. *New Worlds* under John Carnell had been a science fiction magazine, with little to distinguish it from its American rivals except for its publication of ambitious young British writers such as Aldiss, J.G. Ballard, and others. Moorcock's *New Worlds* did not emphasize fantasy *per se* but did stress experimental writing, a greater facility with language and a dissatisfaction with aspects of 1950s science fiction and fantasy, which included an unquestioning faith in human ingenuity and a certain sexual Puritanism. Moorcock offered platforms for writers such as Samuel R. Delany, Thomas M. Disch, Pamela Zoline, Harlan Ellison and, later, M. John Harrison and Christopher Priest (two writers who, from the 1980s onwards, were at the forefront of British fantasy). All of the work of these writers was presented as science fiction, but can often be understood as fantasy. What these writers, collectively known as the New Wave, had in common was a sense of the porousness of a Rabelaisian world: as in the Elric stories, chaos shaped the universes these writers imagined.

Moorcock was a polemical editor, but his vision was stronger than the manifested product. Most of the fictional content of *New Worlds* was science fiction, and hence not technically relevant here, but the review columns of *New Worlds* had a disproportionate influence on British sf and fantasy. Here Moorcock, Harrison and John Clute reconstructed the nature of criticism in the field, and set many of the challenges that later writers of fantasy would try to meet. In the next chapter, for example, we will see how M. John Harrison set out to write a fantasy that would cut across the kind of consolatory conservatism that both he and Moorcock despised.

When Carnell's magazine *New Worlds* was taken over by Moorcock, the sister magazine *Science Fantasy* was taken over by Kyril Bonfiglioli, and two years later transmuted into *Impulse*. One of the editors of this magazine was the writer Keith Roberts, who had begun publishing his stories about the young witch Anita in *Science Fantasy*. But his greatest achievement was a series of short stories for *Impulse* that were gathered together to form the novel *Pavane* (1968). At first sight this looked like a standard alternate history, which some critics would classify as science fiction. It was set in a twentieth-century world from which Protestantism had been expunged after the days of Elizabeth I. But alongside Catholicism were vestiges of a mythical past, such as the dryads. Roberts explored further this idea of ancient powers surviving into a modern world in *The Chalk Giants* (1974) and *Gráinne* (1987), just as Robert Holdstock was to do in his Mythago sequence which began in 1984.

While fantasy for adults was finding a new set of feet, fantasy for children was going from strength to strength. Among the children's writers to emerge in the 1960s there is little obvious pattern. However, writing fantasy for children was still not a vocation, and some excellent writers produced one or two fantasies among a much larger body of work. Alison Uttley, well known for her animal stories about Little Grey Rabbit, produced in 1962 a rather lovely time-slip fantasy, *A Traveller in Time*, in which Penelope finds herself part of the Babington family, assumed to be of their time, but utterly unable to prevent their involvement in the fate of Mary Queen of Scots. Another time-slip novel was Penelope Farmer's *Charlotte Sometimes* (1969), the third fantasy novel about Charlotte Makepeace, in which Charlotte arrives at a modern boarding school and finds herself exchanging places with Clare, at school in 1918. We never get to meet Clare, and the two girls exchange information by leaving notes for each other. In the 1950s Catherine Storr had produced two books about clever Polly and the stupid wolf, and a much larger number of non-fantasy books, but it is *Marianne Dreams* (1964) for which she is best known. In this book a girl being tutored at home due to sickness dreams of a boy in a house she has drawn. When in a moment of jealousy she draws stones with eyes around the house her actions affect his wellbeing, and she must work out how to undo her curse. Norton Juster, an American writer, published *The Phantom Tollbooth* in 1961, a portal fantasy which takes a boy named Milo into a fantastical and fanciful world, the Kingdom of Wisdom, riddled with puns and metaphor. Its two principal cities are the warring Dictionopolis and Digitopolis, representing language and maths. Dodie Smith had already had a hit in 1956 with *The Hundred and One Dalmatians*, an animal story in which two Dalmatians set out to rescue their kidnapped puppies. With the exception that we can understand the dogs, there was nothing fantastical about this book. The sequel, *The Starlight Barking* (1967), begins when the two protagonists (Pongo and Missis) wake to find all humans and animals other than dogs asleep. They are called to London telepathically, by their youngest daughter, who lives with the Prime Minister, and travel by telekinetic swooshing. That night they are visited by the star Sirius, who wishes all earth dogs to join him to assuage his loneliness.

Susan Cooper, most of whose work would be produced in the 1970s, published *Over Sea, Under Stone* in 1965, a rather anaemic Grail hunt, in which three siblings search a seaside resort under the guidance of a Merlin-figure. The four later sequels, starting with *The Dark is Rising* (1974), are very powerful, and we would not advise anyone to begin the series with the first. William Mayne was perhaps one of Britain's most important children's writers, who produced predominantly realist fiction. But his book *Earthfasts* (1966) is considered a classic fantasy novel. Two boys hear drumming under a hill near their homes, and Nelly Jack John, an eighteenth-century drummer boy, marches out of the hill and into the twentieth century. When he goes back he leaves behind a candle which has strange powers and leads one of the boys into trouble. Rosemary Harris began her writing career with a trilogy of books, the first of which is *The Moon in the Cloud* (1968), which uses the story of Noah's flood as its basis. Her later works included both non-fantasy and science fiction.

Elizabeth Beresford's *The Wombles* was published in 1968. The Wombles live on Wimbledon Common; they are small furry creatures who hide from humans, but recycle human rubbish for their purposes. One of the most memorable aspects of them is that they pick their names from maps, and so have names like Bulgaria, Tobermory and Orinoco. The book and its sequels were popular in the UK, but their real success was in the 1970s when they were made into a TV series (1974–5), which ran in a short five-minute slot at the end of children's programming on BBC1. This slot also hosted the French import called

The Magic Roundabout (UK, 1965–77). This stop-motion animation was set in a park, and contained a number of non-human characters, including Dougal the Dog, Brian the Snail, Dylan the Rabbit and two other characters, Florence, a human girl, and Zebedee, a weird alien creature on a spring. The bizarre thing about the show was that it was not translated from the French: instead, the English narrator Eric Thompson made up his own scripts, heavily laden with references to British politics and psychedelia (although the latter is disputed). On the other side of the Atlantic, Maurice Sendak, a writer and illustrator for very young children, was demonstrating the power of the fantastic in picture books. He had been working as an artist in the 1950s, but gained international acclaim with *Where the Wild Things Are* (1963). In this book the child Max's imagination is presented as if it was real, and when sent to bed without any supper, Max transports us to an island of real monsters, where we join the wild rumpus and Max becomes king of the monsters.

Alongside the writers discussed above there emerged a number of authors who had a lengthy career in children's fantasy. Alan Garner began his writing career with the Alderley Edge sequence set in the part of Cheshire where he had grown up and to where he returned after leaving Oxford University at the end of his first year. In both *The Weirdstone of Brisingamen* (1960) and *The Moon of Gomrath*, Colin and Susan encounter figures from various mythological pasts including the Arthurian cycle. In the first book they recover the Weirdstone, a jewel which enabled one hundred and forty Arthurian knights to continue sleeping under the hill, while in the second book Susan is possessed by an evil spirit and the Wild Hunt is allowed into the world. Garner's third novel, *Elidor* (1965) also has analogies to the Arthurian cycle but takes place largely in a secondary world whose entrance is through an abandoned church in Manchester. The last of Garner's novels of the 1960s is *The Owl Service* (1967) which takes place largely in a contemporary Wales and draws on the medieval Welsh story cycle, *The Mabinogion*. *The Owl Service* is a tale of love recycled and a pattern imposed from the past: a figure from Welsh legend who has been imprisoned in a china plate depicting patterns of owls haunts three contemporary youngsters. After *The Owl Service* the tales became less classically fantastic (*Red Shift*, 1973, is a time shift novel) but with the exception of *Strandloper* (1996) also more local. Garner became fascinated with Cheshire and Cheshire dialect as an alternative basis for the fantastic. His linked stories, *The Stone Book Quartet* (assembled in 1983) are an exploration of the power of dialect and the magicality of the geology of Cheshire. This interest has culminated most recently in *Thursbitch* (2003) a novel set in two different times, one eighteenth century and one in the present day, and concerning the power of the remnants of Roman bull worship. The novel is written almost entirely in Cheshire dialect, asserting the power of an unfamiliar (and despised) language to create the sense of the fantastic and challenging the reader to consider why we take for granted the language we do. Alan Garner, as may be evident from that statement, was by the 1990s one of the more interesting critics of children's fantasy writing within the field (see *The Voice that Thunders*, 1997).

The other writer interested in Celtic fantasy traditions and in legends connected more closely with the land than the Arthurian mythos, was Lloyd Alexander. Alexander was an American writer, who served briefly in Wales during the Second World War. This short period had an immense influence on him, and the books that make up The Chronicles of Prydain are very clearly grounded both in the Welsh legends of *The Mabinogion* and in the landscape of that country. In the first book, *The Book of Three* (1964), Taran, an assistant pig-keeper, finds himself searching for his oracular pig, which has been kidnapped by the Horned King. Although the book has many moving moments, it is a relatively straightforward children's fantasy and the delight is frequently in the other characters: Eilonwy, the princess with the red-gold hair and the temper; Fflewddur Fflam, a bard whose harp-strings snap whenever he exaggerates; and Gurgi, a not-quite human creature desperately in search of his own nobility. At first sight these feel like stereotypes, but

Eilonwy is one of the very first really sparky fantasy heroines, mostly working at cross-purposes to Taran, and Fflewddur turns out to have reservoirs of unexpected courage. The later books get darker. In *The Black Cauldron* (1965), Taran's notions of heroism begin to disintegrate as he discovers the degree to which all heroism is contextual and sacrifice is truly painful. In *The Castle of Llyr* (1966), Eilonwy has to make choices between different kinds of power (in ways infuriating to a modern feminist reader), and in *The High King* (1968) there is a final assault on the king of the dead, and Taran and his companions are tested to their limits. Only when all hope is gone and some of his closest friends are dead is Taran elevated to the position of High King and, in a scene reminiscent of the end of *The Lord of the Rings*, faces the departure of magic. The overall trajectory of these novels is clearly influenced by Tolkien, but the fourth book in the series, which we have not yet mentioned, is rather different. In *Taran Wanderer* (1967) Taran sets off to try and find his parentage. He hopes to be proved noble, and thus be able to offer for the princess Eilonwy. The book does not go in quite the direction one expects. Taran is offered adoption by a king, and rejects it; he saves the life of a shepherd who falsely claims to be his father; he gives up his search, and instead three times apprentices himself to different craftsmen among the folk of the Free Commots. In defiance of classic fantasy tradition, Taran proves merely adequate at the trades he takes up (smithing, weaving, pottery). At the end of the book Taran does indeed find out who he is: he is Taran Wanderer.

The author Madeleine L'Engle is one of the few heirs to George MacDonald. She believed in the universal love of God, which caused her books to be banned from some Christian bookshops. Her science fantasies are clearly inflected with her religious belief but the most famous books can be read in complete ignorance of this. The first three Kairos books – *A Wrinkle in Time* (1962), *A Wind in the Door* (1974), and *A Swiftly Tilting Planet* (1978) – are all science fantasy novels in the first of which Meg Murry, her rather fragile brother Charles Wallace, and a high-school acquaintance, Calvin O'Keefe find themselves transported by Mrs Whatsit, Mrs Who and Mrs Which through the galaxy by means of a tesseract, to hold off a dark cloud, which in the very binary philosophy of these books is evil itself. They also find themselves rescuing Meg's father from an alien planet, and learn that Mrs Whatsit is a reincarnation of an exploded star. In subsequent books Meg defends the galaxy from the Echthroi, who wish to destroy the galaxy through un-naming. In *A Swiftly Tilting Planet* Charles Wallace changes the past in order to replace the dictator of a Latin American country with his might-have-been if his ancestor had married somebody else. Summarized in this way, the books feel like science fiction, but to read them in that mode sets them up for failure. To return to the link to George MacDonald, L'Engle is writing in a universe that thrums to the song of God. As in Lewis's work, stars are alive, and moral beings, and dimensional space is a theological rather than an astronomical concept. The books have lasted well, but do suffer for contemporary audiences because of the rather restricted ambitions permitted to Meg, whose role shifts through daughter, sister, girlfriend, wife.

Two writers whose careers as fantasy writers began in the 1960s and went from strength to strength over the next three decades are Joan Aiken and Roald Dahl. Both of them are writers who can be considered as having reconfigured whimsy, taking out its more nauseating traits and adding a wry and wicked spin. Joan Aiken has a reputation as a Gothic novelist for adults, as a fantasy novelist for children, and as a writer of outstanding short stories. Her Gothic novels for adults include *Castle Barebane* (1976) and a collection of linked stories called *The Haunting of Lamb House* (1981). Far better known are her children's novels, of which the first was *The Wolves of Willoughby Chase* (1963). This first novel sets up an alternate England, in which the Stuart dynasty has survived and James III has acceded to the throne in 1832. Britain is riddled with Hanoverian plotters. In the first book two children are made homeless by a wicked governess and assisted in escaping the orphanage and in reclaiming their home by a boy called Simon. In *Black Hearts in Battersea* (1964) Simon becomes embroiled with the Hanoverians and discovers that he is heir to a dukedom. Tucked into a corner of the plot, however, is Dido Twite, child of one of the plotters. It is Dido Twite's adventures that we follow through the remaining ten books. The plots get progressively more outrageous and fantastical, as villains resort to using superguns on Nantucket or stealing a lake in Peru. Outside of what comes to be known as the Dido Twite sequence are other series, including the Arabel and Mortimer series, many of which were read aloud on a children's TV programme (*Jackanory*) in the 1970s, and the Felix trilogy, beginning with *Go Saddle the Sea* in 1978. Aiken also has a Gothic novel set in the same world as the Dido Twite sequence called *Midnight is a Place*, which brought her to wider attention when it was broadcast on ITV. However, despite the popularity of all these books, it is as a short-story writer that Aiken has had immense influence on other fantasy writers.

Tracing Aiken's short stories is extremely difficult. There are over twenty short-story collections in which stories are reprinted, and the reader cannot assume that two collections with the same title, one published in the UK and one in the USA, contain the same stories. Edward James in *The St James Guide to Fantasy Writers* (3rd ed. 1996, p.11) divides her stories into three types: fairytales of traditional type, stories of "magic realism", in which magic appears as an accepted part of daily life, and ghost stories. A classic fairytale from Aiken is "The Rose of Puddlefrattrum" (1972). A leading ballerina slips on a banana skin hidden under the rose petals, breaks her leg, and curses the ballet to be plagued with jinxes until it is performed by one-legged dancers: the "fairy's" curse is undone when robots perform the ballet. A ghost story of Aiken's can be simultaneously sinister and comforting. In "Humblepuppy" (1972) a ghost puppy is found in a box from a job-lot at an auction. The puppy is never seen, but can be felt, whimpering and flinching from an imagined blow. After caring for the puppy for some months, the family leaves it with a vicar while they go on summer holiday, and they return to find that the puppy has switched its affection and has gained confidence at the same time. The story follows exactly the trajectory of the "laying down of ghosts", which one finds in a classic ghost story, but is told throughout with tenderness. "Humblepuppy" is also an example of a technique Aiken pioneered, in which magic becomes an integral part of an otherwise utterly recognizable scene, a sort of alternate 1950s. Many of Aiken's stories are told in a very mundane voice, in which magic is exciting in part because it is presented so ordinarily, but Aiken was capable of writing in a grander style. "A Harp of Fishbones" (1960) tells of a young girl who grows up an orphan, living with a miller beside a river. Occasionally gold appears in the river. One day a large carp tells her to kill it, eat it, and make a harp from the bones. She then follows the river and comes upon a once mighty city where everyone has turned to stone; they return to life when she plays her harp, and she finds that she is a princess of a city which has angered a goddess by falling in love with gold and neglecting her worship. This is a much more moralistic story than Aiken usually writes, and also stands out for its very delicate and intense description.

Roald Dahl's career began in the late 1940s, predominantly with short stories for adults, many of which were televised in 1979 as *Tales of the Unexpected*. His first children's book, *The Gremlins* (1943), has been largely ignored, but in 1961 he produced *James and the Giant Peach*, in which James escapes from his cruel aunts in a giant peach, and travels across the Atlantic with the insects living in the peach. In 1964 he published *Charlie and the Chocolate Factory* and over the next two decades, among other books, he published *Charlie and the Great Glass Elevator* (1973), *The BFG* (1982), *The Witches* (1983) and *Matilda* (1988). John Clute suggests that these do not quite cohere as fantasy, because there is a mildly absurdist wonderland feel to them. In the Charlie books, Charlie moves from a mundane poverty-stricken world into a Cockayne, in which candy grows on trees. In *The BFG*, Sophie spots the big friendly giant, who is a catcher of good dreams, which he sends on to children. Sophie and the BFG set out to defeat the other giants who want to eat children. The book expands outwards into an adventure which draws in the Queen, and the King of Sweden, and the Sultan of Baghdad. However, the book retains the child-like feel that marks out Dahl's writing, in that the punishments meted out to the giants involves eating nasty-tasting snozzcumbers. In *The Witches*, two children discover an organization of witches that aims to wipe out children, while in *Matilda* a five-year-old child who loves to read defeats her indifferent parents, her evil headmistress, and makes friends with the delightful young teacher Miss Honey. Matilda discovers she has telekinetic powers and uses them to terrify the headmistress (and aunt of Miss Honey). Dahl's work is delightful in the power it gives to children, and uses fantasy to emphasize the absurdities of the adult world. *Matilda* in particular shows strong links with *Alice*, in the way in which it depicts adults. However, *Charlie and the Chocolate Factory* has never escaped charges of racism despite several attempts to refigure the Oompa-Loompas. Although their colour has been changed several times, to black pigmies to rosy-white-skinned dwarves to orange skinned with green hair (in *Willy Wonka and the Chocolate Factory*, 1971) and back to brown skinned in the 2005 movie adaptation, in the end it is hard to avoid the fact that they are not permitted to leave the factory and are paid in cacao beans. Furthermore, while Dahl's female children have by the 1980s become spiky and proactive, on the basis of the adult role models in the books they have a future as either saint or witch. This said, however, the books are some of the best fantasy written for children.

Back in the world of fantasy for adults, whimsy continued to hold its position in the American scene. George Selden's *The Cricket in Times Square* (1960) tells of a musically talented cricket who travels from Connecticut to New York City, and makes friends with a small boy whose parents run a newsstand. This animal story sounds like a children's book, and in fact won the Newbery Honor Award, but was very successful as an adult book, with its wise-cracking tone, and fits a tradition of success stories popular in American fiction. One of the finest stories within the whimsical fantastic is Peter Beagle's *A Fine and Private Place* (1961), which he published when he was only 19. This is a very delicate story about a man who lives in a graveyard, two new ghostly inhabitants of the graveyard, and a lonely elderly woman. It throws up many questions about the nature of both life and death, and is notable for the way in which the graveyard seems far less threatening than the "real world" outside its gates. In 1968 Beagle followed this up with *The Last Unicorn*, in which a unicorn who thinks it may be the last of its kind goes looking for others. The book uses a fairytale structure in which the unicorn's encounters function as social satire and commentary upon both life and the nature of fantasy. *The Last Unicorn* might be seen as the first of an emerging counter-narrative to the oncoming Tolkien tsunami, because it was already questioning the assumptions behind the quest narrative. Also working with whimsy was Richard Brautigan, whose counter-cultural works, *A Confederate General from Big Sur* (1957), *Troutfishing in America* (1967) and *In Watermelon Sugar* (1968), are whimsical bordering on the surreal. John Bellairs, later to be known mostly for his children's fiction, produced in this period *The Face in the Frost* (1969), in which Prospero (but not Shakespeare's Prospero) and Roger Bacon go looking for a source of evil. The novel is a picaresque "bracelet" fantasy (in which each adventure could be removed, or another added, leaving the chain of the story intact), which concludes with Prospero finding another wizard in another world, who can defeat their enemy for them. It is the randomness of their adventures that distinguishes this book from the quest tradition: there are no moral gains and there is no sense of personal growth. And finally in this category it is worth mentioning Russell Hoban's *The Mouse and His Child* (1967), considered to be a classic of children's fiction, although in our experience it is not much liked by children despite its popularity among parents and critics. There are two clockwork mice, father and son; after being sold, the child mouse misses his friends in the toyshop and the two set off on a journey, meeting both threatening and friendly characters on the way. The book is full of philosophical discussion and its unflinching description of the harshness of life makes it a very late-1960s book, cousin to the many bitter reflections on war and injustice coming out of literature generally by the end of the decade.

CHAPTER SEVEN

The 1970s

ONE of the most important trends in the 1970s was the move of some science fiction writers across the border into a solid identification (at least on the part of their readers) with fantasy. Some of this was perception rather than a clear move on the part of the author. In the 1960s Ursula K. Le Guin published a number of planetary romances, which emerged from her own grounding in anthropology (her father was America's leading anthropologist in the inter-war period). Le Guin has continued to write science fiction, but the fantasy sequence she began in this period remains her best-known and best-loved work. The first of the Earthsea stories was *A Wizard of Earthsea* (1968), for which she created a full secondary world: islands in a great archipelago, housing many different cultures. As befits a fantasy world there is magic, and there are dragons, but even here there lingers the legacy of the science fiction writer, as it is the science that controls these which provides the impetus for the first and third book (*The Farthest Shore*, 1972) and the most recent two (*Tales from Earthsea*, 2001 and *The Other Wind*, 2001). The principal character is Ged whom we first meet at a School for Wizards, more brutal and lonely than anything Harry Potter experienced. In the first book, *The Wizard of Earthsea* (1968), the arrogant young Ged releases his own shadow and upsets the balance of the world. In the second, *The Tombs of Atuan* (1971) the mature Ged rescues Tenar, a young priestess, from the confines of her religious imprisonment and begins restoring the balance between light and dark, life and death; in the third of the initial trilogy, *The Farthest*

Shore (1972), Ged (now an Archmage) journeys to the underworld in order to mend a new rift in the universe, but does so at the cost of his own wizardly powers.

The Earthsea books offered three very powerful elements. The first was the idea that the Word was powerful and true names incredibly so, an idea about magic which we can see recurring at regular points throughout this century of fantasy literature. The other two are inherently political. Although television and anime adaptations of the Earthsea series have ignored this, Ged is *brown* and so are all his people. Only when he heads out to other lands does he meet people with pale skin. For readers in the 1960s, accustomed to heavily orientalized fantasy worlds, this normalization of the world of non-white people, and orientalization of whites, was shocking. What is unnerving is that it is still a shock for many readers, and evidence from the classroom is that many do not even notice, continuing to read the texts through their own cultural filters. The final, and far less straightforward issue, is Le Guin's relationship to the fictional construction of gender and to the feminist movement within science fiction, much of the argument of which has been played out within these books. The first three books use constructions of gender (for example, that only men can become wizards) which belong very much to the 1950s. Subsequent books very consciously address this. Later the first three books were repackaged for adults while their sequels were clearly intended for adults, but even in its first iteration the Earthsea sequence had a significant impact on adult readers, enough that a writer otherwise entirely associated with science fiction is considered one of the great fantasy writers of our time.

Le Guin's "science fictional" take on building a fantasy world can be seen even more clearly in the works of Roger Zelazny, Marion Zimmer Bradley and Anne McCaffrey. All three created science fiction worlds that became almost indistinguishable from fantasy, and by mid-way within their series were being understood and marketed in this way with the assumption that it was a selling point, indicating the degree to which fantasy was slowly edging ahead of sf in popularity.

The Chronicles of Amber by Roger Zelazny started in 1970 with *Nine Princes in Amber*. The narrator of the first five novels is Corwin, whom we meet in a New York hospital, suffering from amnesia. When he recovers his memory, he continues his struggle to gain dominance within his superhuman family, who are able to travel between an infinite number of parallel worlds. The premise is loosely science fictional, but the execution is affiliated with fantasy and with the trappings of the Gothic (castles, dungeons, magical artefacts, family secrets). The movement between worlds allows Zelazny to construct a fantastical meta-text with a great deal of humour – on one occasion, Corwin's son Merlin takes tea in Wonderland, escaping with the help of a jabberwocky – but he discovers that Wonderland is an LSD-induced hallucination, reinvigorating the link with science fiction. There are ten novels in all, the second five concentrating on Merlin (the last, *Prince of Chaos*, was published in 1991).

Marion Zimmer Bradley's Darkover series began with "The Planet Savers" published in 1958 in *Amazing* (an sf fiction magazine) and published in book form in 1962. Darkover is a planet settled by shipwrecked humans in the distant past of the story and at the time the series opens has been rediscovered by an exploring Terran empire. In the time of their isolation, the original settlers developed a pseudo-early-medieval society, with guilds, modesty laws and rather constricted roles for women. Within the society there is also a group whom the Terrans see as a priestly caste (they are not), marked by red hair and claiming telepathic and telekinetic powers. During the 1960s the Darkover novels were about the clash between cultures of the local humans and the incoming Terrans and one of the things that makes these novels more than averagely interesting is the misunderstandings around the issue of what technology is: the Terrans are far too quick to assume the Darkovans "backward".

From the early 1970s Bradley published a whole series of novels which shifted the focus to the very point at which Terrans had to deal with the nature of the abilities of the Comyn, the red-headed "mage" and "matrix" workers of Darkover, and then later to Darkover during the period of isolation. The effect of this was a series of novels indistinguishable from fantasy. *Darkover Landfall* (1972) returned to the original shipwreck, and explained the origin of the powers of the Comyn as a result of inter-breeding with the indigenous sentient life-form, who just happen to look a lot like fantasy elves and are understood that way by the superstitious (of course) Scottish-descended settlers. In *The Spell Sword* (1974) a stranded earthman is absorbed into a Comyn family; in *The Heritage of Hastur* (1975) a powerful matrix is brought back to Darkover; in *The Shattered Chain* (1976) we see the south of Darkover and a rather determined critique of John Norman's pornographic Gor books (see *Raiders of Gor*, 1971) which were also becoming popular in this period (set on a fantasy world in which women *like* being sex slaves and Earthmen experience true liberation); in *The Forbidden Tower* (1976) four Comyn join together in an effort to restore the "old ways" of power and revive the powers of the Comyn which are understood to have faded. Two novels are entirely set in the time of Isolation: *Stormqueen!* (1978), a tale of a young girl born with the talent to raise the winds, but a talent which is inimical to her own survival, and *Two to Conquer* (1980), a tale of a rogue talent, again involving the transplanting of an Earthman, this time kidnapped by telekinesis from Earth. These last two novels are both tales of the civil wars on Darkover and are interesting for filling in a specific piece of background. When the Terrans arrive on Darkover they are alienated by a piece of consensus law called The Compact: this requires that all weapons bring the user within arm's reach of their target. The solipsistic Terrans assume that this is directed against ballistic weaponry (guns and bombs) and see it as an anti-technology bias. It is in *Stormqueen!* and *Two to Conquer* that we discover that matrix technology can operate at the nuclear level, and it is the *Terrans* who are protected by the Compact, not the "primitive" Darkovans from Terran weaponry.

Throughout the Darkover books there is the constant sense of a science-fictional understanding of the way worlds work which has allowed the books to be read as both sf and fantasy. We will see this positioning later among writers such as Mary Gentle, Steph Swainston, and K.J. Parker, and it produces a very specific inflection to fantasy which is not popular among all fantasy readers, some of whom believe this sense of the logic of the world brings us too close to the mundane. However, at this time Bradley was also writing Tolkienian fantasy actually set in Middle-earth – *The Jewel of Arwen* (1974) and *The Parting of Arwen* (1974) – and while these were not widely available this indicated a longer trend in her career which, after the Darkover books, would move into Arthurian romance.

The crossover of Anne McCaffrey into fantasy was one of reader/audience appropriation. Her early work was all science fiction and indeed her Pern sequence begins with a Hugo Award-winning science fiction story published in *Analog*, the home of the hardest of sf. The conceit of Pern is a planet long colonized by humans, but who in the process of adapting to the conditions of the planet – and particularly the threat of an attack by a corrosive and living rain called Thread, coming from a neighbouring planet – have lost their technological base and constructed a "medievalist" world of guilds, castles and feudal lords. The first book *Dragonflight* (1968) was issued with a prologue proposed by *Analog's* editor, John W. Campbell, which emphasized that this was *science fiction*. This was necessary, because the central and glorious characters of the Pern stories are those ultimate fantasy icons, dragons.

Pern's dragons have been bred from small lizards native to the planet whose capacity for creating fire had been noted by the early settlers. The fire-eating properties of the dragons had proven a low-tech means of fighting thread, which could be destroyed only by fire. To add to the popularity of dragons with Pern's fans, dragons were communicated with through telepathy, but only by an individual who "impressed" a dragon and was paired with it for life; furthermore, dragons could travel through "between", a hyper-space described in fantasy terms, and as we also find out, through time. More than one critic has commented that these books are essentially the girl fantasy of owning a pony of her very, very own, and being able to *talk* to it.

McCaffrey never abandoned the science-fictional rationale, but it is more visible in some novels than in others. The first two novels, *Dragonflight* and *Dragonquest* were shaped by the notion of science and scientific prediction returning to the world, but all knowledge was held by that staple of fantasy novels, the harpers who teach children through song. A later novel, *All the Weyrs of Pern*, took the books back to their sf roots when the harpers/bards and the dragonriders, discover the spaceship on which the settlers arrived, and realize , and welcome that the "fantasy" Pern to which they belong is dying. But in between is a set of novels placed entirely within the world of Pern, and also – not coincidentally – in the harper hall. The Harper books are *Dragonsong* (1976), *Dragonsinger* (1977), and *Dragondrums* (1979). In the first two, Menolly, the daughter of a fisher hall, discovers her musical abilities but hides them because women don't become harpers. She is discovered by a visiting harper and whisked away to the harper hall, where she goes through various trials of fitting in, and eventually emerges as journeyman harper. In *Dragondrums,* young Piemur is devastated when his voice breaks just before he is due to sing a major solo; he is transferred to the drumheights where he annoys the other apprentices by learning the drum rolls that are used to communicate messages across Pern twice as fast as everyone else. An apprentice trick almost kills him and his own curiosity lands him on Pern's South Continent where he foils a plot by the Old Timers, dragonriders brought back from the past in the first book in the series. These three books and sequels written in the 1980s and 1990s feel like full fantasy: they are essentially explorations of the cultural structures of a world very far from ours. The settings and language of the books chime with fantasy also, as each is structured around legends and ballads, particularly *Moreta: Dragonlady of Pern* (1983), which brings to life a teaching song which readers have encountered several times.

Before we leave McCaffrey a final point needs to be made that in the 1970s McCaffrey was one of the writers who were taking to heart the demand for "character". In her work this frequently meant romance which sometimes appeared in forms that are unnerving to modern eyes: smart women are forever falling for muscular men who force them to realise their innate heterosexuality through coerced sex. But hidden away in the Pern books was also something which many readers missed, but which later books acknowledged. On Pern, a gold (female) dragon has a female rider, while all the other colour dragons have male riders. Riders mate when their dragons mate. So far so good. But of all the other colours of dragons (blue, brown, bronze and green) only green dragons are female, and when green dragons mate it leaves open the question as to whether their male riders have sex with the riders of the other dragon. It took until *Moreta* for the obvious to be stated aloud, but for those readers alert for such nuances, McCaffrey's refusal to explain away this logic was an enormously important contribution to the rise of gay and lesbian fantasy in this period.

Norton, Zelazny, McCaffrey and Bradley repopularized the notion of a science fantasy, in which the trappings were fantastical but the paradigm was sf: one of the best of the new writers to pick this up was C.J. Cherryh, who began her Morgaine sequence with *Gate of Ivrel* in 1978. In these books we have gates allowing time travel between worlds, but Morgaine can destroy them with her sword, which in good medieval fantasy tradition has a name: Changeling.

The 1970s also saw the rise of new ways of using history in fantasy. The fantasy of the nineteenth century had tended to use medieval settings while paying relatively little attention to the implications of the medieval context. One of the consequences of Tolkien's work was to turn people's attention to real history and to real legend, and we begin to see fantasy writers consciously exploiting this material in a number of different ways. The two main streams can be divided into an attempt to construct a "real" Middle Ages and to write "real" stories behind "the myth".

When we look at the list of titles we grouped together under the pre-quest medievalist fantasies, what immediately strikes one is the lack of any common ground. They range from pure mythological creation, as in Tolkien's *The Silmarillion* (published posthumously in 1977), through to ironic and humorous riffs on medieval tradition such as the series that Gordon R. Dickson launched in 1976, with *The Dragon and the George*. *The Silmarillion* was edited by Tolkien's son, Christopher, together with the fantasy writer Guy Gavriel Kay, who tried to make sense of the hundreds of fragments, written over a fifty-year period, that Tolkien had left. It begins with an almost biblical description of the creation of Middle-earth and then offers a number of largely disconnected stories of the doings of elves and men in the period before the events of *The Hobbit* begin. Even some dedicated Tolkien fans found it unreadable; however, the principle of its compilation is itself relevant, because this notion of a "found text", pieced together from fragments to become "a truth", becomes one of the classic tropes of the quest fantasy in the next decade. Dickson's *The Dragon and the George* (1976), the start of a series, is as serious in its own way as *The Silmarillion*. The protagonist is a young man from Earth who finds himself in a pseudo-medieval world in the body of a dragon. In a sense this is a Marxist take on fantasy, in that it asks rather rigorous questions about how the world works, from the point of view of one of its victims.

Similarly, these texts range in period from recreations of early Middle Ages pagan ritual as in Tanith Lee's *East of Midnight* (1977), through to the fully fledged chivalry of the later Middle Ages as in Astrid Lindgren's *The Brothers Lionheart* (1973). The inspiration also varies from the world of the Vikings to Celtic-inspired fantasy, such as Patricia McKillip's trilogy beginning with *The Riddle Master of Hed* (1976).

Tanith Lee's *East of Midnight* tells of a young slave pulled by magic into a world of sacrificial royal consorts. The setting feels early-medieval, but the language is often courtly and there is more than an element of orientalism. Tanith Lee wrote nine fantasy novels in the 1970s, and more in the 1980s and 1990s, and she is one of the most talented people in the field today. Her most characteristic technique is to plunder and twist historical periods, so that in her later Venus novels (*Faces Under*

Water, 1998 and others), an eighteenth-century Venice becomes a place of the goddess Venus, subject to her romance and caprice.

Astrid Lindgren is the Swedish children's writer best known outside that country, although mostly for her Pippi Longstocking books. In 1973 she published *The Brothers Lionheart*, a hugely controversial fantasy about the two brothers, Karl and Jonatan: Karl is dying, but when a fire breaks out in their apartment, Jonatan takes Karl on his back and jumps. Jonatan dies, but promises to see Karl in Nangijala. When he dies and finds himself in Nangijala, Karl meets Jonatan settled in a cottage and a community. But all is not well: the community is threatened by soldiers and a dragon. The two boys set out on a journey to kill the dragon, in a quest which owes more to *Beowulf* than to King Arthur. Jonatan is fatally burned by the dragon and the book concludes with Karl taking Jonatan on *his* back and jumping off a cliff so that both can arrive in the next land, Nangilima, together. It is this ending – in which a children's book ends with a young boy committing suicide – that caused the controversy. It is, however, very moving. Lindgren's world feels fanciful rather than full fantasy, because it uses Norse notions of levels of the underworld, seen to a degree in David Lindsay's *A Voyage to Arcturus* (1920) and picked up by Gene Wolfe for his *The Wizard Knight* (*The Wizard*, and *The Knight*, two volumes, 2004) but which is otherwise rather rare.

Probably the most popular and influential of the medievalist fantasies were those in the series begun by Katherine Kurtz in 1970. These books are known as the Deryni series after a race of people with telepathic and other psi powers, and so far there are five distinct trilogies within the series (a phenomenon we will return to when we look at series fantasy at the end of the chapter). The first trilogy (1970–3) concerns Kelson Haldane who, over the course of two weeks, is trying to defend his throne from Deryni rivals while at the same time protecting friends who belong to the same race from the prejudice of others. Later trilogies fill in the story both before and after the time of Kelson. The setting is rather specific in that it corresponds to a history of the British Isles around the year 1100, with an absolutely feudal church and a fairly accurate picture of the physical trappings of the high medieval period. The linguistic details, however, would have made Tolkien weep. In real Britain, our tangle of place names reflects our history of settlement. In Middle-earth, Tolkien devised a whole new set of naming conventions to reflect past settlement histories. Kurtz, while using Tolkien's idea of full creation, selected names from various British settlement traditions, mixing the Welsh arbitrarily with the English and Irish. The result is that instead of being immersed in an "other" world, a reader with an understanding of history (and fantasy attracts many) is constantly irritated (and yes, one of the authors of this book *is* a professional medievalist). If one can ignore this, the mixture of medieval ritual and ecclesiastical ceremony with magic is a fascinating one, and her books have been popular for over three decades.

An alternate mode of creating medieval fantasy can be found in Randall Garrett's Lord Darcy books. In these books the medieval world was a magical one, but the stories – *Too Many Magicians* (1966), and two collections, *Murder and Magic* (1979), and *Lord Darcy Investigates* (1981) – are set in the twentieth century in a world in which the Plantagenet Empire never fell and in which King John had never ruled and Richard I was succeeded by his nephew Arthur. These stories are witty investigations in which the medieval mind-set extended into the present provides much of the pleasure.

M. John Harrison, John Brunner, Patricia McKillip and Phyllis Eisenstein all used a relatively conventional chivalric setting but their characters tended to be displaced in these settings, wanderers through their world rather than part of it. M. John Harrison (*The Pastel City*, 1971) uses a chivalric setting of knights and chargers but set at the end of the world and framed by ennui. The protagonist is a knight errant, whose magic fails him, and eventually he turns away from the world. In John Brunner's *The Traveller in Black* (1971), the traveller moves across a landscape of magic, trying to move the world from the region of Chaos (magic) to Order (unavoidable consequence). Both Harrison and Brunner use characters who cut across the medievalism which surrounds them, puncturing the carefully constructed notion of another time, another place.

McKillip's Riddle Master trilogy, which began with *The Riddle Master of Hed*, in 1976, concentrates upon Morgon, prince of a small island. He is a "land-ruler": he is aware of everything (every animal and every rock) in his realm – an animist notion that we will see becoming more common in the work of fantasy writers in the 1980s and 1990s. When he sets out to claim his bride, his ship is attacked by shape-changers and he loses his memory and powers of speech. The rest of the trilogy is about discovering his place in the world and he ends by becoming the High One, who oversees the land-rule linkage between monarchs and their realms. Phyllis Eisenstein's protagonist in *Born to Exile* (1978) is a wandering minstrel, with the ability to teleport, whose loose adventures take him across the land. In *Sorcerer's Son* (1979), the child of two magic users, conceived in rivalry and hatred, sets out to find his father, and in the process undoes the social order that relies on enslaved demons.

Some "medievalist" fantasies of this period are set in the present, frequently hovering on the borders of horror. These fictions were and are about the legacy of the past disrupting our sense of what is "normal", the sense that our natural selves and our link to nature is always lurking. Alan Garner's *The Owl Service* (which we discussed in the previous chapter), his 1973 *Red Shift*, Penelope Lively's *The Wild Hunt of Hagworthy* (1971) and the 1973 movie, *The Wicker Man* (dir. Robin Hardy) all deal with the eruption of pre-Christian powers into the modern world. Lively's story is about a town taken over by the ritual it chose to enact on a May Day. *The Wicker Man* is an even more frightening tale of a small Scottish island that chooses paganism over Christianity. Garner's *Red Shift* is based on the ballad of "Tam Lin". All three of these books are about re-configuring tales, re-evaluating stories, and the power of story in shaping human behaviour.

The 1970s saw some exceptional contributions to the tradition of retelling of the fantasies of the past, above all myths, legends and fairytales. *The Rocky Horror Picture Show* (1975, dir. Jim Sharman), a retelling of *Frankenstein*, was perhaps the most subversive – and the one with the most staying power – but there were many more conventional approaches. Evangeline Walton added three more volumes to the retelling of *The Mabinogion* that she had begun before the Second World War. Thomas Burnett Swann produced a series of texts exploring ancient Greek setting, including *The Forest of Forever* (1971) and *Cry Silver Bells* (1977). Three standout writers, including two who wrote relatively little fantasy, were William Goldman, Elizabeth Marie Pope and Robin McKinley. William Goldman was a very prolific writer in other contexts but *The Princess Bride* (1973, filmed 1987) is his one fantasy. This book purports to be a retelling of a true history, only the originating book does not exist and neither does the country. Goldman has combined the traditions of swashbuckling cinema, classic fairytale constructions and a wicked sense of humour, and the whole book is a meditation upon story-telling; its nearest cousin is possibly William Thackeray's *The Rose and the Ring*. Elizabeth Marie Pope's *The Perilous Gard* (1975) takes place in England in the 1500s, and is a reworking of the Tam Lin story. Kate discovers an underground route to Faerie and has to save a young man called Christopher from the pact he has made with the Queen of the Fairies. This novel is one of the first to choose the Elizabethan period as a setting for fantasy.

More classically, Robin McKinley's first book was *Beauty* (1978), a retelling of the Beauty and the Beast fairytale, which transposes the story into a real-life setting. In this version Beauty is actually very plain and her name, an embarrassing childish nickname, is one she would love to dispense with. The story maintains the magic, but is reinterpreted to readers as prosaically as possible. McKinley has written several more retellings, including a second retelling of Beauty and the Beast, *Rose's Daughter* (1997), and most memorably *Deerskin* (1993), in which the story of the princess whose father falls in love with her (Perrault's "Donkeyskin") is rendered graphically alongside a story of a kind Moon goddess. In the 1980s McKinley also wrote two stories called *The Blue Sword* (1982) and *The Hero and the Crown* (1984). Although not in themselves retellings, these stories are precisely about the retelling of history and the way in which myth narrative is constructed and becomes powerful. At the end of McKinley's *The Blue Sword* the protagonist has to choose between life with an immortal or with a mortal man. There is a sudden moment of shock when one realizes that she has chosen both. We are in a different kind of fantasy, one in which suddenly many of the assumptions of courtly romance taken for granted in much of the fantasy literature of the previous one hundred years are gone, and we are on unstable sexual ground. How did this happen?

The effects of feminism were felt in science fiction from the mid-1960s onwards, although not all the writers whom feminists now embrace would have been comfortable with the term. Similarly in fantasy, while there are some writers from the 1930s (C.L. Moore, Leslie F. Stone) who are recognizably feminist, many of the female writers we have already talked about would have rejected the term. Even a writer such as Marion Zimmer Bradley, who in the 1980s would produce some hard-core lesbian separatist fantasy, in the 1970s was still writing plots structured around heteronormative romance. Yet seemingly out of nowhere, several books and at least one film (*The Stepford Wives*, dir. Bryan Forbes, screenplay by William Goldman, 1974) in the 1970s broke through and well beyond the conventional parameters of gender assumptions in fantasy literature. We go from fantasy in which women barely exist or are prizes, to independent Amazons and homosexual warlords almost overnight. Two of the greatest writers in science fiction, Joanna Russ and Samuel R. Delany, each produced in the second half of this decade books which could be considered as either science fiction or fantasy, but which in terms of the tropes they played with were clearly informed by, and arguing with, the fantasy traditions. Joanna Russ's *The Adventures of Alyx* (1976) is a collection of linked stories about a small wiry adventuress, who has at some point abandoned her husband and who moves through the world taking on jobs as they arise. Sometimes she defeats the men around her, sometimes she is compromised, but always Alyx remains fundamentally herself. In a number of her adventures Alyx critiques the narrative structure to explain why it is patriarchal nonsense (although she never uses this term). Reading these stories one is continually unnerved by Alyx's casual reactions to matters of honour and glory: all the things that matter in fantasy seem a bit silly and childish to Alyx. Samuel R. Delany's *Tales of Nevèrÿon* (1979) is also a collection of tales about Gorgik, a brown man of a respectable family, who is captured and taken to work as a slave in a context where most slaves are pale-skinned. Gorgik is the classic muscular giant of sword-and-sorcery (the kind Alyx rather fancies but tends to discard); but he is also bisexual. Delany took the well-recognised homosexual subtext of much sword-and-sorcery imagery, which many critics have noted, and by making it the actual subject matter produced a much more grown-up sexuality, one which was highly politicized in terms of the social structure of Nevèrÿon. The Nevèrÿon tales, like the stories of Alyx, set out to unpick taken-for-granted narrative causalities within the sword-and-sorcery/fantasy genres. It is as if once one begins to question the taken-for-granted of gender and sexuality, everything one thinks one knows about history, politics and economics becomes unravelled. These two books have been enormously influential in creating space for fantasy authors who wish to produce radical constructions of society.

The degree to which these new, radical ideas were accepted by the fantasy community was shown by the World Fantasy Award voted to Elizabeth A. Lynn for her *Watchtower* (1979), the first of the Chronicles of Tornor. This book starts like any conventional fantasy: a castle is lost to an invading barbarian; the prince, Errel, and his vassal, the graceless and narrow-minded Ryke, escape. But assisting their escape are two apparent hermaphrodites, Sorren and Norres. In this society, hermaphrodites are considered strange but within the social body (like hijira). Barely has the reader recovered from this shock (Ursula K. Le Guin's *The Left Hand of Darkness*, with its hermaphroditic population appeared as recently as 1969 and was still considered *outré*), than we discover that in fact they are two women, specifically two women in a sexual relationship with each other. The four protagonists then travel to the home village of the women where Ryke is further shocked to discover that women are respected equally alongside men and that this society has no leaders and no warriors. All the pillars of his patriarchal world are rendered here as unnecessary and perhaps slightly childish. The greatest blow that Ryke receives, however, comes from within: Prince Errel, in any other fantasy the locus of all hopes, doesn't actually want his principality back and cedes it to Sorren. In the sequel, *The Dancers of Arun* (1979) Sorren is long dead, and several generations have lived and died. The protagonist is a distant descendant of Sorren and the story focuses both on his discovery of telepathic abilities and on his homosexuality. Just in case you thought you could relax now, this relationship is with his brother, rendered normal, loving and natural within the text. Alongside these radical reworkings of fantasy, we also have the work of Angela Carter, whose approach to fairytale in the 1970s, collected in *The Bloody Chamber and Other Stories* (1979), ripped any remaining lace and taffeta from the courtly tales of Perrault. Carter's versions of the fairytales involve trickery, rape and mutilation: Grimm written in silk, velvet and blood. Although her work is not strictly feminist (feminists frequently get short shrift in her work) later writers in this area such as Nalo Hopkinson and Margo Lanagan are clearly working in the same vein [sic].

Previously, when we talked of a "series", we meant a lengthy run of books originating in a single book that happened to become popular. Examples of this include Andre Norton's Witch World or Robert E. Howard's Conan stories; sequels are written and the story of the main character and, if the series continues, other characters may be added. Although we hesitate to suggest that the change was ever planned, when Piers Anthony created his Xanth series, he appears to have created a very different kind of series fantasy, and one which would be a template for other authors (most notably Terry Pratchett). We are here going to dub this "theatre fantasy": the fantasy world provides a theatre stage on which stories can be played out. In the first book, *A Spell for Chameleon* (1977) Bink is expelled from Xanth for having no magic and during his adventures meets a woman whose beauty, temper and intelligence wax and wane with the phases of the Moon – making literal men's perception of women's menstrual cycle. Some of the books combine flippant joking with meditations on philosophy and logic. *Golem in the Gears* (1986), for example, contains an extensive discussion of a game-theory concept known as Prisoner's Dilemma.[13] Once the Xanth series got going however, it was increasingly the *world* that was of interest rather than the characters. This is not to dismiss the stories and plots of the early books, all of which are memorable, but by the third or fourth book of a thirty-two book series (numbers 33 and 34 are due in 2009 and 2010) we realize that we are in a game. What can the author do with the world he has created? Xanth is a world of magic, structured around puns. Its inhabitants live in an animated environment in which a firm grip on puzzles, crossword techniques and riddles is essential for survival. It is a theatre, and in each book we get to watch a different story performed. One element in the development of these books was a growing closeness between Anthony and his readers. Many of his books end with a discussion of correspondence and a list of those who had provided useful puns. In this way readers have helped build the world and again contribute to the sense that it is the world that matters.

Another writer to construct a theatre world was Robert Lynn Asprin, with his MythAdventures series (begun in 1978 and with several in press at his death in 2008). In these books a protagonist moves through different kinds of worlds, each of which has its own rules for magic and technology. They are puzzle books in which negotiating the worlds is

---

13   A two person bargaining game in which there are three outcomes. Two prisoners are held incommunicado: both confess and are punished; both refuse to confess and both escape, or one confesses and the other holds out leading to the hold-out being punished only. This game is the basis of all succeeding logic and bargaining games and underlies much international negotiation.

the game. Each of the books contains the word *Myth* in its title, usually as a mispronunciation for another word, creating a pun, as in *Myth Conceptions* (1980). Another theatre world created by Robert Lynn Asprin was the "shared universe" of Thieves' World. Prior to this series, writing in someone else's world was either the purview of amateurs, or of professional writers writing for hire (novelizations of *Doctor Who* or *Star Trek* for example). Asprin's *Thieves' World* is something else and its impact is such that it requires us to introduce you to a new idea, the "creator copyright universe". This simply means that a writer is using a world *he or she* has created. Before the late 1970s this would have been taken for granted. By the end of the century however, many sf and fantasy authors are writing in two contexts, within their own "creator copyright" worlds, but also in "licensed" worlds such as the extremely profitable and professional *Star Trek* and *Star Wars* franchises, in ways which are *not* novelizations of scripts, but which allow the authors to stage any story within the licensed world, sometimes in ways which are subversive of that world's ideology.

Thieves' World was Asprin's creation. It is a stage set which he has loaned to other writers in order to create a collaborative performance. Most of the Thieves' World stories are set in the city of Sanctuary, a rundown spot on the edge of a great empire, inhabited by criminals, sorcerers, gods and other standard fantasy characters. The tone is drawn from Leiber. Asprin created Thieves' World as a project to which he could invite writer colleagues to contribute: the idea was that he established the ground rules of the world, but the characters and plots they staged in his "theatre" was left to contributing authors. He was in effect an "actor-manager" of his fantasy world. The writers included such well-known names as Poul Anderson, Marion Zimmer Bradley, John Brunner and C.J. Cherryh. There were twelve anthologies in all between 1979 and 1989, during which most of the authors created lengthy story lines for their own characters, but it was quite normal for one writer's protagonist to have a walk on part in another writer's story. Each author's story cycle could run across several anthologies. Marion Zimmer Bradley eventually left the series but took her character Lythande with her, and also in the 1990s opened her own Darkover series to a similar collaboration with her fans, a number of whom moved on to construct their own "creator copyright" universes. There were official novels in the series too, and in 1981, a Thieves' World role-playing game was launched by Chaosium which allowed its fans as well as its official authors to create new narratives.

Of course, *Sanctuary*, the Thieves' World game, was not the first of the major fantasy RPGs (role-playing games). That honour goes to *Dungeons and Dragons*, a set of rules for creating a fantasy adventure first released by Gary Gygax and Dave Arneson in 1974. The impact of *Dungeons and Dragons* is huge: by creating a *system* of game play, it made possible game play among strangers. This book does not have room to list all the major games that have emerged from it, but *Dungeons and Dragons* helped to create LARPing (live action role play in which players physically represent the characters they are playing) and fed into the nascent computer industry whose gaming arm is now dominated by fantasy games using very similar role-playing rules to *Dungeons and Dragons*. These games have moved from text based multi-user dimensions (MUDs) through to the vivid animation and "virtuality" of *World of Warcraft* (a sword-and-sorcery game) and *Second Life* (a live action environment). Among writers, fan-fiction in which amateur writers swap stories set in other people's universes, often to a highly professional standard, over the internet has become a form of literature in itself. We will discuss that when we consider the role of the internet in chapters nine and eleven.

In 1977 two books and two movies appear like giant icebergs in the ocean of fantasy: whether you regard them as incredibly beautiful objects of the natural sublime or ship wreckers depends entirely on what kind of fantasy you like. George Lucas's *Star Wars* was a fairytale movie set in "a galaxy far, far away". Steven Spielberg's *Close Encounters of the Third Kind* revisioned elves as small grey creatures come from another planet to play us a bar of music, and return abductees. Terry

Brooks published *The Sword of Shannara*, the first in a continuing series which has kept at least two fantasy publishing lines going, and Stephen R. Donaldson's *Lord Foul's Bane*, the first in the chronicles of Thomas Covenant. All four of these texts are *quests*, quests for something so magnificent that securing it will change the course of history. Between them, these texts determined not so much what would be written in the next thirty years but what would dominate the book shelves of Barnes and Noble, Waterstone's, and other chain book stores. The era of the multi-volume quest fantasy had arrived.

George Lucas's *Star Wars* and its two sequels had all the trapping of science fiction, but its structure – as Lucas has described – is taken straight from Joseph Campbell's *The Hero with a Thousand Faces*. Specifically it is a *Bildungsroman*, in which the protagonist is discovered as an unknown, deals with various trials, tribulations and challenges, to emerge at the end as a hero. The text is also a fairytale of the uncrowned hidden prince and his companions. There is nothing subtle about these movies, but they captivated millions and sparked a revival of the cinema of the fantastic. Spielberg's *Close Encounters of the Third Kind* is a more complex movie, essentially science fiction in its rhetoric and trappings, in which we see a series of vignettes as individual characters move along their own path to the eventual meeting with the aliens/elves/gods. This vignette structure, in which we follow separated individuals towards a common goal, will turn into one of the recognizable tropes of the quest fantasy, as it becomes quite obvious to writers of quest fantasies that this is a really easy way to expand a novel into a trilogy. Although technically these two films stand outside this book (they are usually marketed as sf) their popularity was clearly connected to the dramatic reaction among fantasy readers to the work of Brooks and Donaldson.

What is perhaps most astonishing about the first volumes of the series by Brooks and Donaldson is the degree to which Tolkien's work is visible. Brooks sets his series in a far-future, dying, post-scientific world, but the protagonist, Shea, lives in The Vale (The Shire) and is visited by a great wizard called Allanon (Gandalf) who tells him the story of the wars between Men, Dwarves and Elves. Shea's destiny is to recover a thing of power (destroy a ring) with a band of companions (two elves, two men – one of whom is a Prince who keeps regretting his own lack of princeliness – and a dwarf). *The Sword of Shannara* feels as if someone had set out to produce a scaled-down model of *The Lord of the Rings*. Indeed, this is what Terry Brooks himself said in 2003:

> ...in 1965, I read J.R.R. Tolkien's The Lord of the Rings and I thought that maybe I had found what I was looking for. I would set my adventure story in an imaginary world, a vast, sprawling, mythical world like that of Tolkien, filled with magic that had replaced science and races that had evolved from Man. But I was not Tolkien and did not share his background in academia or his interest in cultural study. So I would eliminate the poetry and songs, the digressions on the ways and habits of types of characters, and the appendices of language and backstory that characterized and informed Tolkien's work. I would write the sort of straightforward adventure story that barrelled ahead, picking up speed as it went, compelling a turning of pages until there were no more pages to be turned.[14]

Numerous episodes recall Tolkien: there is a great tentacled monster in a pool watching over caverns of treasure and Allanon fights an evil being over a chasm and they both fall into a pit, although Allanon survives. The ending, however, is different, and sets the pattern for those whom China Miéville calls "The Tolkienistas". Where Tolkien's heroes were attempting to get rid of the thing of power, Brooks's protagonists, and the protagonists of endless quest fantasies to come after, are *competing for* the thing of power. Tom Shippey wrote, "Anyone who had not read *The Lord of the Rings* might find it highly innovative – but I doubt that many of its original readers fell into that category. What *The Sword of Shannara* seems to show is that many readers had developed the taste (the addiction) for heroic fantasy so strongly that if they could not get the real thing they would take any substitute, no matter how diluted" (Shippey, *J.R.R. Tolkien: Author of the Century*, p.320). The Shannara

---

14   Terry Brooks, *Sometimes the Magic Works: Lessons from a Writing Life*. New York: Del Rey, 2003, p.188.

books are still being written, and have moved away from this straight imitation, but the legacy of the first book is powerful.

On the face of it, Stephen Donaldson created something very different from Tolkien. The world of Thomas Covenant deliberately sets out to reverse some of the expectations of the fantasy genre: in our world Thomas is a leper, ostracized, isolated, and increasingly mentally ill. When he finds himself in another world, he is ill prepared to accept the role of saviour that is thrust upon him. A doubting Thomas, he commits rape and treachery, partially because in this world he is not a leper and can maintain an erection, partially because he doesn't believe the world he is in is real, and also because the bit of him that does believe it, refuses to believe he is good or pure enough for this world. The elements which are reminiscent of Tolkien, however, include the plot and the settings. The plot is pretty thin stuff: the world is threatened by a dark lord, and Thomas is the only hope for salvation because he and the dark lord share a mental link. The setting of the world maps onto Middle-earth: at the beginning we have a cave-wight recovering a talisman (much like Gollum and his ring), Tolkien's ring-wraiths appear as "ravers", Lothlorien appears Woodhelven, and the Donaldson's giant Saltheart Foamfollower is a walking oak tree reminiscent of Tolkien's Ents, who laments that his race is dying out. The heroine, Lena (the woman he rapes), is described in language worthy of elvish beauty and, as Michael Moorcock points out in *Wizardry and Wild Romance*, the landscape is both direct from Tolkien and oddly muted: "Deserts and mountains are vast and forests are dense" (p.66); all are psychoactive, so that the mental health of Covenant and the physical health of the land are intertwined. As the series progressed (there are two trilogies and two volumes of a planned quartet were published in 2004 and 2007), the connection with Tolkien became more tenuous. In the second trilogy Donaldson began to critique the colonialist politics of the portal fantasy, and where in the first volumes Covenant is oblivious to the pain he causes, and Donaldson too often seems to justify it, in later volumes Covenant's ability to heal the land is increasingly tied to his ability to recognize it and its people as real.

Up to the 1970s, while there are many different types of fantasy, there is no real sense of separate fantasy sub-genres and separate audiences, with the exception perhaps of the ghost-story market. The 1970s, however, sees what we can think of as speciation, in which certain aspects of the field become recognizable marketing categories in their own right. By the end of the 1970s at least one of these marketing categories (the quest fantasy, "in the tradition of J.R.R. Tolkien") was threatening to become so powerful as to overwhelm the presence of other forms.

Two sub-genres of fantasy separating themselves thoroughly in the 1970s were horror and the animal fantasy. Horror fiction had a separate existence from the fantastic at least from the late eighteenth century: even when the cause of the horror is supernatural, horror fiction is mostly staged in a world we recognize, and hence has an appeal to readers for whom other worlds have no interest. Horror fiction is also peculiarly cyclical. Its popularity tends to rise and fall as new taboos are identified, and are in their turn exhausted. At the beginning of the 1970s the ghost story, which was often constructed around the revelation of very domestic secrets, had gone into decline (reading the ghost stories of the mid-twentieth century, it is astonishing how cosy and domestic they seem). The revival began with the publication of Stephen King's *Carrie* (1974).

Carrie is radical in a number of ways. First, instead of sex being the taboo and the pressure that leads to the eventual haunting, sex and sexuality are discussed openly by all the characters. Repression becomes the subject-matter rather than the context. Second, Carrie's powers are made obvious to the reader almost from the beginning. The reader is adopted into the viewpoint of the omniscient narrator, and the rhetorical structure of mystery which shaped the work of writers in the 1920s and 1930s is missing. Third, King deployed a genre form that was still relatively new: the true crime story. The text is marshalled from an assemblage of evidence that spirals and closes in on the protagonist, rendering the structure of the story superbly suffocating. Carrie is far less trapped by the insanity of her mother than by the narrative causality of community expectations.

In the 1970s King wrote four more novels, including *Salem's Lot* (1975) and *The Shining* (1977), and another ten in the 1980s alone. Many of these became movies, most memorably *Carrie* (dir. De Palma, 1976) and *The Shining* (dir. Kubrick, 1980). Not all of Stephen King's horror is supernatural, but telepathy and, typically, powers of supernatural coercion are hallmarks of his work. His most fantastical work is a series of seven books known as *The Dark Tower* (1982–2004), which combines an Arthurian quest fantasy with psychological horror, all set in a feudal American West.

By the 1990s Stephen King dominated the horror market worldwide. The filming of Stephen King's books gave a huge fillip to the horror movie industry, and horror became the form of fantasy most likely to appear on the cinema screen. While judging horror cinema retrospectively is difficult because the efficacy of special effects is vulnerable to audience sophistication, the past thirty years have seen increasingly sophisticated and subtle uses of horror in the movies (both in terms of scripts, and psychological understandings). The situation in the bookshops, however, is more problematic. King's huge popularity did initially prompt publishers to speculate in horror fiction, but by the late 1990s his dominance was so great that the horror section in bookshops frequently consisted of several shelves of King and very little else. One consequence is that currently some of the very best horror writing in the early twenty-first century was being published by thriving small presses rather than by major publishers.

The careers of a number of popular horror writers began in the 1970s. In America there was Anne Rice, whose 1976 novel *Interview with the Vampire* became a cult classic; Chelsea Quinn Yarbro, whose *Hôtel Transylvania* (1978) was the first of numerous novels to feature the aristocratic vampire Saint-Germain; and Charles L. Grant, whose series about ancient evils rampant in small-town Connecticut began with *The Sound of Midnight* (1978). The most critically acclaimed of the new American writers of the 1970s is Peter Straub. Not all of his horror-writing is fantastical, but of his early work *Julia* (1975; *Full Circle* in the UK, 1977), *If You Could See Me Now* (1977) and *Ghost Story* (1979) are sophisticated ghost stories, and *Shadowland* (1980) is the tale of an adolescent drawn by a magician under the influence of a supernatural power. With *Shadowland* Straub introduced one of his favourite unsettling characteristics, which we find also in two of his most recent books, *lost boy lost girl* (2003) and *In the Night Room* (2004): requiring the reader to question constantly what is and isn't real. Peter Straub and Stephen King have also been very effective collaborators, producing *The Talisman* series, *The Talisman* (1984) and *Black House*, which had the misfortune to be published on 15 September 2001. Straub's work has demonstrated the degree to which horror remains a fiction of *language*. Although there is an ongoing argument about the degree to which horror should be confined by the term "affect" fiction, Straub is the master at constructing his affect in the emotional interstices of the lines.

Perhaps more significant for the history of horror fantasy, however, is what was happening in Britain. Ramsey Campbell was writing ghost stories throughout the 1960s, and stories inspired by Lovecraft, but in the 1970s he picked up on the growing conspiracy element that was infecting both American and British culture, and also focused on the nature of evil. Campbell, even more than King, was interested in exploiting the cracks in the moral order that were emerging as organized religion was losing its hold and New Age religions were increasingly visible. His best-known work of this period was *The Doll Who Ate His Mother* (1976), a story of an evil child born as a result of Satanism. This, of course, is very similar to the plot of the extremely popular movie *The Omen* (Donner, 1976): both of these texts probably have their roots in growing anxieties about illegitimacy and promiscuity in the 1970s. With Campbell, however, there is always a doubt about whether evil is something external or inherent in human nature, and several later novels explore the nature of madness. But his writing skilfully evokes terror, and he always does this much more subtly than his contemporary, James Herbert, whose over-the-top stories of mutant rats (*The Rats*, 1974) or a malignant fog which turns people into vicious killers (*The Fog*, 1975) were nevertheless very popular. The most important British horror writer of the 1980s, Clive Barker (inspired to write when fellow Liverpudlian Ramsey Campbell visited his school to talk about horror-writing) blended Campbell's intelligence with Herbert's visceral nastiness, and burst onto the scene in 1984 with the first three of his six *Books of Blood*, stories which explored many different kinds of horror. After Barker directed the movie *Hellraiser* (1987), based on his own short story, he became one of the most influential modern creators of horror.

The final trend of the 1970s lies as far from the terrors of Campbell and Barker as it is possible to be: the renewal of the animal story. Between the publication of *The Wind in the Willows* and the 1970s, the animal fantasy had been understood as being entirely for children. To an extent animal fantasy in the 1970s was still the preserve of children's fiction. Robert C. O'Brien's *Mrs Frisby and the Rats of NIMH* (1971) continued the tradition with a rather lovely story about mice and rats who have escaped from a government laboratory. However, the most successful children's writer of animal fantasy in the 1950s, 1960s, and 1970s was not actually a novelist but the animator, puppeteer and writer, Oliver Postgate and his collaborator Peter Firmin (animator and model maker). With the exception of *Noggin the Nog* (1959–65), a tale of Norse heroes which did contain an anthropomorphised cormorant, all of Postgate's works were anthropomorphic fantasies. *Ivor the Engine* ran through 1959, and then again in 1975–7; *The Clangers*, small knitted beings who lived on a moon, ran from 1969–74; and *Bagpuss* ("a saggy old cloth cat, baggy and a bit loose at the seams," who minded a junk shop) and which ran in 1974 and in 1999 took first place in a BBC poll of favourite children's television. However, at the beginning of the 1970s two books changed our perspective. Richard Bach's *Jonathan Livingston*

Seagull (1970) was a New Age allegory about a seagull who wishes to rise above the squabbles of his daily existence, exhausting himself to learn more about the possibilities of flight. One day he meets two gulls who take him to a higher plane. By 1972 this book had sold over a million copies, and it was filmed in 1973. Its popularity clearly has far more to do with its "inner meaning" than its status as an animal fantasy, and this element may also help explain the even more surprising success of Richard Adams's *Watership Down* (1972).

Seen in one way, *Watership Down* is simply the tale of a bunch of rabbits seeking a new home. As an anthropomorphic fantasy, it clearly spawned an entire sub-genre, most of which are ongoing series such as William Horwood's *Duncton Wood* (1979; moles), Brian Jacques's Redwall series (1986 and still going; mice and rats, but in a medievalist setting), Tad Williams's *Tailchaser's Song* (1985; cats) and Gabriel King's *The Wild Road* (1999; cats again). To give you a sense of the degree to which this has become a separate genre, we quote here from the Google blurb for *The Wild Road*: "in the grand storytelling tradition of *Watership Down* and *Tailchaser's Song*, comes an epic of adventure and danger, of heroism against insurmountable odds, and of love and comradeship among extraordinary animals". What distinguishes such books from *The Wind in the Willows* and other animal fantasies before the 1970s is their attempt at biological and ecological accuracy: this is the case even when, as in Jacques, the animals are treated as little aliens in a full fantasy world. This is not the random fancy of inserting a toad into the English gentry.

Watership Down is a quest fantasy, and also a highly mystical text. The rabbits of the text have their own religion and culture, and the epic adventure is interspersed with intensely philosophic moments. The book is classically structured in terms of Greek notions of heroism: there is a Hercules figure, an Apollo, and a Ulysses. The message of the book is the need for all of these elements in the psyche. The communities that the rabbits meet in their search for a home have each made the mistake of concentrating on only one of these attributes. The book is saved from any chance of becoming twee by the intense concentration on the realities of rabbit existence, from the threat of myxomatosis (only just diminishing in the 1970s), to the destruction of warrens by gassing or levelling for housing development. When we meet an apparently "utopian" rabbit community, it turns out to be a group of rabbits bred for human consumption. The failure of rabbit to return to the British menu after the threat of myxomatosis died out may owe much to the success of Adams's book and the 1978 animated movie (dir. Martin Rosen).

The animal fantasy remains popular, but not all authors accept its assumptions unquestioningly. Although not strictly an animal fantasy, Michael de Larrabeiti's controversial Borribles trilogy (1976–86) is a direct successor of *The Borrowers*, but has more in common in structure and attitude with a book like *Watership Down*. In the Borribles books, feral children grow pointed ears, and live in the London streets in a colony system. We include them here, because the Borribles, as their name suggests, remind one starkly of very badly behaved Wombles. Indeed, the comparison is intended by the author: the Borribles' enemies in the first book are called Rumbles, whose names are slightly changed versions of the names of Wombles. They are all slaughtered. The Borribles are skinny, tough thieves: anti-authoritarian and incredibly threatening. To many critics this book *was* about animals, since accepting it as a critique of inner-city deprivation was too discomfiting. One recent manifestation of the animal fantasy, and perhaps indicating the degree to which it is (for now) worn out, is the sardonic *The Amazing Maurice and his Educated Rodents* by Terry Pratchett (2001), in which a talking cat and a group of talking rats go around from town to town with a "stupid-looking kid", playing "the Pied Piper trick".

The crucial change in the 1970s, as we have described, is that whereas prior to this fans of fantasy could be assumed to read many different kinds of fantasy fiction, by the end of the decade we can see a clear separation into distinct strands. The rest of this book will attempt to show the ways in which these strands have remained close enough together that it is still plausible to see fantasy as a literary braid.

CHAPTER EIGHT

The 1980s

*I*F we are to contend that quest fantasies became the dominant tradition in the 1980s, we need to explain the difference between quest fantasies and the older sword-and-sorcery. Superficially, the two types can look similar, making use of medievalist or other kinds of pre-industrial settings, purple prose, and a sense of moral order to the adventure. However, quest fantasies are usually structured by some kind of destinarian inevitability – sometimes in the form of a prophecy, other times a simple narrative causality drawn from fairytales. Quest fantasies come to an end, usually with some kind of healing of the land, and either a restoration or dissolution of magic, whereas sword-and-sorcery fantasies always have room for another adventure. One consequence of this is that quest fantasies tend to the structured trilogy (or quartet, or quintet, or in the case of Robert Jordan twelve volumes), while sword-and-sorcery frequently accretes as sets of linked, previously published short stories. We can conceive the quest fantasies as having a story *arc* while the sword-and-sorcery books are linked adventures.

One new trend to appear in the 1980s was fantasy films which closely resembled the book form of the genre. There are a number of quest fantasy films in the 1980s: Jim Henson's *The Dark Crystal* (1982) is the adventure of a small Gelfling who leaves his forest and becomes involved in the magical politics of his world. Jen heals the crystal, destroys the evil race who rule the world and restores the stricken world to its former beauty. The film used large puppets for its characters and was largely successful in conjuring up a fantastical world and creating the quest structure with its sense of small beings against large odds. A much more interesting puppet (Muppet) movie was Jim Henson's *Labyrinth* (1986), based on the old fairytale of the goblin king who steals a baby. This movie was a mixed success, but has had a very sustained life on DVD, in part because of the stunning portrayal of the goblin king by David Bowie and the wonderful Escher-like goblin castle.

The Neverending Story started life as a children's book by the German writer Michael Ende (1979, trans. 1983). The tale of Bastian, a fat bookworm who discovers another world in which he is a fit and active hero who must try to heal the world in the form of the sick child Empress, was initially distinguished by being published with multi-coloured ink. The book is Oz-like, consisting of a series of encounters with fabulous beings and tasks. The movie constructed its wonders with the aid of large puppets but Michael Ende disliked it so much he disowned it. Although the theme tune did well, the movie itself was not hugely successful.

Ladyhawke (dir. Richard Donner, 1985) is a fantasy folk tale of two lovers, condemned by a curse. He is a man during the day and a wolf at night. She is a hawk by day and a woman by night. They become involved with a young peasant thief, who helps them to defeat the Bishop who cursed them. A rather intimate fantasy, this is a medievalist fantasy closer to sword-and-sorcery; it could conceivably be an adventure within a Conan collection, a coincidence as this decade also saw two Conan movies. *Conan the Barbarian* (dir. John Milius, 1982) is best known for launching the acting career of Arnold Schwarzenegger (although it was not his debut) but is actually quite a good movie, in which Conan travels across the landscape seeking revenge for the destruction of his village when he was a boy. The introduction of the revenge motif was an indication of a wider shift in American culture; the simple premise that the more civilized/stronger had the right to use violence (think of the Western genre) was receding and there was at least a tentative realization that some kind of motive was needed. The second Conan movie, *Conan the Destroyer* (dir.

Richard Fleischer, 1984), is much lighter in tone, but does contain far more of the sorcery of Howard's original.

The most conventional of the literary quest fantasies in the 1980s was the much-loved Belgariad sequence by David Eddings. A sequence of five books, it begins with a brief prologue about the creation of the world and the dissension between the gods. The first book, *Pawn of Prophecy* (1982), opens with the boy Garion almost drowning. Garion lives on a farm with his aunt Pol; he is as ordinary and mud stained as they come, although perhaps more thoughtful. When his aunt receives a mysterious message that drags her off, she leaves with Garion and the local smith. The three of them travel with Mr Wolf, and in the first three books Garion learns about the big wide world, the maimed god, the working of magic, and the overarching prophecy that concerns his family. At the end of the third book he discovers that he is the High King of the world. In the next two books he and his dryad wife mobilize the armies of half the world against the other half, in order to kill the maimed god. The book has the classic trajectory of the quest fantasy. There is both a personal and a cosmic conclusion. It starts small, humble and cosy (like Tolkien's Shire); companions are collected and information gathered; there are many red herrings, but any information found in an ancient text or passed on by an elderly mage with a long beard is likely to be correct. One other aspect of these books that becomes typical is the notion of a restricted structure of magic. In these books it is the Will and the Word, the right word and enough will, and the limitation is that the attempt to unmake anything will destroy the magician. One of the things that prevent the Eddings books being simply a collection of clichés is that they are frequently very amusing. Many of the characters are extremes of medievalist romance, and like many other quest-fantasy writers, Eddings has acerbic comments to make about feudalism which prevent the books becoming too complacent.

A more challenging sequence is *The Fionavar Tapestry*, a very widely read trilogy produced by Guy Gavriel Kay (the first is *The Summer Tree*, 1984). This is both a portal and a quest fantasy, beginning with the five main characters attending a lecture at the University of Toronto by Professor Marcus, who turns out to be a mage from the land of Fionavar who has come to bring them back with him. The three volumes trace their adventures in this land, which they eventually save from its dark lord. Guy Gavriel Kay is well-versed in medieval literature and Fionavar is the land where all Earth legends have their origin. The books of the Fionavar Tapestry weave in Norse, Celtic and English legend, and towards the middle of the second book begin to draw in the characters from the Arthurian cycle. There are some aspects of the texts typical of the form: as with Thomas Covenant, each of the main characters turns out to have an attribute in Fionavar which will prove crucial to the land's well-being: one takes the King's place hung upside down on the summer tree for three days and three nights, while one is a seer. There is also the trick developed by Tolkien and found in almost all quest fantasies of separating out the characters: for most of the second book their adventures are independent and personal, coalescing into cosmic significance only at the end.

Other notable sequences include work from Jennifer Roberson, Tad Williams and Freda Warrington. Jennifer Roberson's Chronicles of the Cheysuli began with *Shapechangers* in 1984: all eight novels are held together by the playing out of a prophecy and the struggles of protagonists to avoid being caught up in the process of its fulfilment. The prophecy runs over one hundred years, and is an attempt to breed a new race: at the very end it comes within a whisker of failure when the final link in the chain refuses to breed. Freda Warrington's Blackbird quartet (*A Blackbird in Silver*, 1986) tells of a great battle against a world-destroying serpent, and the world that is constructed in the aftermath. In Michael Scott Rohan's The Winter of the World quartet (*The Anvil of Ice*, 1986) the world-destroyer is the ice itself, advancing southwards in a prehistoric ice age. Tad Williams's Memory, Sorrow and Thorn began in 1988 with *The Dragonbone Chair* (1988) and continued with volumes almost as long individually as entire quest trilogies from earlier writers. Memory, Sorrow and Thorn is another tale of a kitchen boy

(Simon) caught up in a cataclysmic war between humans and immortal Sithi, shaped by prophecy and magic. Like many of these books there are companions, there is magic to learn, there is adulthood to grow into, and finally a healing of the land through the long-lost swords of power (Memory, Sorrow, Thorn); and Simon becomes King. Yet the predictability of the form is part of its pleasure.

The writers who work with quest fantasies know that certain patterns are demanded to make the form work, but are aware that the long journeys which fill the pages provide an unparalleled canvas for the description of fabulous people and places. These books are epic, and function best if understood as riffs on a theme. Their originality is in the variation, and in the choice of instruments rather than in the musical form. However, in the hands of real hacks (that is, people writing to a franchise) the quest form is easy to exhaust. The 1980s saw the emergence of book series that were intended to tie in with gaming conventions. Steve Jackson, co-founder of Games Workshop, developed a line of *Fighting Fantasy* books (59 in the series so far) which drew on Dungeons and Dragons characters and structures, while Tracy Hickman and Margaret Weiss went in the other direction, producing the Dragonlance series (over 190 books so far) which were intended specifically to attract people who had previously encountered fantasy mostly through the game *Dungeons and Dragons*. The early Dragonlance books were novelizations of games actually played.

The Jackson and the Weiss/Hickman books are very derivative, but writers also used the game formula as the context for original novels. Ian Watson's *Queenmagic, Kingmagic* (1986) was based on chess: the courtiers of the two warring nations (King, Queen, Bishop, Knight, etc.,) each have their own modes of magic and their own methods of magical transportation. In *The True Game*, Sheri S. Tepper structured her planetary hierarchies and conflicts through formal games. Each player has attributes, hierarchies are decided by formal moves, and there is formal game playing going on throughout the three trilogies which form the series. The Peter series begins with *King's Blood Four* (1983) and is succeeded by the Mavin Manyshaped trilogy, beginning with *The Song of Mavin Manyshaped* (1985), perhaps the best known of the sequence and certainly the most uncomfortable, telling as it does the escape of a young child from her family in which a shortage of women has led to serious and legitimized sexual abuse.

Quest fantasy is a large category and there are forms that have the structure of quest fantasies, but play rather different notes. One form of the quest fantasy is less cataclysmic and more domestic: authors use the structure of the quest, but emphasize the *Bildungsroman* aspects, producing books which can be summarized as the rise to or fall from power of a protagonist against the background of great events. Mercedes Lackey's *Arrows of the Queen* (1987) and its two sequels (*Arrow's Flight*, 1987; *Arrow's Fall*, 1988) fit this pattern. These are the stories of the choosing and training of the Queen's Own Herald, Talia. She has the Gift of Empathy and other senses and these both arouse hostility and help her in her rise. In these kinds of books we frequently learn a great deal about the trade for which the protagonist is training. Some of the most popular books in this vein are the stories for young adults by Tamora Pierce about Alanna, a young woman who rejects her destiny as a magic user and takes her twin brother's place to train as a knight. The first in the series is *Alanna: The First Adventure* (1983) and by the fourth volume (*Lioness Rampant*, 1988), Alanna has met the Great Mother Goddess, defeated her magical enemies and become the King's Champion, the first female to hold the position. The book's appeal is at least in part because of the extensive instruction in strength training it gives to young female readers – these are very empowering books. Raymond E. Feist's *Magician* (1982, but separated into two volumes in the US, *Apprentice* and *Master*, 1986) combines the *Bildungsroman* model with a portal fantasy from one fantasy world to another, and complex court politics. Unlike many other books in this field, *Magician* is a book about the growth of a mage/Merlin figure rather than of a king. Pug is a kitchen boy who is trained as a magician but is captured by invaders from another world – reached through a magical portal –

where he serves as a slave for years before climbing the hierarchy. When courtiers from his own world find him, he is dragged back, becomes embroiled in the civil war, and becomes advisor to the new king. At the end Pug heals the land by blocking the rift or connection between the two worlds, preventing the other world from invading once more. This book became the beginning of a longer sequence known as the Riftwar, still being constructed as sets of trilogies. Linked trilogies have become increasingly popular as a way of maintaining the continuity of marketing while periodically refreshing the franchise.

There are also in the 1980s a number of attempts to subvert the quest fantasy. In Geoff Ryman's *The Warrior Who Carried Life* (1985), a woman whose life has been destroyed by warfare has herself turned into a man in order to wreak revenge. Gradually she realizes that there is another way. The book abandons the kind of epic conclusions of most quest fantasies and looks instead to explorations of gender and pacifism. Julian May's *Saga of Pliocene Exile* (beginning with *The Many-Colored Land* in 1981) is a quest fantasy sequence in which the initial portal opens onto the past and the beings from "Celtic" mythology are actually aliens marooned on earth. Two species, the Tanu and the Firvulag, compete for Earth. Both have magical powers, but the Tanu wear torcs which enhance them. Our protagonists land in the middle of this strife and generate resentment among the humans that causes them to join the war against the Tanu. These books are perhaps the first of the quest fantasies to be highly sexualized, and the first to really address the idea that an encounter with faerie is dangerous, an idea that will become more common in the 1990s as Elizabethan ideas of fairy folk as wilful and vicious begin to replace the Victorian, Pre-Raphaelite notions of elves and fairies as fundamentally good and wise.

R.A. MacAvoy's *A Trio for Lute* began as a fairly traditional fantasy with a young boy who is the son of a wizard (*Damiano*, 1982), but is set in Renaissance Italy rather than medieval England or France. Where it diverges from most 1980s quest fantasies is that it incorporates a clear Christian mythology: Damiano's guide is the Archangel Raphael, and by the third book (*Raphael*, 1984) the book turns to the cosmic struggle between the Archangel and his brother, Lucifer. With the exception of Gene Wolfe – who does it so subtly it is unnoticeable and who will be discussed in greater detail later – no other writer of the period makes such direct use of the Christian tradition (although Orson Scott Card's Alvin Maker sequence, beginning with *Seventh Son* in 1987, is inspired by his Mormonism and in 1990s James Morrow and Philip Pullman, among others, will begin to see Christian mythologies as a useful source for modern fantasy).

Gene Wolfe was one of the most admired writers of the 1980s, above all for his *The Book of the New Sun*, which began in 1980 with *The Shadow of the Torturer*. This four-book series (to which a fifth was added in 1987) is accepted as fantasy by many casual readers. Like many quest fantasies the books describe the travels and rise to prominence of a lowly servant. Severian, however, is an apprentice torturer. Wolfe confuses the matter further by having Severian relate his own experiences based on his perfect memory and utter conviction of righteousness in his work. Wolfe is playing with us, even though it takes several readings to realize this, and to come to the conclusion – as many critics have – that Severian is a Christ-figure and that the whole story is suffused with Wolfe's own Catholicism. And by the by, the story is set in the far future and is, by the fifth volume, very clearly science fiction. Critics such as John Clute and John Crowley see this as one of the great science fiction books of the twentieth century; yet it is a landmark in the history of fantasy too. Severian of the perfect memory was mirrored in Wolfe's other great fantasy series, beginning with *Soldier of the Mist* (1986), in which Latro, an ancient Greek warrior, never has any memory of the previous day when he wakes up. The reader is as puzzled, and intrigued, as Latro, as together they struggle to make sense of the world in which he lives, and try to distinguish between the mortals and immortals he meets.

Some of the best-selling books of the decade were retellings of the Arthurian cycle. The most literal of them were Stephen Lawhead's *Taliesin* (1987), *Merlin* (1988) and *Arthur* (1989). Lawhead added a second trilogy, *Pendragon* (1994), *Grail* (1997) and *Avalon* (1999), two prequels and a sequel, respectively. Most of the books are based securely on the medieval Arthurian tales, particularly the versions ascribed to Geoffrey of Monmouth, but there are numerous chronological inconsistencies in Lawhead's books which make it clear that he is not attempting a historical reconstruction such as Rosemary Sutcliff's *Sword at Sunset* (1963). The mention of potatoes may be historical ignorance (or a nod to Tolkien, who had them in parts of Middle-earth), but the books begin with the destruction of Atlantis and there are genuine historical characters ranging from the fourth century AD to the seventh, all of whom find a place in Lawhead's life of Arthur. The first book of the sequence is particularly interesting because it focuses on the bard Taliesin, a somewhat hazy historical figure who here is rendered as the father of Merlin. David Gemmell's two books *Ghost King* (1988) and *Last Sword of Power* (1988) tell of Merlin, a member of a group of mages who preserve the knowledge held by the lost kingdom of Atlantis. Uther Pendragon becomes the great hope of the campaign against the powers of darkness.

Marion Zimmer Bradley's *The Mists of Avalon* (1979) was a feminist re-telling of the Arthur cycle, told from the point of view of Morgaine and the interests of Guinevere (here rendered as Gwenhwyfar), Viviane and Morgause. Arthur is constructed as a space between their needs and desires, and the roles they play in the cycle. It moves the interest of the stories to women's experiences and marginalises much of the warfare and courtly activity which is usually central to the tales and also turns the tale of Christianity over-throwing paganism into a tale of gender warfare: the women are nice, gentle worshippers of the mother-goddess, while the men are vicious, misogynist, hypocritical Christians. Medieval scholars react with extreme irritation, but the book was hugely successful and led to a lengthy series written with Diana L. Paxson, a noted writer of fantasy and of pagan spiritual works.

A much more eccentric take on the Arthurian cycle was Jack Vance's Lyonesse Trilogy (*Suldrun's Garden*, 1983; *The Green Pearl*,

1985; *Madouc*, 1989). As with Lawhead's trilogy, there is a link made between Atlantis and Arthur, but Vance's version is far more fantastic and infused with faerie. The action takes place mostly on islands west of Cornwall, supposedly two or three generations before Arthur. The first volume lovingly builds up the adolescent heroine Suldrun, only for her to commit suicide halfway through the novel – although she reappears as a fairly interventionist ghost later on. The plot is intensely complicated and the names are misleading, but running through this tale of changelings, magicians and lost princes is a sequence haunted by the history of Arthur as laid out by T.H. White.

The most radical use of the Arthurian cycle in the 1980s was in Robert Holdstock's *Mythago Wood* (1984). In one sense this is not an Arthurian book at all. It is the tale of a family who live on the edge of Ryhope Wood, an oddly threatening and difficult to negotiate stretch of forest. The father of the family is a psychologist, and has become fascinated with the concept of *mythagos*, heroic legendary characters from our own collective unconscious, who both shape human action and are shaped by it. When his father disappears, Stephen Huxley goes looking for him in the wood, and discovers that the wood generates these mythago beings. The tale which structures the first half of the book is Guinevere's relationship with and betrayal of Arthur. Guinevere as a figure appears several times, each time in relationships with different men; she may have been Stephen's mother Jennifer, who had died several years earlier, but she also appears as Guiwenneth, as Gwyneth and as Gwyn. Guinevere also appears as a goddess and as a warrior. Stephen's mythago role appears to be as the liberator of the land from evil, but in a stroke of genius the dark lord/outsider is Stephen's brother Christian, thus also replaying the mythago of Cain and Abel and exposing the outsider-protagonist's role in quest fantasies to scrutiny. One of the most important themes running through this book is the connection of the protagonists to the land. The actions of Stephen and Christian affect whether the wood sickens or thrives, so that when one is buried in the land one becomes both a spiritual and a physical fertilizer. Later books by Holdstock extend the themes of the mythago. *The Hollowing* (1993) is inspired by *Sir Gawain and the Green Knight,* and the title story of the collection *Merlin's Wood* (1994) embroils a family in the struggle between Merlin and Vivian. A new book in the series, *Avilion,* was published in 2009.

At the end of the 1970s, sword-and-sorcery was clearly being eclipsed, but ironically, it was also increasing in sophistication and – as we saw with the work of Russ and Delany – was becoming a far more knowing genre which both plundered and critiqued its own past. One of the cleverest stories perhaps is "Sláine", a strip written by Pat Mills and drawn by Angela Kincaid, Mike McMahon and Massimo Belardinelli from the 1980s onwards for the comic *2000 AD. 2000 AD* was predominantly a science fiction comic, but in Sláine it produced one of the classic sword-and-sorcery heroes. Narrated mostly by Ukko the dwarf, this is the tale of how Sláine, berserker warrior, came to rule the Tir-Nan-Og. Sláine's rages, which have to be contained by special armour, are particularly spectacular and are fuelled by the power of the earth feeding through his body.

Some sword-and-sorcery books set out to imagine what an alternative to the big, white, muscled lunk would do to the plot of a sword-and-sorcery tale. Charles R. Saunders, an African American writer, produced a trilogy beginning with *Imaro* (1981) which originally had as a cover quote, "The Epic Novel of a Black Tarzan". This was removed to appease the Edgar Rice Burroughs estate, but is a fair description of the novel and its sequels. These novels were set in a pre-colonial, magical Africa, and set out to critique the colonialist structures of the Tarzan books. P.C. Hodgell's *God Stalk* (1982) tells of a wandering warrior and her band, attempting to confront a dark lord, but continually hampered by the sexism of the society in which she lives. Glen Cook's *The Black Company* (1984) tells sword-and-sorcery from the point of view of the mercenaries who make up a villain's army (a grunt's eye view, appropriate for a man who spent much of his life working at General Motors). Steven Brust's Vlad Taltos series (*Jhereg*, 1983) introduces the voice of a hard-boiled detective (linked telepathically to his dragon-like jhereg) to tell the story of criminal life in a world dominated by magic users and idiot warriors. David Gemmell's Drenai sequence, beginning with *Legend* in 1984 – one of the best selling fantasy books ever – tended to focus on the roles of individual soldiers and war leaders within a much larger conflict. Gemmell does have the fantasy tropes of dark enemies aided by mystical forces, but these aren't usually the business of his protagonists. Gemmell was a religious writer, whose books were structured around issues of loyalty, honour and redemption. As a Christian he believed in the possibilities of redemption even for the most evil, and this coloured his work. Some of these ideals have been seamlessly incorporated into modern High Fantasy, even where the Christian message itself has been ignored.

And of course, there is Terry Pratchett, whom we will discuss in greater detail in chapter ten. Although his Discworld series very quickly moved away from its concentration on sword-and-sorcery, Pratchett began the series with *The Colour of Magic* (1983) and *The Light Fantastic* (1986) in which the rather bedraggled and hopeless wizzard (*sic*, because he can't spell either) Rincewind, leads the tourist Twoflower through a world inhabited by Hrun the Barbarian (who can think without moving his lips), Herena the henna-haired harridan (who wears nice, practical brown leather), Cohen the elderly Barbarian who believes the best things in life are "hot water, good dentishtry and shoft lavatory paper", and Death, who rides a real white horse because the skeletal one kept falling apart. By the time Pratchett had finished, there was very little of the sword-and-sorcery genre left to take seriously, although this hasn't stopped anyone.

It is too easy to suggest an improvement in literary quality when what one actually means is a refinement in sensibility, but in the 1980s there genuinely does seem to be an increased concern with the literariness of fantasy. In 1973, Gabriel García Márquez's *One Hundred Years of Solitude* had been translated into English. It is difficult to track direct influences, but there was a growing sense that fantasy could be literature, of the kind that could be reviewed by mainstream journals. Two authors who benefited from this were Jonathan Carroll and Joyce Carol Oates. Jonathan Carroll published his first novel, *The Land of Laughs*, in 1980, a story about a young schoolteacher researching the life of a favourite author of children's books; the book slides into fantasy as a dog begins talking to him and his life blends into that of the author whom he is researching. Carroll is very much part of the fantasy world, and has been shortlisted over the years for the World Fantasy Award, the Hugo and the British Fantasy Awards, and in interview is perfectly ready to describe himself as a fantasy writer, but his work is frequently labelled "magic realism", and read metaphorically. In contrast Joyce Carol Oates was in the 1980s very much part of the literary establishment, having been published since 1964. In 1980 she published *Bellefleur*, a Gothic saga about multiple generations of a New York State family. Previously this book might have been understood entirely within mainstream constructions, but it quickly attracted the label "magic realist". In 1985, Isabel Allende's *The House of the Spirits* was translated into English, a similar tale of fantastical events and civic decline across several generations of a family. Magic realism, as it was becoming understood in the English-speaking world, required the creation of a world like ours in which magic was a natural element. Rather than looking to indigenous American writers such as Faulkner the term was applied to a range of writers, some of whom came from the British and American mainstream and used the fantastical to create metaphorical resonance (such as Jeanette Winterson's *Oranges Are Not the Only Fruit* (1985), in which the tale of a young lesbian growing up in northern England is punctuated by fable), and some of whom came from other cultures, and their blend of different traditions was co-opted under this label. Suniti Namjoshi's *The Conversations of Cow* (1985) introduces Suniti, "an average middle-of-the-road Lesbian separatist" to Bhadravati, a Brahmin Lesbian cow, in a Canadian suburb. Others came from the fantasy ghetto, and saw a way to write a more ambiguous version of the fantastic. These writers included John

Crowley, Christopher Priest, Megan Lindholm and Carol Emshwiller, who each in their very different way demonstrated how the everyday could be infused with an air of the fantastic.

John Crowley's *Little, Big* (1981) can be understood as (in John Clute's terminology) an edifice fantasy. However, where most edifice fantasies are about castles (Otranto or Gormenghast), Crowley's vision is of an American domesticity: an entire family shaped by a house and by the house's liminal position on the borderlands with Faerie. The book has the classic trajectory marked out by Gabriel García Márquez and Isabel Allende for a magic realist novel: it maps the decline of the power of generations with the decline of their relationship with Faerie and with the decline of order in the City. The novel is a braid of characters' lives, held together by the observations of Smoky Barnable, who arrives as a young man to marry the daughter of the house, Daily Alice Drinkwater, and it is Smoky's death at the end that signals a full crossing-over into Faerie and a revival of the connection between the house and its inhabitants. However, it is the language of the book that makes it stand out. Crowley returns us to the distant view and the fine detail of the Pre-Raphaelite writers. Even when we think we are in the real world, the language is of a fantastic landscape. In 1987, John Crowley followed this up with *Ægypt* (now renamed *The Solitudes*), the first of a fantasy sequence only finished in 2007 which may, in retrospect, be regarded as one of the greatest works of fantasy of our time. The four books are similarly set in a "real America" (intercut with passages from a novel about John Dee and Giordano Bruno) but are permeated by a sense that the world we see is not the only reality, and that the magical world that existed before the Scientific Revolution may be about to return.

Christopher Priest already had an established reputation as a science fiction short-story writer and novelist, but in the 1980s his work began to shift towards a form of magic realism in which the walls of the world became increasingly permeable. Ideas made mechanical in a science fiction text such as *A Dream of Wessex* in which machinery projects the protagonist into another world, were rendered fantastical in *The*

Affirmation (1981) where a writer's own writing appears to be achieving the same ends. In *The Glamour* (1984) a man suffering traumatic amnesia begins to recall memories of an underworld of invisible presences.

Megan Lindholm's *Wizard of the Pigeons* (1986) is a very odd novel. It can be read as pure fantasy: a tale of an urban wizard helping to keep Seattle free from demons. In this reading when Wizard comes under attack the gritty reality of the Vietnam War and its fallout is part of a dizzying delusion. Alternatively, this is a novel of poverty and mental illness, in which Michael Ignatius O'Brien survives only because he has retreated into a fantastical world in his own mind. The reason the book is so special and is so often cited is that there is an extraordinarily effective reading that balances both of these and in which we are in a world in which the magical and the real exist side by side.

Magic realism offered new opportunities to feminists, as one could once more write fantasy that did not have to have the air of rationality and reality that had become the norm in the genre. We have already mentioned the work of Jeanette Winterson. In Carol Emshwiller's *Carmen Dog* (1988) women are turned into dogs, and vice versa, much to the confusion of male observers. Ellen Galford, an American writer who has lived in Scotland since the early 1970s, produced three feminist magic realist novels, the first of which, *The Fires of Bride* (1986), tells of a young artist who ends up living on a Scottish island and whose scrap-metal sculptures revive the former goddess Bride.

Stepping away from fiction that is strictly magic realism, there is what we might call "conversational fantasy". In the 1980s we get a number of texts in which people stand around talking about magic or the magical worlds they find themselves in. R.A. MacAvoy's *Tea with the Black Dragon* (1983) is a story about a young woman who gets into bad company and is kidnapped, but the pleasure of the story is in the conversations her mother has with an elderly gentleman she meets in her hotel, who turns out to be an ancient Chinese dragon. Similarly, Woody Allen's *The Purple Rose of Cairo* (1985) is a metastory of the Depression and the poor prospects for women, but all its delight is in the conversation between Cecilia and Tom, a character in a film who breaks out from the screen into Cecilia's world. The nature of reality is still the theme in Joanna Russ's "Mr. Wilde's Second Chance" (1987), but with a very different meaning. In this "posthumous fantasy", Mr. Wilde finds himself in limbo. A very courteous gentleman leads him to a jigsaw puzzle of his life. Wilde completes the puzzle, and creates a life in which he never meets Lord Alfred Douglas, remains happily married, completes many more plays, and dies at home. Receiving the congratulations of the courteous gentleman, Mr. Wilde contemplates this picture before sweeping it off the table, choosing his own reality. The narration of the tale is essentially a conversation about modes of truth. One very quirky novel of the period is the epistolary fantasy *Sorcery and Cecelia or The Enchanted Chocolate Pot Being the Correspondence of Two Young Ladies of Quality Regarding Various Magical Scandals in London and the Country* (1988), by Caroline Stevermer and Patricia C. Wrede. This novel was written as a letter game, and is a delightful confection of bitchiness and fantasy, but is not in the slightest bit whimsical.

The 1980s welcomed two film directors as clear contributors to original fantasy (rather than adaptations or, like the films discussed above, reiterations of the genre). Terry Gilliam directed three movies in this decade, all of which are regarded as outstanding by genre critics (although film critics tend to take a long while to realize that a science fiction or fantasy film has any merits). In *Time Bandits* (1981) a bunch of dwarfs on the run from the Supreme Being burst into the bedroom of a boy called Kevin. When the Supreme Being arrives they escape into a black void and take Kevin with them. Using the map of wormholes they have stolen they engage in a glorious smash-and-grab raid across history. *Brazil* (1984) is a science fiction dystopia in which one of the characters maintains his sanity through imagining a fantastical utopia, into which he retreats when he is tortured. Finally, in the 1980s, was *The Adventures of Baron Munchausen* (1988), an adaptation of a German fantasy classic from the eighteenth century, which had already been filmed three times before. The film was financially disastrous, because

Columbia Pictures was being sold at the time and failed to invest in the distribution, and it is uneven (and possibly a bit too long), but is arguably one of the best fantasy movies ever made, because the movie feels as if it loves fantasy. In the 1990s Gilliam made another three genre movies: *The Fisher King* (1991), an urban fantasy based on Arthurian myth; *Twelve Monkeys* (1996), a science fiction movie, and *The Brothers Grimm* (2005), which entwines the story of the brothers with the stories which they collected.

The other filmmaker to endear himself to genre fans in this period was Tim Burton. The first of his fantasy movies was *Beetlejuice* (1988), a comedy horror movie in which a happily married couple are killed on their way to their new home, and find themselves as ghosts. Unfortunately the house is quickly sold, and the new tenants are unbearable. Against the advice of their ghost social worker, they seek the help of a freelance "bioexorcist" to drive out the new residents. Betelgeuse, however, has an agenda of his own. In 1989 Burton produced *Batman*, the first of the revisionist superhero movies, and in 1990 the steampunk fairytale *Edward Scissorhands*, a revisioning of *Frankenstein* set in a sugar-coated 1960s suburbia. Burton's fantasy career continued through the 1990s, with *A Nightmare before Christmas* (1993), an animated movie in which Jack Skellington of Hallowe'en Town tries to take over Christmas (with the best of intentions); *James and the Giant Peach* (1996), an adaptation of Roald Dahl's book; the execrable *Mars Attacks!* (1996); *Sleepy Hollow* (1999), an adaptation of Washington Irving's classic ghost story; *Big Fish* (2003), a magic realist "fish story"; and *Charlie and the Chocolate Factory* (2005), another Dahl adaptation.

One of the hallmarks of Gilliam and Burton was a certain quirkiness, a willingness to rifle and recombine different sub-genres and elements of the fantastic. The literary equivalent of Gilliam and Burton are the friends Tim Powers and James Blaylock who in the 1980s helped create the sub-genre known as steampunk. Blaylock's first series, which begins with *The Elfin Ship* (1982), at first sight seems a fairly standard quest fantasy with its elves and magicians. But the setting and sensibility of the books are a nineteenth century in which magic exists alongside technological advances that our own Victorian period did not see. This is the essence of steampunk which was developed further by Blaylock in *Homunculus* (1986), in which our hero is opposed to a reanimator of corpses, and comes across a dirigible piloted by a skeleton, an alien starship and all kinds of science fiction and fantasy clichés, brought together in a very original way. Tim Powers's first novel was *The Drawing of the Dark* (1979) in which King Arthur was reincarnated as a soldier of fortune defending Vienna against the Turks. However, Powers's most characteristic book is *The Anubis Gates* (1983). This is technically a science fiction novel in which the protagonist travels back to the early nineteenth century of Lord Byron's London, but the phantasmagoric atmosphere of his imaginary London and the almost Dickensian array of characters makes this much more fantasy than science fiction. The idea of bringing fantasy back to Victorian times and to Victorian London was becoming increasingly attractive, specifically to writers crossing the sf/fantasy divide. William Gibson and Bruce Sterling's steampunk sf novel, *The Difference Engine* (1990) and Colin Greenland's *Harm's Way* (1993) are some of the best on the sf side of the divide. One of the most influential fantasy stories of this kind (and which may have influenced Michael Swanwick's *The Iron Dragon's Daughter*, 1993) is Lucius Shepard's novella, "The Man Who Painted the Dragon Griaule" (1984) in which an artist works out that the way to kill a dormant dragon is to poison it with paint, but who creates a work of great art, and is simultaneously poisoned by the dragon, and lives to see entire industries and industrial systems created to support his great work.

The popularity of nineteenth-century London in the works of Powers and Blaylock points us towards a growing interest in the urban environment as a setting for the fantastic. Ellen Kushner's *Swordspoint* (1987) is a Ruritania: a tale of political, social and sexual intrigue set in a faux seventeenth century. The prequel, *The Fall of the Kings* (2002), with Delia Sherman, is more explicitly about the interaction of magic with the "modern" world, a theme we shall see in other books in chapter eleven. More archetypal of what has come to be known as "urban fantasy" are Emma Bull's *War for the Oaks* (1987) and Charles de Lint's *Jack the Giant Killer* (1987). In this new urban fantasy, the fairies and elves of rural Britain upped sticks and, often following the Irish migrations, moved to the cities of North America.

In Emma Bull's book a young musician, a woman, living in Minneapolis is pulled into a battle between two fairy courts; in Charles de Lint's a lonely young woman is pulled into a battle between two fairy courts, this time in a city in Canada. Both books have a system of Faerie that has migrated from the Old World to the New; both books rest on the premise that humans have something special to offer to Faerie. The pleasure in these books is very much about the ways in which the authors interpolate Faerie with the urban environments of their choice. In both cases and in the sub-genre of urban fantasy that develops from these two books, an additional element is that the protagonists continually feel themselves to be (and indeed may in reality be) on the edge of madness.

Charles de Lint has been one of the major proponents of this form of fantasy, setting many of his fantasies in the imaginary town of Newford. His most recent books include *The Blue Girl* (2004) in which a newcomer to Newford develops a friendship with a ghost and finds fairies invading her dreams, and a Young Adult book, *Little (Grrl) Lost* (2007) in which a girl moving to the suburbs meets and befriends an urban punk fairy. Mark Helprin's *Winter's Tale* (1983) is very different. It tells of a young man, Peter Lake, arriving as an immigrant child in New York, who is adopted by the Baymen of the Bayonne marsh. When grown he is sent to Manhattan, where he lives as an ordinary man, but one for whom the miraculous periodically intercedes. At one stage in the novel he disappears for several years, and when he returns he can hear and see things that nobody else can. When New York begins to burn, he comes into his full power, eventually achieving Christ-like abilities. There are elements of the Fisher King in this tale (reiterating American fantasy's fascination with Arthur) and although in many ways totally unlike Bull and de Lint's work it repeats the idea that America must import its magical salvation from the Old World. The year 1984 also saw the release of the hit movie, *Ghostbusters* (dir. Ivan Reitman) which brought ghosts in from the haunted mansion to the streets and high-rise buildings of New York City. *Ghostbusters* also brought exorcism in to the realm of rationalized fantasy as the bell, book and candle fell before the new technology of the charged waves and a metal ghost safe.

In Britain, the most visible forms of urban fantasy were in the comics. Artists such as Bryan Talbot and writers such as Neil Gaiman and Alan Moore were developing a vision of Thatcherite Britain, which was dark and grimy, and which coloured both past and future, much of it in the still active *2000 AD*. Perhaps the best remembered was the *Sandman* series, which takes place in Hell, Faerie and Asgard among other places, but mostly in the realm of Morpheus. Although not strictly urban fantasy, the images are clearly influenced by the developments in urban fantasy, and the sense of a world permeated by the fantastic and particularly by faerie. *The Sandman* (1989–96) demonstrated what could be done with comics and is one of the important texts in the development of the graphic novel in this period. It remains incredibly influential, and drew in the talents of a range of artists, most notably Dave McKean and Charles Vess who have both become very important fantasy artists with very different visions of the urban fantastic. In the United States, this dark vision was encapsulated in Frank Miller's *The Dark Knight Returns* (1986) a revisioning of *Batman*, which Tim Burton later translated onto the screen.

One author who is almost too eclectic to be pigeonholed is Diana Wynne Jones, ostensibly a writer for children and young adults but today with a huge adult following. If one were to put her in an overall category, then "urban fantasy" is perhaps the most appropriate, given that most of her books were set in post-eighteenth-century-style worlds or occasionally in industrializing landscapes, and that in one or two of her books the nature of industrialization and modernization were the things at stake. Jones's first fantasy novel was published in 1973, *Wilkins' Tooth* (US, *Witch's Business*: a bowdlerized version), a fairytale set in a small town.

She wrote four books in the 1970s, which included *The Ogre Downstairs* (1974), in which a magical chemistry set is introduced into the lives of two sets of children just amalgamated by a new marriage, *Eight Days of Luke* (1975), in which a very lonely boy accidentally conjures up Loki and becomes involved in Norse legend, and *Dogsbody* (1975), in which the star Sirius finds himself trapped on Earth in a dog's body, as the pet of Katherine, who is a dogsbody in her uncle's house. All three books take quite old tales and ask how they would play out in a contemporary setting. Each time it is the tale that gives way to the demands of the contemporary, and it is this that makes Jones's work distinctive.

Jones has been extraordinarily prolific in the last three decades (46 books to date), but it is in the 1980s that she produced some of her most exciting work. As we cannot discuss all of it, we will discuss here three of the most interesting: *Archer's Goon* (1984), *Fire and Hemlock* (1984), and *The Magicians of Caprona* (1980). *Archer's Goon* is set in a small suburb, and is a story of Howard and his younger sister, usually known as Awful. Their father Quentin is a writer and a polytechnic lecturer and their mother is a school music inspector. As the story starts, Howard arrives home to find a goon sitting at the kitchen table, who wants "Archer's 2000". As Howard investigates what the 2000 are (words) and who Archer is, he discovers that his town is run by seven sibling wizards, all of whom are trapped apparently by the words that Quentin has been writing for Archer for thirteen years. *Archer's Goon* is a classic Jones screwball comedy, although a pretty sinister one. Howard discovers that he isn't quite who he thought he was and Quentin's words turn out to be powerful in ways none of them expected. Words and the power of words connect *Archer's Goon* to the otherwise completely different *Fire and Hemlock*. The former book is structured by a series of theses or propositions; the latter is structured by four paintings, T.S. Eliot's *Four Quartets* and approximately thirty children's fantasy books, which are mentioned by name in the text. *Fire and Hemlock* is a story of a young man caught by the fairy queen and the girl Polly he meets when she is just nine years old and whom he grooms to rescue him (a sinister aspect to the tale that Jones acknowledges). The ballads "Tam Lin" and "Thomas the Rhymer" are the background, but this is a new iteration and not a retelling. In this version the fairy queen is defeated because Polly has the resources of the contemporary world, and crucially the power of words. *The Magicians of Caprona* is a Romeo-and-Juliet story set in a faux Renaissance Italian city-state and is part of the Chrestomanci series, which began with *Charmed Life* (1977). In this sequence there are many alternate worlds stacked in series. In one world, where magic is possible, abuse of this knowledge is controlled by the Chrestomanci, a nine-lived enchanter. Chrestomanci is peripheral to *The Magicians of Caprona*, which is about what happens to the city-state when its two great magic houses fall out, and how it is saved by four children and two cats. Two of the children have rather peculiar magic, which draws the reader's attention to what we might understand as Jones's core message: magic is the right word at the right time. Part of the charm of this book, however, is also the degree to which we get to know the city of Caprona from a number of different perspectives. Currently Jones's best-known work is *Howl's Moving Castle* (1986), adapted by Studio Ghibli's Hayao Miyazaki (2004). Although the film is wonderful in its way, it is no longer Jones. Miyazaki dispensed with most of Jones's characteristic humour and rather ramshackle approach to authority, and, crucially, Sophie Hatter no longer has the power to talk life into inanimate objects.

The Chrestomanci sequence can be seen as alternate history in which magic works. Two others books like this were David Brin's *The Practice Effect* (1984) and John M. Ford's *The Dragon Waiting: A Masque of History* (1984). In *The Practice Effect*, an earthman goes through to another world in which goods are perfected by being used or practised (a crude chair sat on for many years will gradually evolve into a piece of designer furniture). John M. Ford's *The Dragon Waiting* is an alternate history that combines a blend of folklore, various historical figures such as the Medicis and the Sforzas with complicated plots around Edward IV and Richard III of England.

The idea of mixing folklore with English politics is explored brilliantly in Brian Stableford's *The Empire of Fear* (1984). One of the new modern vampire novels, in *The Empire of Fear* the story begins in seventeenth-century London at the time of the rise of modern science. Edmund Cordery, mechanician to the court of the still-thriving Richard the Lionheart, develops a microscope and through this hopes to discover the secret of the longevity of the vampires who form the aristocracy of this alternate world. In this world vampirism turns out to be a sexually-transmitted disease (which exposes the sexual proclivities of certain members of the aristocracy).

Chelsea Quinn Yarbro has been one of the most successful modernizers of the vampire mythos. In 1978 Yarbro published the first of her Saint Germain novels, *Hôtel Transylvania* (1978) set in the early eighteenth century. The immortality of her vampires allows her to use numerous historical settings, so that *Blood Games* (1980) is set at the time of Nero, while *Tempting Fate* (1981) is set during the Russian revolution. Anne Rice also continued her vampire series, which began with *Interview with the Vampire* in 1976, after a ten-year delay. In 1985 she published *The Vampire Lestat*, and in 1988 *The Queen of the Damned*, two books which earned her a leading place among the vampire writers and kick-started a genre which would develop into the paranormal romance in which the emphasis is on flirting (and more) with the monster (vampires, werewolves, etc.).

Tucked away in the UK is an unexpected girls' comic called *Misty* (1978–84), remembered with fond nostalgia by its readers. *Misty* broke with the standard "nice" stories of UK girls' comics at the time (which were on the verge of oblivion – they were almost all gone by 1990). Instead it published tales of the supernatural and horror "related" by the comic's masthead icon, Misty, who looked a lot like a vampire. The female author of this book remembers it as damn frightening, and the single annual on her shelves confirms that no punches were pulled. Many of the tales were of the "unexpected" kind, and happy endings were few and far between.

Among children's books, Margaret Mahy's *The Changeover* (1984) is one of the most interesting, and tells of a young girl on the edge of adulthood who believes her brother is being taken by a witch. Her only option is to become a witch herself. In the movies, one of the more interesting vampire stories is *The Lost Boys* (dir. Joel Schumacher, 1987). In this version of the trope, American boys who move to California and find themselves being drawn into vampire gangs, set out to destroy the vampires.

A more radical take on vampires was offered by Suzy McKee Charnas and Joanna Russ. In *The Vampire Tapestry*, by Charnas (1980), five linked novellas form a single narrative about Dr Weyland, who slowly emerges as an apparently immortal vampire. Joanna Russ's short story "My Dear Emily" (1987) follows the traditional tale of a girl seduced by a vampire, but when she has to choose between her love for him and her love for her best friend, the story takes a sharp turn and she abandons the vampire to the fire and sets out to turn her friend into a vampire. The most radical revisioning of the vampire trope came from a new writer, Storm Constantine, whose Wraeththu series (beginning with *The Enchantments of Flesh and Spirit*, 1987) can also be read as science fiction: in a devastated world, gangs of young boys roam the streets, but these are not boys, rather they are Wraeththu, hermaphroditic (but sexual) successors to humanity who can survive the ecological damage and who infect others through the transfer of blood. The Wraeththu destroy humanity by converting human males and killing human females, and are themselves dependent on regular sex for reinvigoration. The Wraeththu books acquired a cult following, particularly among the Goth subculture, and Constantine is one of the writers to have a fandom that can be considered separate from fantasy. Finally, we should mention the outstanding horror anthologists of this period, David Hartwell, who published the historical anthology *The Dark Descent: the Evolution of Horror* in 1987, followed by *The Color of Evil*, in 1990, and Stephen Jones who edited *Best New Horror* in 1990 which was the beginning of a series (edited initially with Ramsey Campbell) which has lasted to the present day.

CHAPTER NINE

The 1990s

*I*N the 1990s the fantasy genre continued to diversify and although older forms continued, they took on new dimensions, which means we have not always chosen to continue with the same category names. Urban fantasy, for example, has here been retitled indigenous fantasy, both to embrace the growing interest in local rural and urban landscapes and to take on board the degree to which magic was being localized by many writers. Similarly, while horror continued as a genre, the 1990s saw the emergence of the label "dark fantasy" which was something other. One element that we will draw attention to is the growing number of Canadian, Australian and British writers appearing in our lists. The late 1990s in particular was to see the start of the "British Boom" first in sf, but later in fantasy, which was rapidly accompanied by the growing availability of fine writing from Canada and Australia.

The only sub-genre that seems to have been eclipsed in this period was sword-and-sorcery. As we shall see in the next chapter, at least one author was also making it his business to ridicule sword-and-sorcery: this may not have been the reason for its decline but it certainly helps to explain the revisioning of sword-and-sorcery in the 2000s.

Medievalist fantasy became really big business, and in the case of the three most successful authors of the period, even if they had started with the intentions of writing a quest trilogy, commercial pressures persuaded each of them to extend their story into an apparently indefinite series. Also noticeable was how large these books became: if one stacks fantasy books by date order, up to 1977 they were relatively slim at 250 pages. After that, they expand to 500. In the 1980s, the medievalist fantasies ballooned, often reaching 1,000 pages (after which binding becomes a problem). We have been told by more than one editor that this was encouraged because it serves two para-literary purposes: first, the author's name and the title can be more visible by being written horizontally, and second, that publishing fat books is a deliberate attempt to physically crowd out other authors from the fantasy shelves in book shops. (Later, it would become fashionable to create spines in which stacking the sequels together forms a picture, as an encouragement to buy the whole series.)

Before discussing medievalist fantasies, we should mention perhaps the best critical book on medievalist fantasy, ever. In 1996 Diana Wynne Jones entered the lists with *The Tough Guide to Fantasyland* and a properly sharpened lance. *The Tough Guide to Fantasyland* purports to be a "Rough Guide" to the world of medieval quest fantasies. It envisions Fantasyland™ as ordered specifically for the adventurers, whom she terms "Tourists". *The Tough Guide* is ordered alphabetically, and offers such helpful comments as:

Horses are of a breed unique to Fantasyland. They are capable of galloping full-tilt all day without a rest. Sometimes they do not require food or water. They never cast shoes, go lame, or put their hooves down holes, except when the Management [the author] deems it necessary as when the forces of the DARK LORD are only half an hour behind.

Maps. No tour is complete without a Map. Further, you must not expect to be let off from visiting every damn place shown on it.

Prophecy is used by the Management to make sure that no Tourist is unduly surprised by events, and by GODDESSES AND GODS to make sure that people do as the deity wants. All Prophecies come true. This is a Rule.

Stew: ... the staple food in Fantasyland...Stew seems to be an odd choice of staple food, since, on a rough calculation, it takes forty times as long to prepare as steak.

In 1998, Jones published *The Dark Lord of Derkholm* which fictionalized this scenario: it is a fantasy world which has been taken over by a travel agency which sends package tours through from Earth each year causing economic and cultural devastation common to many Earth tourist spots. Seen through Jones's eyes, rather too much of medievalist fantasy has a faintly ludicrous feel as if it has been staged for our convenience: we only ever see Temples, never lavatories.

The three major medievalist writers of the 1990s are Robert Jordan, Terry Goodkind and George R.R. Martin. Robert Jordan's The Wheel of Time sequence began in 1990 with the publication of *The Eye of the World*. Jordan was still writing the twelfth book in the series – none of them less than eight hundred pages – when he died in 2007. *The Wheel of Time* sequence is an eternal champion tale set in a classic Fantasyland™: in order to defeat Shai'tan (Satan) the wheel of time periodically spins out a champion called the Dragon. The sequence itself concerns one such champion. *The Eye of the World* proceeds in archetypal quest fantasy fashion, in that we first meet the young man who is going to save the world (at least temporarily) at home in his small village. The story then proceeds by gathering companions, with various attributes and fates, who then travel across the world (see **Maps** above) accepting much of what they are told as gospel, until something else they are told supersedes it, when that becomes gospel. The characterization is thin, with most characters having one trait, continually referred to in order to tell them apart (our red-haired priestess for example, continually pulls her braid). Even some of the die-hard fans of the series (and there are millions) had begun to tire of the endless travels back and forth across the world and the continually delayed climax.

Terry Goodkind has his medieval world too, in the series called The Sword of Truth (*Wizard's First Rule*, 1994), and his Dark Lord and a characterless hero suitably called Richard Cypher (suggesting that he is not unaware of what he is doing). For the first few hundred pages (of 836) we follow the story of a young male and his love for a teenage girl and we might be persuaded that we are in a young adult fantasy as written by David Eddings. However, in chapter 40 Richard encounters a Mord'Sith, one of the Dark Lord's torture maidens. Naturally she is dressed in red leather, the better to hide the blood stains and she proceeds to torture him over a period of several months in order to render him her submissive sex slave. In 2007, the eleventh in the series was published, *Confessor* (which went to number two on the *New York Times* bestseller list), by which time Richard has discovered that his real father is the Dark Lord, has been elevated to head of the empire, and opens up a new, non-magical world, for people who so desire to emigrate to. The intervening plots are extremely tangled and involve things characteristic of these kinds of fantasy, a great deal of travelling and a certain amount of ritualizing of the unpleasant: torture is rarely about securing information, and almost always about satisfying the lusts of a Dark Lord. One of the interesting idiosyncrasies about these is the presence of North American fauna (chipmunks) in an otherwise staple European fantasy world: as Richard gives them to the torture maidens in an attempt to humanize them, this may be an oblique statement about the New World's civilizing role in relation to the Old. Or maybe not.

George R.R. Martin has the highest critical reputation of the three authors considered here, deservedly so, and has won both juried and popular voted awards. Martin was already established as a science-fiction writer when in 1996 he published the first novel in the The Song of Ice and Fire sequence (*A Game of Thrones*); the fifth, *A Dance with Dragons* is due in 2009. What distinguishes Martin from Jordan and Goodkind (and many other medievalist writers) is that he depicts a plausible and internally coherent medieval world largely free from the clichés that Jones satirized in her *Tough Guide*. The fifteenth-century Wars of the Roses are probably what inspired Martin, and there is certainly much more detailed politics and warfare in these books than there is of magic and sorcery. George R.R. Martin's more realistic and hardcore mode has influenced a number of new writers including the Canadians Steven Erikson and Scott Bakker.

Other notable writers working in medievalist fantasy worlds include K.J. Parker (British), Tanya Huff (Canadian), Patricia McKillip and Robin Hobb. K.J. Parker's Fencer trilogy is set in a medieval city-state facing off against plains barbarians. In the first book, *Colours in the Steel* (1998) we get an intimate look at the *way* that such a city-state functions through the eyes of a barbarian chief who is figuring out how to bring it down. Parker's books are notable less for their medievalism than for an engineer's eye view of the world (which becomes a theme in itself in his third trilogy known as *The Engineer Trilogy*); his system of magic functions almost like levers and screwdrivers on the world. In the Fencer sequence, there is no overt magic at all, yet the characters are aware of the *possbility* of magic, while in the Engineer sequence there is apparently no magic and yet magic lingers in the air. The fascination in the books, and in the two trilogies that have succeeded these, are less the setting than the tightly constructed spirals of family and courtly vendetta expressed metaphorically in the testing of metal, the building of siege-engines and the construction of grand strategy. Parker's work is also infused with a cynicism that means that any character stupid enough to construct a classic "fantasy trajectory" for themselves is almost certainly doomed.

Tanya Huff is currently better known for her paranormal detective stories but she also produced a highly regarded four-volume medievalist sequence beginning with *Sing the Four Quarters* (1994) in which the ability to produce magic and music are intimately linked. Better known as medievalist fantasists are the American writers Patricia McKillip and Robin Hobb. Patricia McKillip, whom we discussed in chapter seven, has been particularly prolific and throughout the 1990s and 2000s has continued to appear on the Locus best fantasy lists. In this period she wrote the Cygnet duology (*The Sorceress and the Cygnet*, 1991 and *The Cygnet and the Firebird*, 1993) which uses a medievalist setting for reworking fairytales, while commenting on the nature of story: swordswomen and dragons take their place next to swans and phoenix. McKillip also published a number of standalone books in the 1990s such as *Winter Rose* (1996), a retelling of the Tam Lin story, which can be placed alongside the equally excellent *Thomas the Rhymer* (1990) by Ellen Kushner. Slightly off topic, it is worth noting that one of the really excellent retellings of the 1990s was Geraldine McCaughrean's *Fire's Astonishment* (1990), which retold the story of the Laidly Worm (a Northumbrian folktale) and set it in a very plausible early Middle Ages, in a world in which Christianity is not yet fully accepted.

Robin Hobb was discussed in chapter eight in her other incarnation as Megan Lindholm, writer of slightly off-beat urban fantasy. In the 1990s she published two acclaimed medievalist trilogies, the Farseer trilogy starting with *Assassin's Apprentice* (1995) and the Liveship Traders trilogy, starting with *Ship of Magic* (1998), set in the same world and loosely linked. The first of the trilogies is about the rise to power of the bastard child of an aristocrat but there are several differences to the usual trajectory. First, the titles are misleading, *Assassin's Quest* is the third book and not (as one of us, schooled in reading quest fantasies in which "quest" is *always* the middle book and the third volume ends with a coronation, thought) the second: the correct order for the unwary is *Assassin's Apprentice*, *Royal Assassin* and *Assassin's Quest*. Second, Fitz does not become King. He even dies and has to be brought back. For once we have a hero content to spend his life as the sidekick, even if it is as a very powerful one.

An author who set out to gently subvert the medievalist fantasy is Barbara Hambly. In the 1980s she produced two medievalist sword-and-sorcery sequences, but also *Dragonsbane* (1985), in which John Aversin, tall, skinny and with glasses, is the last successful slayer of dragons in the kingdom. Hambly produced several sequels to this – *Dragonshadow* (1999), *Knight of the Demon Queen* (2000) and *Dragonstar* (2002) – and also the somewhat subversive Windrose Chronicles in which Antryg Windrose is exiled from his own world to Earth. The two most unnerving books of this period, however, make up the Sun-Cross duology. In the first book, *The Rainbow Abyss* (1991), we open on a world in which wizards are being persecuted. The protagonist works with his master to open a portal to another world, which seems to be crying out for a revival of magic. The second book, *The Magicians of Night* (1992), begins when Rhion wakes in the other world. At first, as any traveller through a portal, he is dependent on what he is told for his understanding of the world around him; only very slowly does he realize the nature of the people for whom he now works, and we realize that they are Nazis and that this is 1940. In the course of the two books, Hambly sets out to challenge our readings of medievalist fantasy, and the way in which we as reader function in portal fantasies.

Greer Gilman's *Moonwise* (1991) is probably the most radical book here, if only for the language it employs. The high language of nineteenth-century medievalism has long been abandoned, and most medievalist fantasy is told in a contemporary voice. In *Moonwise* Greer Gilman takes an old tale of ritual and earth magic and relates it with a "pitch and density of language reminiscent of Gerard Manley Hopkins" (Clute, p.411). Gilman may be the only author to write an entire novel using iambic pentameter, as she has done in her most recent book, *Cloud and Ashes* (2009).

Perhaps the most enterprising of our medievalist writers from the 1990s is Guy Gavriel Kay whose Fionavar Tapestry we discussed in the last chapter. In the 1990s he wrote major fantasy novels set in four different types of medieval world. *Tigana* (1990) is about a group of rebels trying to win back their homeland in a world that resembles late medieval Italy. *A Song for Arbonne* (1992) is in part a rewriting of a story of the Crusades against the Cathars and is set in France. *The Lions of Al-Rassan* (1995) takes place in a world resembling Spain at the time of the medieval reconquest of Islam, and finally in the 1990s he wrote *Sailing to Sarantium* (1998) and its sequel, *Lord of Emperors* (2000). In these books we follow the adventures of a mosaicist employed by the emperor in Sarantium to decorate his magnificent new church. Kay uses the fantasy form to comment upon "real" history. His emperor, Valerius II, is clearly the sixth-century Justinian and Sarantium is a thinly disguised Byzantium. In a fantasy context Kay can use supernatural intervention and visions in a way which actually gets us closer to the sixth-century mind than he could in a standard historical novel, in that the reader's expectations are closer to those of the protagonists than would be the case in the "realist" mode, where it is very hard to avoid condescension with respect to historical belief-systems.

Not all medievalist fantasy available in the UK was Anglo-American. Fans interested in anime were already aware of Hayao Miyazaki, but the wide release of the medieval fantasy *Princess Mononoke* in 1997, a period drama about the conflict of human industrialization and the intervention of the gods of the forest, destroying the polluting industries, brought Miyazaki to wider attention. The visual language of the movie was hugely influential, and the awareness of different fantastical traditions did much to invigorate medievalist fantasy in the next decade.

Although medievalist fantasy has remained popular, by the 1990s other periods were becoming increasingly attractive as contexts for fantasy. The texts we are looking at are quite different from medievalist fantasy. Where the medievalist worlds were mostly separate from ours, those authors working with the material provided by later periods tended to set their stories in facsimiles of our worlds, or to begin at least ostensibly in our world. The novels are closer to alternate history than to the full fantasy of the medievalists, and also have a great deal in common with the "urban fantasists" of the 1990s, whom we will consider later in the chapter, in that magic tends to be intricately connected to the polity.

Mary Gentle's *Rats and Gargoyles* (1990), Peter Ackroyd's *The House of Doctor Dee* (1993) and Michael Swanwick's *Jack Faust* (1997) are all very different books, but they share a vision of an urban fantasy in which the Renaissance is under challenge either by the author or the characters. Mary Gentle's *Rats and Gargoyles* is a full fantasy, the first of her *White Crow* novels, set in a faux seventeenth century. This is a world in which rats rule men, and gods walk the land. Although this world is wholly fantastic Gentle is drawing on the intellectual history of the sixteenth and seventeenth centuries with its belief in hidden secrets either preserved in the writings of Hermes Trismegistus or else preserved by secret societies such as the Rosicrucians. Gentle's world is confronted directly in a number of fantasies, most notably in this period, by Ackroyd and Swanwick. In Ackroyd's *The House of Doctor Dee* the protagonist comes to believe that he is a homunculus created by Doctor Dee. John Dee has proven one of the great staple characters of modern fantasy, appearing in the works of Charles Maturin and H.P. Lovecraft, and more recently in Umberto Eco's *Foucault's Pendulum* (1988), John Crowley's *Ægypt* sequence, Michael Moorcock's *Gloriana* (1978), Lisa Goldstein's *The Alchemist's Door* (2002), Michael Scott's *The Alchemyst: the Secrets of the Immortal Nicholas Flamel* and Liz Williams's *The Poison Master* (2003). Michael Swanwick's *Jack Faust* is a new take on the Faust story. In this case Faust's pact with Mephistopheles involves an attempt to avoid the kind of industrialization we live with. Faust gets to live through the consequences of his desires at high speed, and the reader gets to consider whether this might indeed be the best of possible worlds.

In 1992 John Whitbourn published *A Dangerous Energy*, the first of a series of books set in an England where Elizabeth I died of smallpox in 1562. Mary Queen of Scots succeeded to the English throne from where she launched a counter-reformation; however, this is also a world with magic, where incubi and succubi really exist and it is truly possible to make a pact with evil. The substance of this and the other books (*Popes and Phantoms*, 1993, and *To Build Jerusalem*, 1995) are the secret plots of reformers and puritans, marginalized by the return of the Old Order. Whitbourn's books trace the alternative history of England not infrequently traced out by English Catholics' hopes and fears in the years before the failure of the Jacobite uprisings, and he completed the set with *The Royal Changeling* (1998) which is essentially a story of Jacobite rebellion and propaganda (the only other Jacobite fantasies are those by Joan Aiken). Whitbourn's work was very different to his contemporaries, and he and Mary Gentle were to an extent both harbingers of the New Weird, a movement in British fantasy that we will deal with in the last chapter.

Although the French Revolution has been a very attractive period to people writing time travel novels, it has not attracted fantasy writers. A singular exception was the very unusual *The Porcelain Dove* (1993) by Delia Sherman. In a small town far from Paris, a corrupt Duke (and magician) is cursed that his family will never be happy until they find the porcelain dove. Told from the point of view of the maid, much of the novel is a story of how the family deteriorated over a long period of time, losing its virtue and its sense of self as the world outside it spiralled towards revolution. The tone of the book is elegiac, and elegant, but it describes truly awful events. It is a shock when the revolution finally breaks out, and the daughter of the house leaves in search of the porcelain dove, sealing up the entire family in the castle. They do not sleep for a hundred years, but they are held apart from events, immortal, never aging.

At the end of the 1980s we saw the emergence of a new publishing category. By the 1990s horror fiction was going through one of its periods of exhaustion. Dark fantasy as a concept seems to have been both a strategy to reinvigorate the market, and also a reaction to the increasing emphasis on blood and gore in horror movies. Some writers' work was simply reclassified. Tanith Lee had always been understood as a horror oriented fantasy writer, and the new label might have been shaped just for her. In the 1990s she produced the Unicorn series (*Black Unicorn, Gold Unicorn,* and *Red Unicorn,* 1989–97, full fantasy novels), the Blood Opera series (*Dark Dance, Personal Darkness, Darkness, I,* 1992–4, modern Gothic urban fantasies) and the Venus series set in a dark and Gothic eighteenth-century alternate and pagan Venice (*Faces Under Water, Saint Fire, A Bed of Earth,* and *Venus Preserved,* 1998–2003).

Dark fantasy in general has a nineteenth- or twentieth-century setting and a fondness for some of the traditional icons of fantastic folklore such as the vampire and the werewolf. However, it is not "fright" fiction and traditional sympathies are realigned. Dark fantasy also tends to be "immersive" fantasy where horror is "intrusion" fantasy (see Mendlesohn, 2008: immersive fantasy is where we are in a complete other world to which the protagonist belongs; in intrusion fantasy, the fantastic *intrudes* or invades our world). In much dark fantasy, the supernatural is already known to exist, and an accommodation has already been reached, often on a societal level. Much dark fantasy can be read as "alternate world" in much the same way that the work of Keith Roberts and John Whitbourn could be read this way. It is often a form of rationalized fantasy. One element in this was that the early 1990s saw the influence of AIDS on fantasy literature. A number of "dark fantasy" tropes which had hitherto been used to discuss racial and sexual taboos, were now pressed in to service to address the social consequence of this frightening new disease.

One of the earliest manifestations of dark fantasy was Brian Stableford's *Empire of Fear* discussed in the previous chapter: in the 1990s Brian Stableford began his David Lydyard trilogy, with *The Werewolves of London* in 1990. The young protagonist travels to Egypt in 1872 and is possessed by a strange power; on his return to London he becomes involved in plots by occultists and meets the legendary werewolves of the tale. In *The Angel of Pain* (1991) it is 1893 and Lydyard's visionary powers are becoming more oppressive. He finds himself caught up in the great occult event of the late Victorian era, the reawakening of fallen angels. The final volume, *The Carnival of Destruction* (1994) begins in 1918 when Lydyard becomes aware that the angels plot to bring apocalypse to the world. In the early 1990s Stableford also produced two more rationalized versions of the vampire legend, *Young Blood* (1992) which looks at the link between vampirism and mind-altering viruses, and *The Hunger and Ecstasy of Vampires* (1996) where H.G. Wells's time traveller goes to a future ruled by vampires.

Two other British authors who sought to place vampires into more modern settings were Freda Warrington and Kim Newman. Warrington's *Blood Wine* sequence (*A Taste of Blood Wine*, 1992) staged an epic battle between a vampire and his maker on the battlefield of the First World War and the drawing rooms of 1920s Cambridge, interweaving a tale of attraction in which lust for love and lust for blood become hopelessly confused in a precursor to the paranormal romance which will dominate the form later in the decade. In the same year, Kim Newman published *Anno Dracula*, the first of a series of alternate history vampire novels, set in a world in which Count Dracula is real, has not been killed, and has married Queen Victoria. There is a threat that the vampires are going to take over the country and the Jack the Ripper murders are, in this novel, an attempt to prevent vampire prostitutes from "converting" their clients. The sequel, *The Bloody Red Baron* (1995), takes place during the First World War, at a time when the Germans are trying to create ace pilots out of the undead, one of whom becomes known as the Red Baron. Newman's works are meta-textual in that a number of fictional characters make an appearance. That both Newman and Warrington set their tales during the First World War is not wholly coincidental: at the end of the twentieth century Britain was mourning some of the last of the veterans of that war, and there was a revival in public display. The language and poetry of the war, with its emphasis on the blood draining out of the land, is peculiarly easy to appropriate.

One new development in dark fantasy was the private investigator who worked among the paranormal. The mode of engagement varied: Tananarive Due's Jennifer in the African Immortals series is dragged into the world of the supernatural by killings committed by her immortal husband in *My Soul to Keep* (1997). More common among the new fiction however, was the full fantasy world in which the supernatural lives alongside us, in full moonlight if not daylight. In Tanya Huff's *Blood Price* (1991) the first of a series, Vicki Nelson an ex-detective, pairs up with a vampire romance writer to investigate a series of murders in the city of Toronto, which involve werewolves and other supernatural beings.

The most successful of this kind of fantasy in the 1990s was Laurell K. Hamilton's Anita Blake sequence, a phenomenon which may or may not owe something to the release of the *Buffy the Vampire Slayer* movie in 1992 (and which we will soon discuss). The first in the sequence is *Guilty Pleasures* (1993), which sets up a world in which vampires have been acknowledged and their presence legitimized in the United States, leading to an influx from Europe. Vampires can take their place in society, as long as they don't break the law. If they do, they are taken down by vampire hunters. Anita Blake is one such, despite her diminutive height. Blake is a good Catholic girl, whose faith often rescues her, but is excommunicated because she is a professional zombie raiser: at the start of the series, the vampire hunting is merely a side-line. Although vampires have been accepted, shape-shifters (who are created through contagion via blood and sex) are not, and one of the main shape-shifter characters is socially crippled by his fear of being outed, again picking up on the AIDS fear of the 1990s. The first few books are essentially detective novels, but running through them are romantic complications. Anita finds herself courted by the Master Vampire of the city of St. Louis, but also by the head werewolf. Like any Catholic girl would, she gets involved with both and spends the next sixteen books (the most recent, *Blood Noir*, 2008) feeling guilty about it, dealing with the werewolf's anger and the unfortunate psychic bond the three of them set up. The books lose interest in the detective element and are increasingly concerned with the politics of the paranormal denizens of the city, which just happens to be played out in Anita's bed, often accompanied by whips and chains. By book ten, the readership of these books, while still growing, began to change. Many early fans simply could not handle the quite explicit descriptions of consensual sadism and also sexual abuse in the later books. In the 2000s there will be an explosion of books picking up on the paranormal romance aspect of these books, such as Charlaine Harris's The Southern Vampire Mysteries (*Dead Until Dark*, 2002; series ongoing).

The outstandingly successful paranormal investigator/paranormal romance of the 1990s was, of course, *Buffy the Vampire Slayer*. The original 1992 movie, directed by Fran Rubel Kuzei with a script by Joss Whedon, is widely considered a mess, but its core idea of a cheerleader who discovers that it is her job to save the world from vampires and all things that go bump in the night was intrinsically amusing. What was not expected was that the TV series, which began in 1997 (created and supervised by Whedon) would turn out to be one of the most thoughtful, witty and subtle shows on television. The basic premise is the same, and over seven seasons there were a number of individual stories in which Buffy beats the monsters, but there are several major story-arcs, including a romance with a vampire, whose restored soul has placed him on Buffy's side, and later a second relationship with another vampire who is prevented from killing by a chip in his head. Both relationships become contexts for the exploration of the nature of free will and of good and evil. *Buffy* traded in ironic awareness of the fictional world: when Dracula appears, he is defeated easily because as the characters say, "we've read the book". We could quite easily write an entire chapter on *Buffy*, since we are both hardcore fans, but sadly there is not the space. One thing worth noting, however, is that Buffy created an entire new mythology around vampires and other aspects of the supernatural, and many young writers have simply picked up on these ideas, apparently oblivious to earlier traditions.

At the very end of the 1980s Ellen Datlow, one of the best short-story editors in the field, began collaborating with Terri Windling, herself a talented author and editor, to produce a *Year's Best Fantasy and Horror* anthology for St Martin's Press. This anthology showcased some of the best in dark fantasy and helped to shape the sub-genre. Since 2003 Windling's role has been taken by Kelly Link and Gavin Grant, and the series is ongoing. Its covers, however, have always been painted by Thomas Canty, whose work revived Pre-Raphaelite faerie; he also did the covers for Datlow and Windling's collections of modern fairytales, the Colors of Fantasy series.

The Colors of Fantasy series began with *Snow White, Blood Red* in 1993. These were collections of original fairytales, sometimes loosely based on traditional ones, such as Gahan Wilson's "The Frog Prince" (1993), and sometimes inspired by fairytale structures and tropes, but otherwise original tales, such as Neil Gaiman's "The Troll Bridge". Six volumes were published in this series, with the last one being *Black Heart, Ivory Bones* (2000), a generally more sinister collection. Some of the very best authors in the field contributed to these series, including John Brunner, Susanna Clarke, John Crowley, Nalo Hopkinson, Pat Murphy, and Gene Wolfe, in the process transforming what fantasy writers felt that they could do with fairytales. We can see much the same process going on in the novel in this period. Where previous work with fairytales had been predominantly in the area of retellings, authors in the 1990s began to use fairytale and fantasy structures to write absolutely modern stories in which knowledge of the structures was the exoskeleton of the story rather than the story itself.

The first and one of the most impressive of these books is Geoff Ryman's *"Was ..."* (1992). *"Was ..."* is the story of two people, a young man dying of AIDS, who sets out to discover the ruby slippers from the MGM musical *The Wizard of Oz* and an elderly woman dying in an old people's home, who tells everybody she was the original Dorothy, and that Baum had stolen her story. Although this book is very much "contemporary literature" it is infused with immanence. There is always a sense that Glinda the Good is just around the corner waiting to grant wishes, and that Dorothy will find her way back to Oz. A very different approach to using faerie can be found in Patrice Kindl's *Owl in Love* (1993). This is a tale of a frog prince, told from the frog prince's point of view. Owl is a wereowl, and when she meets her true love her kiss will transform him into (or at least help him realize that he is) another wereowl. The story itself is set in a high school, and Owl's problems are about the difficulty of fitting in, when the bread on a mouse sandwich makes her feel ill, and the tail keeps falling out. Jane Yolen's *Briar Rose* (1991) is even further from the fairytale than Ryman's *"Was ..."*. On one level this is a story about the concentration camp at Chelmno, one of the most horrific of the Nazi death camps, from which very few survived. The camp was in a castle, surrounded by barbed wire. Inspired by this, Yolen used the story of Sleeping Beauty (asleep in a castle surrounded by thorns) to deepen the sense of horror and threat felt by the protagonist, a descendant of a rare Chelmno survivor.

There are more straightforward approaches to the modern fairytale. In Elizabeth Ann Scarborough's *The Godmother* (1994) Rose Samson wishes for a fairy godmother to save all Seattle, and is a bit taken aback when one promptly arrives, a very modern godmother capable of dealing with the modern world. Rachel Pollack's two protagonists in *Godmother Night* (1996) also acquire a godmother, but this is Death, who rides a Harley Davidson and helps them to cope with life as lesbians in a hostile society. In Holly Lisle's *Sympathy for the Devil* (1995) a nurse bargains with God to give the inhabitants of Hell a second chance, in a story reminiscent of many of the slick fantasies of the 1930s and '40s. John Barnes's *One for the Morning Glory* (1996) is an utterly original fairytale in which a young man is rendered only half of himself after he sips the wine of the gods. In his travels to find his other half he is accompanied by various companions, each with their own attributes, who had turned up at court while the hero was a small child. This is clearly a fairytale and not a quest fantasy, following very closely the tropes and rhythms of classic fairytale as described by Vladimir Propp. Neil Gaiman's *Stardust* (1998, filmed 2007) tells of a young man who lives in a town on the edge of Faerie, who crosses the wall to find a falling star to bring home to his fiancée. *Stardust* is a classic tale of a lost prince, a rescued heroine, wickedness and witches, clearly influenced by the work of Hope Mirrlees, whom we discussed in an earlier chapter. Patrick O'Leary's *The Gift* (1997) is a story about story-telling, about a king and about a boy being cursed, drawing heavily on the specifically American fairytale imagery created by Baum and to a certain extent the darker world of the Grimms. China Miéville's debut novel, *King Rat* (1999), is a Pied Piper story set in the grimy streets of London and told from the point of view of a young man who discovers that his true father is a wererat and that he is the result of rape. Of the texts discussed here Miéville's is the most brutal, and in some ways also harks back to the Grimms in its construction of faerie- and folklore.

The best-known "re-teller" of the 1990s is probably Gregory Maguire. Already a well-known children's writer, Maguire published *Wicked: The Life and Times of the Wicked Witch of the West* (1995), which set out to dismantle the Wizard of Oz's narration of the witch and consider how "wickedness" is created in both reality and conception. Maguire's take on the tale reinvigorated many of the political themes of Baum's tale and showed an unusual awareness of early-twentieth-century American politics (such as the resegregation of Washington). *Wicked* was made into a very successful stage musical in 2003 that watered down much of this but handled the fantasy meta-text very well. Since then Maguire has published the fairytale retellings *Confessions of an Ugly Stepsister* (1999) and *Mirror, Mirror* (2003) among other titles.

Two movies which came out in this period that could loosely be included here are *The Mask* (1993, dir. Charles Russell) and *Groundhog Day* (1993, dir. Harold Ramis). In *The Mask* a young man with no confidence finds a mask that transforms his personality and allows him to change the behaviour of those around him, much like the gifts in fairytales. In *Groundhog Day* an utterly arrogant and selfish weather presenter finds himself forced to relive the same day over and over again; he constantly tweaks it until he has not only got it "right" but, in the process of doing this, has transformed his character. This tale is clearly a tale of a fairy curse and a punishment; only when he gives his lunch to a stranger and acts like a fairytale hero can he be released from the curse.

Examining these modern fairytales leads us to a development in fantasy which, while not wholly new, becomes pronounced in the 1990s: the increasing use of local landscape and local mythologies, if necessary, creating myth-structures from the whole-cut cloth of the modern world, a mode we have labelled "indigenous fantasy". Graham Joyce's *The Tooth Fairy* (1998) might have been discussed in the previous section. In this story a young boy wakes up and sees the Tooth Fairy at the bottom of his bed, and over the course of the book has various increasingly scary encounters with the fairy. But the story is set very firmly in the

English Midlands, against a background of attending school, finding his first girlfriend, and hanging out with his mates, and the conclusion to the book demonstrates the degree to which he has imposed his own childhood ideas on a being who cannot resist them. The Tooth Fairy of this book is not *our* tooth fairy, but something quite Other.

In the 1990s a number of authors worked to generate new kinds of fantasy linked to their own sense of place and their own notions of the fantastic. In Britain a number of writers stand out. Ellen Galford, who in the 1980s wrote *The Fires of Bride*, followed this in 1990 with *Queendom Come* and in 1993 with *The Dyke and the Dybbuk*. *Queendom Come* is an anti-Thatcherite fantasy in which a depressed Scottish doctor accidentally revives a Boudicca-like figure to rescue Britain in its time of need. Unfortunately this pagan barbarian gets on rather well with the Prime Minister, and eventually our protagonist and the queen's sidekick conspire together to lock both up in a magical prison. At one point in the novel the Prime Minister finds herself confronted by the rather irritated ghosts of martyred witches and other problematic women. In *The Dyke and the Dybbuk* a North London lesbian Jew finds herself dealing with a curse laid on her great-great-grandmother who had ditched her girlfriend in favour of a good marriage.

Ben Okri is a Nigerian writer who has spent much of his childhood and adult life in London. In 1991 he produced *The Famished Road*, set in Nigeria, which won the Booker Prize. It is narrated by Azaro, a child who has never lost his ties to the spiritual world, which is constantly trying to take him back. Christopher Priest, an author associated with New Wave science fiction in the 1960s, produced a notable fantasy in this period: *The Prestige* (1995; adapted as a movie, 2006, dir. Christopher Nolan). The protagonist lives in a house to which he seems to be connected and in which at some point in the past two stage-magicians had met. Much of the novel is made up from an autobiographical statement from the first magician, and the diary of the second which, between them, tell of their rivalry and deathly competition, involving teleportation and replication of human beings. Diana Wynne Jones returned to form with a novel for adults called *A Sudden Wild Magic* (1992), which imagined the island of Britain protected by a circle of witches who strongly resemble your local mad cat woman and that nice lady who runs the crystal shop down the street. The outstanding British indigenous fantasy novel of this period, however, is M. John Harrison's *The Course of the Heart* (1992), a novel about three people who perform magic while at university, and are haunted by its consequences. One of them seems to recover, but watches as the other two are consumed by their attempts to keep the magic at bay. They do this by creating a tale of yet another world, but this seems to fuel the latent magic so that our world becomes overlapped by both the fictional text and the magical world. In this novel the streets of Manchester ripple with threat, ghosts appear outside cottages, but nothing is truly connected, in the same way that there are few connections between people in the postmodern world. Harrison's argument seems to be that our world is unreal and fantastical, and we render it real in our heads for our own peace of mind.

Over in America Thomas M. Disch produced a series of bitter satires of the institutions of American society through the medium of horror and fantasy. In *The Priest: A Gothic Romance* (1994) a Minneapolis priest engages in a number of indiscretions, not the least of which is that he frequently becomes possessed by a medieval bishop of the Inquisition. In *The Sub: A Study in Witchcraft* (1999), Diana Turney is a teacher hired by an elementary school as a replacement for two teachers fired for Satanic abuse. However, Diana is a wiccan, and quickly discovers that she has magical powers, which she uses to take revenge on the men in her life. Rebecca Ore offers a slightly different take on witchcraft in *Slow Funeral* (1994) in which Maud Fuller, who has avoided dealing with her witch relatives, heads home to live with her dying grandmother. The book is rooted in Appalachian life. Terri Windling looks to a different type of indigenous tradition in *The Wood Wife* (1996), in which Maggie Black moves to Tucson and becomes aware that she is surrounded by magic and magic users. As she becomes bedded down in the Arizonan landscape, she becomes aware of the local spirits and local folklore. Similarly in Louise Erdrich's *The Antelope Wife* (1998), a soldier chasing a dog that carries an Ojibwa baby strapped to its back becomes the key image in a modern tale of Ojibwa families living in present-day Minneapolis. In Erdrich's book different worlds exist overlaid by each other, while stories cross time, linked by artefacts from the past. Jonathan Carroll, who had produced *The Land of Laughs* in 1980, in the 1990s published *Outside the Dog Museum* (1991), *After Silence* (1992) and *From the Teeth of Angels* (1993). All of these books have a Rabelaisian quality, frequently mixing the slick fantasy style, in which people make pacts with the supernatural, with the anarchy of Lewis Carroll. Jonathan Carroll seems fascinated by the afterlife, and all his books have an element of "posthumous fantasy".

Four writers who contributed to a very distinct kind of American fantasy in this period are Elizabeth Hand, James Morrow, Michael Swanwick and Sean Stewart. Beginning with *Passion Play* (1992) and proceeding with novels such as *Mockingbird* (1998) and *Galveston* (2000), Sean Stewart constructed a magical realism in the American South, in which the gods of carnival live in and among the citizens and must be appeased. *Galveston* tells the tale of a small island flooded by both water and magic which must come to terms with its new relationship to the supernatural. Elizabeth Hand's first novel *Winterlong* (1988) had been set in a post-apocalyptic Rabelaisian future America in which pagan gods roamed. In the 1990s she published *Aestival Tide* (1992), *Icarus Descending* (1993), *Waking the Moon* (1994), *Glimmering* (1997, an sf novel), and *Black Light* (1999), as well as a collection, *Last Summer at Mars Hill* (1998). Of these, *Waking the Moon* and *Last Summer at Mars Hill* are most distinctive. *Waking the Moon* is about a young freshman at a Catholic university who is accidentally brought within the orbit of a group of secret masters, who are involved in a centuries-long conspiracy to hold back a pagan goddess. Sweeney Cassidy's boyfriend becomes involved with a woman called Angelica, who by the end has become an avatar of the goddess. The book is distinctive because although it draws on the Greek story of the Bacchae, it is in part precisely about the

Americanization of older traditions, in this case Hand uses the Bacchae in part to critique the place of goddess-worship in American feminism.

In the 1990s James Morrow produced a number of very highly regarded books that satirized Christianity by placing God (and the body of God) in very American contexts. In *Only Begotten Daughter* (1990) a celibate lighthouse-keeper near Atlantic city becomes father to a female messiah, who can walk on water and raise the dead. In *Towing Jehovah* (1994) the archangel Raphael reveals that God is dead and his two-mile-long body is floating in the Atlantic and a super-tanker is hired to tow the body into the Arctic to preserve it from decomposition (a prime concern of American morticians everywhere). In the sequel, *Blameless in Abaddon* (1996) the body has been incorporated into a religious theme park. Morrow tackled the question of religion in numerous different ways in short stories throughout the late 1980s and 1990s and these were collected together into *Bible Stories for Adults* (1996).

Finally, one of the most inventive novels of the decade was Michael Swanwick's *The Iron Dragon's Daughter* (1993). Swanwick has discussed how this novel came out of a visit to England and his admiration for the degree to which English writers wrote from their own landscape. Searching for a distinctly American landscape he was struck by the image of a train coming out of a tunnel and transformed it in his mind into a great iron dragon, a weapon of war. *The Iron Dragon's Daughter* is set in a parallel faerie America. This is an industrialized, urban fairytale in which no one cares what happens to the changeling Jane, rescued from a dragon factory by a dragon with an agenda of his own. She stumbles through a lethal university system and the social structure of faerie before finding her way back into the human world. In 2008, Swanwick published a sequel, *The Dragons of Babel*, in which a young boy discovers he is a lost prince of this fantasy land, which in practice is somehow not quite what those of us conditioned to fairytales expect.

There are a number of writers and texts we want to mention whom we cannot easily link to the loose categories above. The 1990s saw, for example, two new sword-and-sorcery TV programmes, at the very time at which the genre was neglected in the written form. *Hercules: The Legendary Journeys* (produced by Pacific Renaissance Pictures Ltd, 1995–99) shamelessly rifled tales from the Greek myths and was a witty and pleasant take on these stories. However, its spin-off, *Xena: Warrior Princess*, from the same stable (1995–2001) was a great cult hit. Using essentially the same premise, *Xena* did not restrict itself to Greek myth but plundered stories from the ancient world totally indiscriminately (with Xena being present at the siege of Troy one week, and meeting Julius Caesar the next). Some of its appeal was due to the relationship between Xena and her sidekick Gabrielle. At some stage the producers became aware that the show was attracting a large gay following, but instead of trying to evade the homoerotic subtext as previous television programmes had done, the script-writers played up to it, and increasingly presented Xena and Gabrielle as soul-mates. At the cinema, one of the best fantasy movies of the 1990s was Anthony Minghella's *Truly, Madly, Deeply* (1991), in which a woman cannot let go of her grief for her partner, so he comes back as a ghost and sets about persuading her to move on, mostly by moving in his ghostly friends. The movie is mostly set in a small apartment and for much of the time the ghost sits and shivers; although deeply moving, this is not a sentimental story, unlike the romantic drama *Ghost* (dir. Jerry Zucker), which came out the year before.

Writers who produced interesting books in this period were Lisa Goldstein (*Dark Cities Underground*, 1999), Maggie Furey (*Harp of Winds*, 1995), Monica Furlong (*Juniper*, 1991), and Michael Bishop (*Brittle Innings*, 1994). Two writers working in dark fantasy were Nina Kiriki Hoffman (*The Thread that Binds the Bones*, 1993) and S.P. Somtow (*Riverrun*, 1991). One of the best children's writers working in the 1990s was K.A. Applegate, who as Katherine Applegate was far better known for long series of romances, but had already produced a lengthy sf series called *Animorphs* (1996–2001, 54 books). Her *Everworld* sequence for young adults (1999–2001, 12 books) traps five teenagers in a particularly scary pocket universe, inhabited by exiled gods. It is often overlooked in the general and unwarranted disparagement of "series books" for younger readers. Tom Holt became very popular in Britain in this decade for his humorous rewritings of familiar fantasy settings. He had begun in 1987 with *Expecting Someone Taller*, in which the world of the Norse gods erupts into modern England, and in the 1990s he dealt with the Flying Dutchman, Arthur, Faust, Ali Baba, among others. Also interesting is Caroline Stevermer's *A College of Magics* (1994), a quirky Ruritanian romance set in a young ladies' finishing school which turns out witches, and *Good Omens: The Nice and Accurate Prophecies of Agnes Nutter, Witch* (1990) by Neil Gaiman and Terry Pratchett, a story of what happens when the Antichrist really *does* come and a book of prophecies is approached by somebody with the mind of a crossword puzzle addict. In this book the kind of great plans which structure so many fantasies come up against the hard reality of incompetence and good intentions.

At the end of the 1990s, fantasy – as this chapter demonstrates – was healthier and more diverse than ever, yet in the public eye three British writers had come to dominate perceptions of fantasy: Terry Pratchett, J.K. Rowling, and Philip Pullman. In the next chapter we will describe how this came about.

CHAPTER TEN

Pullman, Rowling, Pratchett

*A*s we look back at the 1990s, three writers seem to stand out from the field, not so much for their contribution to the nature or form of fantasy literature as for their contribution to the marketing of fantasy and to the public perception of the field. In the early 1990s Terry Pratchett was *the* best-selling author in Britain. Each year he produced at least one hardback, and one hardback was reprinted in paperback. Both could be expected to reach the top ten in their respective lists. By the end of the 1990s, J.K. Rowling had become the best-selling author in the world and the twelfth richest woman in Britain. In 2001, Philip Pullman became the first author to win the Whitbread Award with a book written and marketed specifically for children (with *The Amber Spyglass*, 2000, last of the His Dark Materials trilogy).

We are going to take these authors out of order, for the simple reason that Pullman and Rowling have finished the sequences for which they are known, while Pratchett's sequence is still ongoing.

Philip Pullman's first children's novel was *Count Karlstein, or The Ride of the Demon Huntsman* (1982), in part a novelization of the fantasy opera *Der Freischütz* by Carl Maria von Weber. He followed this up with a number of other works for children and young adults, some of which were fantastical and some of which (the Sally Lockhart series for example, 1985–94) were not. Perhaps his most successful standalone book has been *I Was a Rat!* or *The Scarlet Slippers* (1999) which tells the story of one of the rats on Cinderella's coach who, having been turned into a page boy, misses out on his chance to become a rat again, and has to survive in this human world. One reason the book is notable is because Pullman has discussed it often in the context of his discovery that many British children are unaware of the classic European fairytales (or know only the Disney versions).[15]

Pullman's reputation was established with the publication of three novels known collectively as *His Dark Materials*. *Northern Lights* (1995: US, *The Golden Compass*) introduced Lyra, an unattached child wandering the corridors of an Oxford college in an alternate world. Lyra is a ward of the college, and we begin the books with the assumption that she is an orphan. For the reader, the most immediate awareness that we are in a different world is not that Jordan College does not exist but that every character is accompanied by an animal familiar known as a dæmon. Children's dæmons change species according to mood and need; around puberty, however, the dæmon settles down into a single form. This element is the major hook of the books, both in terms of their popularity and the story itself, but is also the element which has led some critics to feel uneasy as the forms dæmons take seem to reinforce social hierarchies (servants tend to have dog dæmons) and heteronormativity (almost all dæmons are of opposite sex to the host and the one servant with a same sex dæmon is regarded with suspicion).

The three books – *Northern Lights*, *The Subtle Knife* (1997) and *The Amber Spyglass* (1999) – have several levels of plot: the intimate children's plot of travel and adventure; the adult story of challenging God's order; and a Miltonesque tale of war in heaven. The children's tale is of Lyra and Will, children from two different worlds. Lyra sets out from the Oxford college initially to find out why her friend Roger and other children have been kidnapped off the streets. She is chased by Mrs Coulter and later by her father Lord Asriel. Mrs Coulter wants the alethiometer, which had been given to Lyra by the Master of Jordan College. Lord Asriel is experimenting with the substance known as Dust, which can be seen to gather around children as they approach puberty, and which

---

15   Some of this of course is because many of the children *aren't* European.

he is convinced has something to do with the sinfulness of the world. Both Mrs. Coulter and Lord Asriel are out to challenge the Authority; in both cases their challenge focuses on divorcing children from their dæmons (intercision). Mrs Coulter does this in the service of purity, while Lord Asriel is looking for a way to release energy. At the end of the first book this tears a hole in the world, and it is through this that Will comes, from a world haunted by soul-sucking shadows. Before Will comes through to Lyra's world, however, he has a series of adventures during which he acquires "the subtle knife", which allows him to cut his way through worlds. He joins up with Lyra and they aid each other in escaping from Mrs Coulter, who has chased them into a world called Cittàgazze where the invisible shadows of Will's world are manifest. At the end of the book Will finds his missing father, who unfortunately is almost immediately killed by a witch, whose love he had failed to return. Lyra takes responsibility for this and tells Will that she will support him in his adventure. In the third book Lyra spends much of the time asleep in a glass coffin in which Mrs Coulter has placed her for safekeeping, having discovered that Lyra is her daughter by Lord Asriel. Will gets to travel through another hole in the world to our world, where he finds the Catholic scientist Mary Malone, and takes her into yet another world, in which there are fantastic aliens with wheels instead of feet. Meanwhile, the third level of the story becomes clearer, as angels become involved in the adventure and, towards the end of the book, the two children accidentally kill God (both of us – one an atheist, one a believer – feel it should have been deliberate).

A full summary of the books would take an entire chapter and is quite unnecessary. The books are written on an epic scale – there are witches, talking bears wearing armour made from meteorites, wild flights with gypsies, and thrilling escapes – and the tone is similarly epic, with pauses in the vernacular narrative for characters to sit by fires and tell lengthy stories of origins and heroes. In the third book Lyra experiences a descent into Limbo in which the ability to tell these types of stories will prove the key to escape for all of Limbo's inhabitants. The books are also militantly anti-Christian and deeply philosophical. The first of these aspects was toned down in the 2007 movie *The Golden Compass* (although even so the prior publicity rendered the movie a flop in the States), but at the end of *The Amber Spyglass* we discover that Lord Asriel does not wish to destroy Dust as we had assumed, but wishes to preserve it. His opposition to the church is because "sin" (associated with the acquisition of Dust in puberty) is the origin of originality and free will.

The intelligence, complexity and *density* of Pullman's trilogy lie at the heart of its popularity both with young readers and with critics. These are books to be chewed over. They have never reached the sales figures of J.K. Rowling's *Harry Potter* series, but then they are very clearly written for the Reading Child (the child who actively wants to read), rather than the child reader (who appears commonly in the educationalist literature and whom educationalists and librarians wish to persuade to read). Pullman's books are very susceptible to re-reading, because they are loaded with Greek myth, theology, literary references, and scientific speculation: they are books to grow up with. Similarly, the texts offer a great deal to adults, particularly those concerned with theology. Pullman's direct and vocal attack on C.S. Lewis, both in the construction of the books and subsequent discussion, has drawn significant attention. Pullman has engaged in debate with the Archbishop of Canterbury at the National Theatre (*The Daily Telegraph*, 17.3.05) and the books appear on apologetics courses to help trainee ministers hone their argumentative skills against those pesky atheists.

However, not all of the atheists are too happy about Pullman's work either, despite the assumptions of critics such as Peter Hitchens (see his article in *The Spectator*, 18.1.03). There are several problems. As we have already mentioned, the dæmons create a peculiarly reified vision of class and sexuality. There is also an uncomfortable element of misogyny in the books. More than one female reader was taken aback at Lyra's passivity in the third book. Mrs Coulter is the classic devious female reaching into male domains. Of the witches, those who love well are nice, those who love poorly are vicious. The gypsy woman we meet is lovely because she is a caring mother. The female scientist is also posed in a maternal role. There are no women just being people. The nicest female character is Hester, the dæmon of the aeronaut Lee Scoresby who dies when he does (one of the two most heart-rending moments of the book). This is ironic, given that many of Pullman's attacks on his predecessor, C.S. Lewis, have been focused on the character of Susan Pevensie, and Lewis's apparent condemnation of her femininity (see the discussion in chapter four). Furthermore, not all atheist readers cheer (as Hitchens suggests) at the death of God, or the attack on the Church as it is constructed: for some readers it is too blunt an instrument, for others, the religious tone of the books means that by the end of the series the attack on religion dwindles to an attack on the established church, and an argument for reformation rather than demolition.

Although Pullman's reception has been generally favourable among the literary intelligentsia, when he won the Whitbread prize in 2001 some critics reacted as if the sky had fallen in, and the brains of the British were turning to mush. This response was tied to the success of one of the other writers in this chapter, J.K. Rowling, and to a much wider sense that a seismic change in literary taste was taking place. In summary, British readers were rejecting "literary fiction" with its emphasis on psychological complexity, style and a mode of "adulthood" which was often encapsulated in a narrative of acceptance and suffering, and turning instead to texts which offered plot and story, or a rattling good adventure.

We can see this most evidently if we look once more at the surveys of favourite books in 2003. In the BBC's "Big Read" survey, Tolkien took top place as he did in many surveys at the end of the twentieth century, even in Australia and Germany (in Hungary he slipped to number three), much to the pain of those championing the classic novel. Pullman's trilogy appeared at number three. Only two classic novels of emotion, *Pride and Prejudice* and *Jane Eyre*, made it into the top ten and Jane Austen may have been riding on the success of the

BBC adaptation (1995) which was available by this time on DVD. Among places 11–20, the split between fantastic and mimetic fiction is about half and half. However, this is distorted because an arbitrary rule was imposed that no author could appear twice in the top twenty. Places 22, 23, and 24 are therefore occupied by J.K. Rowling, who had also appeared at number 5.

The first book, *Harry Potter and the Philosopher's Stone* (US: .... *Sorcerer's Stone*), appeared in 1997. Much has been made of the number of times it was rejected by publishers, but this is not uncommon for many books that go on to be critical or commercial successes. Bloomsbury only printed one thousand copies of the first edition, also not unusual for a first novel, and specifically one printed at a time when fantasy for children had been considered unfashionable for some time. Writers such as Diana Wynne Jones, Lloyd Alexander and Susan Cooper found it hard to publish in the 1990s: "realism" was considered to be what children wanted and this is reflected in the "realist" cover of the first Rowling novel, a boy against a steam engine.

The seven books that make up J.K. Rowling's Harry Potter sequence tell the story of Harry Potter whose parents have been killed by Lord Voldemort, once a pupil at Hogwarts school for wizards, and now the hidden threat for all right-thinking wizardry. Lord Voldemort believes those not born into wizarding families should be discriminated against and that Muggles (non-wizards) should rule Muggles. This is complicated by our discovery that he is a half-Muggle himself. On Lord Voldemort's side are some of the aristocratic families; against him are aligned most of the teachers in the school, some of Harry's parents' friends, and eventually Harry (from one of the oldest wizarding families in the country) and his friends (one of whom is Muggle-born). The first three books can be read as standalone adventures; after that, we are into a linked trajectory of epic conflict. Alongside this – and clearly part of the appeal – is a tale of high jinks at a rather old-fashioned boarding school, complete with inter-house and inter-school sports, specifically a broomstick version of polo called quidditch. Elements which clearly appeal to readers are the sports, the sorting hat which chooses which house each child will go into, and the magic.

Harry Potter and the Philosopher's Stone is frequently described as a sleeper hit, "discovered" by children and spread by word of mouth, but in fact it won the Smarties prize within months of publication, and was shortlisted for the UK Carnegie Medal, the most prestigious of the UK children's literature awards, in the same year. The books rapidly built up commercial momentum, and by book four, queues at the shops prior to the day of release had become the norm. The seventh and last of the Harry Potter books (*Harry Potter and the Deathly Hallows*, 2007) sold more than eleven million copies in the first twenty-four hours, making it the fastest-selling book on record.

The obvious question to ask is why J.K. Rowling's work had such an impact and such an effect on the market. The main issues are the plots, the accessible writing style, and the nature of the market which Rowling entered which can itself be considered both in terms of what was on offer and the relative lack of fantasy available at the time, and the internationalization of the market.

The basic story outline is not particularly new: there had been wizard and witch schools before – Diane Duane and Jill Murphy are the best known practitioners, along with Jane Yolen's *Wizard's Hall* (1991), in which Henry goes to school thinking he has no talent, has a friend with red hair and finds that the pictures on the walls of the school speak and move. There had been great conflicts against evil before (see previous nine chapters); the fantasy world had been entered from King's Cross Station before by a lonely orphan living with hostile guardians (see Eva Ibbotson's *The Secret of Platform 13*, 1994); furthermore, Harry Potter looks remarkably like Julian in Enid Blyton's *The Naughtiest Girl Again* (1942). The magical creatures of the novels are common to many different fantasies and mythologies. On a series of even more critical notes, Harry is a cipher whose role is to walk through fantasies while his friends mostly do the work; the portrayal of the very bright Hermione is rather patronizing (she is often sidelined or mocked and spends a lot of time telling Harry he is braver and cleverer than she); and the magic system is incoherent.

The comparison to Enid Blyton may be the crucial one. Prior to the appearance of Rowling, it was Blyton who had for generations dominated the children's market in Britain and the British Commonwealth (of which more in a moment). Although other writers, such as Roald Dahl, were immensely popular, Blyton sold to children of all abilities and to their parents. Her stories were "rattling good reads" of adventure, told in very straightforward language, and were all about *groups* of children each of whom was given quite obvious attributes. It is the space vacated by Blyton as her work attracted increasing ire from left-wing parents, librarians and teachers, and also simply became too old fashioned and un-updatable (one current crop of students commented on how slow the books were), which Rowling seems to have filled. This is seen also in the way her initial popularity built through word of mouth, one child to another. These were books marketed by peer-to-peer networks. Bloomsbury's marketing campaigns came *after* the books were already successful and may have created the gigantism we see today, but were not directly responsible for Rowling's success. However, there were other things on Rowling's side.

In 1997 as we have already said, there was very little fantasy for children on the market and the Potter books seemed much more original than they really were. That first non-fantasy cover, with Harry and a steam-engine, also struck a note with a longing for nostalgia and for an "old England" that had disappeared and was about to be replaced by British PM Tony Blair's "Cool Britannia". This nostalgia runs throughout the books which at times seem to be set in 1950s Britain, up to and including the familial financing and social arrangements of Harry's best friends, the Weasleys. The construction of an adventure in the context of many children together may well been even more fantasy/wish-fulfilment than the quidditch game, in a society where the single child is an ever more common norm. Over and above all of this, however, were the changes in the marketing and distribution of books, and particularly children's books, which took place in the 1990s.

Prior to the 1990s, the world's book markets were very regional. Crucially, the US market was separate from the market we can call (loosely) the British Commonwealth. Unless a UK book received a separate US deal, it was unlikely to be available in the USA. The reverse was less true as some shops imported US books (particularly bookshops which specialized in crime or in sf and fantasy) but the books were always expensive and limited in distribution. This division was particularly sharp in the children's book market: although some very famous authors travelled (C.S. Lewis in one direction, E.B. White in another), generally speaking, US and British Commonwealth children had very different reading experiences. Within the Commonwealth, while UK children did not tend to get many Australian, Canadian or Indian books, these countries and others were flooded by the output of British publishing houses. This all changed when the publishing houses began to merge across national boundaries: by the 1990s, international publishing cooperation was the norm. Many authors still have separate publishers in the US and the UK but this is coming under pressure: although agents continue to try and sell separate rights, increasingly rights are "bundled" so that a publishing house may seek world rights for both print and electronic versions of a text (even where they don't intend to use them). Even more important to readers, however, was the launch of Amazon.com in 1995. Prior to this, many fans of a particular "foreign" fiction simply did book swaps with each other. With the launch of Amazon, and its willingness to stock books from the UK on its US site, fans of particular books could buy direct (although UK book buyers seem to be more willing to use .com than US buyers are to use .co.uk). Finally, and perhaps crucially, in 1997 the UK abandoned the Net Book Agreement by which book cover prices had been fixed: discounting of large book runs, and the creation of loss leaders was now possible. As the supermarkets moved into book selling, the latest Harry Potter novel became a major means of bringing people into stores: the last three Harry Potter novels have been sold by many British supermarkets and major chain book stores at a loss (to the detriment of many independent bookshops). The growth of online piracy of novels always affected science fiction and fantasy fiction to a greater degree than other areas of fiction (the fans tend to be more technically astute) and the success of Rowling's novels provided a perfect testing ground for pirates. This in turn created publicity for the books as Rowling and her publishers attempted to keep the lid on "the next Harry Potter" novel and others attempted to leak complete copies on to the internet. In addition, J.K. Rowling's publishers have acquired a reputation for litigation to protect the books from illegal copying, alleged plagiarism, and various forms of commentary. These moves have underlined the feeling that Harry Potter has become a commercial product as much as a literary success.

All of the above relates primarily to the commercial success, but the Harry Potter novels also generated a huge culture of "fandom". We have not yet discussed the rise of fan fiction in this book. Fan fiction is written by readers to extend the universe of the world they love. It is not new, and before the rise of commercial copyright much of it would simply have been absorbed into tale cycles such as those associated with Arthur or Robin Hood. The modern manifestation is linked to the availability of portable reproduction facilities, dating from the end of the nineteenth century (with the mini-printing-press). In the 1960s mimeograph machines supported the rise of fan magazines generally and the circulation of fan fiction in particular, most notably that linked to *Star Trek*. Harry Potter coincided with the rise of the internet and easily constructible websites; both fanzines and Harry Potter fan fiction migrated very rapidly to this medium. Much of this was from child fans – the intended audience – but for the first time external critics could see the degree of adult interest in a children's series (and as we note above, they were quite hostile). Many adults liked the books because they told good stories, something notably absent from books shortlisted for major literary awards. Many adults simply welcomed the chance to buy books that shared the values of the kinds of movies which dominated the Best Movie lists. For others the ever-inventive, detailed fantasy world appealed and for still others the straightforward tale of good and evil.

Bloomsbury responded to the combination of adult interest and adult embarrassment by rolling out "adult" covers, with sober black-and-white pictures (a strategy now applied to a number of authors, including Pratchett).

Some of the adult fan fiction and commentary that Harry Potter generated was relatively straightforward enthusiasm for the series, but some of it was specifically adult in nature. There are two sides to this, often produced by the same people. Most notorious, perhaps, is the "slash fiction". Slash fiction originated in *Star Trek* fandom. In these stories, two characters not together in canon, are brought together, and discover that they are in love/lust, and have sex. Frequently they are both female or both male: classic *Star Trek* slash is about Kirk and Spock. Most of this fiction is written by women and before the publication of Harry Potter they tended to focus on television programmes (*Buffy* and *Blake's 7* are two of the most popular, but there are many others). Harry Potter slash fiction has been particularly problematic because so many of the characters are underage, and one of the commonest linkings is Harry Potter and Snape, the schoolmaster who dislikes him.

The fan fiction interest in Harry Potter has supported the rise in academic studies. The earliest academic work on Rowling was quite closely focused on the texts (Lana Whited, ed., *Harry Potter and the Ivory Tower*, 2002), but in the past five years studies of the fan community, its products, its social networking, and its interaction with creator copyright fiction have generated whole new academic networks with interesting things to say about living in a world in which reading is no longer a lonely pursuit.

Harry Potter has not been unequivocally welcomed: apart from those decrying the decline in the intelligence of the reading public and academics, and fans of fantasy (like ourselves) who can't quite see the appeal, the Harry Potter books have attracted a good deal of opposition from a wide range of religious groups. Protestants in the United States have claimed that the books encourage children to dabble in witchcraft (they have been the subject of at least three local book burnings, and there is a Catholic family guide to Harry Potter and several books discussing the spiritual meaning of Harry Potter from both supportive and hostile positions). Orthodox churches in Greece and elsewhere have campaigned against them, and they have been banned in schools in the United Arab Emirates. None of this has prevented the juggernaut. In 2001 the first of the books was filmed, and a range of Harry Potter merchandise produced. Rowling has maintained control over the contents of the films, resisting the kind of bowdlerization which has afflicted other adaptations of children's books (and also insisting that the entire cast be British). One laudable effect is that the movies are as multi-cultural as the books (that is, not wonderful in that only minor characters are non-white, but also not all-white like most of the rest of the fantasy universe). So far there are five movies, but unlike the ill-fated attempts to render Narnia on the TV screen and the radio over the years, it looks as if the series will be completed.

The success of J.K. Rowling's work has been crucial to the health of children's fantasy: many extremely good established authors have been brought back into print (Diana Wynne Jones's books were repackaged by HarperCollins as "Hotter than Potter") and many new authors have been treated with greater respect (in terms of hardback publication, and high quality covers and marketing) than used to be the case with children's fantasy. We will deal with some of these authors in the next chapter.

Philip Pullman's reputation in the fantasy world rests on three books, J.K. Rowling's on seven. Terry Pratchett has to this date published thirty-six books in his Discworld series, and two separate trilogies of children's fantasies. Twenty-two of these were published in the 1990s which is why, for want of a better decision, we have placed him here, between the 1990s and the 2000s. However, Terry Pratchett began publishing in 1965. Of the three writers discussed here, he is the one with the strongest links to science fiction and fantasy and he has always maintained a close relationship with his own fans. Pratchett's first science fiction convention was in 1964. In the mid-1960s he wrote articles for science fiction fanzines with one of the authors of this book, and his first two adult novels were in fact science fiction (although his first book, *The Carpet People*, 1971, was a children's fantasy which crosses Tolkien with Mary Norton's *Borrowers*). In *Strata* (1981) Pratchett conceived the idea of far-future builders of planets and one of their projects was the building of a flat, disc-shaped world. In 1983 Pratchett published the first of his fantasy series set on the Discworld, a flat earth which rides through space on the back of four elephants who stand on the great A'Tuin, a turtle (a cosmological conceit found in several traditions, attributed above all to one of a number of Hindu creation myths).

The Discworld series begins as a series of parodies of different types of fantasy. The first two, *The Colour of Magic* (1983) and *The Light Fantastic* (1986), riff on many different types of popular fantasy. The books are sword-and-sorcery, with barbarian warriors drawn straight from Robert E. Howard, but landed with uncooperative swords, and the problems of old age. Littering the text are in-jokes for readers of Anne McCaffrey (dragons which are only as brilliant as your imagination) and H.P. Lovecraft (the mystical number 8, and seriously tentacled gods living in the dungeon dimensions and the abandoned temples of Discworld), among others. In the next few books however, the targets became more specific and where the first raided the closets of fantasy almost at random, books such as *Mort* (1987), a tale of Death's Apprentice, *Wyrd Sisters* (1988), based very loosely around the story of *Macbeth*, and ~~Faust~~ *Eric* (1990), a story of a boy who wants to raise a devil, began asking some of the awkward questions avoided by the original authors of the taproot stories. The books acquired a sense of purpose, which lifted them up above the "theatre fantasy" tradition of which they are a part. This was first evident with *Guards! Guards!* (1989), the eighth in the series.

Guards! Guards! begins with a trademark pastiche (perhaps of an Ed McBain novel), as the main character, Captain Samuel Vimes of the City of Ankh-Morpork Night Watch, lies drunk in a gutter and considers his love for a city which only ever kicks him. The book proceeds with the recruitment of a new officer from out of town, the arrival of a dragon, and the victory of the Night Watch – made up of complete losers – over both the dragon and the conspiracy against the Patrician. *Guards! Guards!* introduced some of Pratchett's most successful characters, and although not the first hint at the character clusters which would develop, perhaps the best of the character debut novels. In what has become known as the City Watch sequence (eight books so far), Samuel Vimes is the point of view character: principled, suspicious of hereditary authority but not exactly enthused by his own class, irascible, and resentfully sober, Vimes has risen from the position of a street captain to be Commander of the Watch and Duke of Ankh-Morpork, partially on his own merits but partially, as he acknowledges, through his marriage to Lady Sybil Ramkin, one of the richest women in the city. The books' success is not least because Vimes is perpetually both at odds with, and yet the best supporter of, the Patrician, Lord Vetinari, who is at his most viciously amusing when teasing Vimes.

The City Watch sequence is currently the most popular of the Discworld fantasies but they are run a very close second by the Witches sequence, which began weakly with *Equal Rites* (1987) the story of a girl who wants to be a wizard, but which took out of that book the imposing Granny Weatherwax (a sort of Vanessa Redgrave figure) and gave her as companions the joyously vulgar Nanny Ogg (perhaps Miriam Margolyes?) and the incredibly vague, hippy and hopelessly optimistic Magrat (Jane Horrocks?). The insertion of possible actresses for a much hoped-for movie is not just self-indulgence: one of the appeals of the Discworld books has clearly been the degree to which fans love being able to visualize these books and recognize in them not so much stereotypes, as archetypes. Of the remaining books, the main other series are based around Death (a walking skeleton) and his grand-daughter Susan (a rather pragmatic governess); around the wizards, particularly the ever resourceful Rincewind, who can shout "Help!" in every language on the disc; and around Tiffany Aching, a witch born on the chalk hills (where witches do not normally grow), who is in many ways a young Granny Weatherwax.

There are also some standalone novels, of which our favourites are *The Amazing Maurice and His Educated Rodents* (2001, discussed in chapter seven), *Small Gods* (1992) and *Monstrous Regiment* (2003). *Small Gods* is set some time in the past of the Discworld in a desert culture dominated by a rather unpleasant "church". The book opens on a not very bright novice monk hoeing the garden, who is horrified to realize a small tortoise is talking to him. The tortoise turns out to be his incarnated god, who can't figure out why he hasn't come back as a stamping bull. As the novice (Brutha) and the god (Om) set out to discover what has gone wrong, we are taken through a philosophical discussion about the nature of gods, of worship, of organized religion and the interaction between them. In *Monstrous Regiment* Polly, a barmaid in Borogravia, cuts her hair and joins the army to find her brother. This time we get to think about patriotism and the nature of masculinity (the first can be found among scoundrels, the second resides in socks). These two books are representative of the whole: if the Discworld has gone from strength to strength (rather than petering out as many theatre fantasies do) it is not because they are funny (although they are) or because the characters have become so interesting, but because Pratchett has used the story-lines and the characters to poke and prod at the "givens" of our own world, of the stories we tell about it, and of the fantasy worlds many of his colleagues write.

Pratchett, like Rowling, has his own fandom that exists separately from fantasy fandom. There are many people who do not read fantasy, but read Pratchett. His demographic is astonishing: although noted for attracting boys to reading, the latest survey (by Eve Smith, Liverpool John Moores University) confirms what fans know, that they range in age from 11 to 80 years old and the adults are predominantly professionals, although the books maintain appeal across all social classes. Pratchett's fandom has been assiduous in running conventions (the bi-annual UK Discworld convention is the largest), and buying figurines, computer games, comic books and tie-in books, such as Stephen Briggs's maps and dramatizations, and the Science of Discworld books (three so far) produced by Jack Cohen and Ian Stewart along with Pratchett himself. *The Science of Discworld* books are interesting in themselves because unlike their equivalents in other series (such as the science of *Star Trek*) they are *not* books which explain Discworld. Instead, the Wizards of Discworld attempt a number of thought-experiments by building themselves a round world in order to figure out such important questions as why people don't fall off. We get to accompany them on this educational journey. Naturally academics have got on the bandwagon, but the astonishing thing has been the success of the academic books. *Guilty of Literature* (Butler, James, Mendlesohn, 2000) sold out and went into a second edition; the Pocket Essentials guide to Pratchett (Butler, 2001) similarly sold out, and the latest book by Andrew M. Butler, an unofficial companion, is also doing well. In 2008 for the first time there was a set of academic papers given at the Discworld convention. Some of this is explained quite simply: those academics who have chosen to write on Discworld were fans first and foremost.

The marketing of Pratchett has been rather different than that for either Pullman or Rowling. To begin with, the books were sleeper hits, passed from hand to hand, often by university students (some of whom went on to be academics, see above). By the 1990s, however, Pratchett was the best selling UK author and is currently the seventh most popular non-US author in the USA (although his work was slow to spread in America). Pratchett is the only author who has had more than one title in the Neilsen Bookspan top 5,000 UK sellers ever since the list began in 1995. He has three: *The Colour of Magic*, *The Light Fantastic*, and *Mort*. Yet unlike Rowling and Pullman, Pratchett was not quickly embraced by the literary establishment. Librarians loved him, but often for functional reasons: boys wanted the books, and one of the most charming characters is the Librarian, an orang-utan who finds his prehensile feet very useful for climbing shelves, who knows the mysteries of the book catalogue, who can rip the head off recalcitrant borrowers and who, like most librarians, is paid peanuts. Yet programme after programme on the TV or the radio would introduce "Britain's most popular comedic novelist" and it would *not* be Pratchett. And although his Johnny series (about a young boy in suburban England) was a TV success, it was only with his OBE in 1998 and his Carnegie medal for *Maurice* in 2001, after thirty years of writing and more than a decade of dominating the bestseller lists, that he joined the establishment in a single bound. His comment on receiving the OBE for services to literature was "I suspect 'services to literature' consisted of refraining from trying to write any." Yet in the BBC's Big Read survey, Pratchett was one of only two authors with five books in the top hundred: the other was Charles Dickens whose London is uncannily evoked by the increasingly nineteenth-century city of Ankh-Morpork.

Pratchett continues to write, and while he has few emulators, as we shall see in the next chapter the current crop of city fantasies owe a great deal to Pratchett's view of the world. Similarly, while sword-and-sorcery makes an impressive reappearance in the twenty-first century with the work of China Miéville, Scott Lynch and Sarah Monette, it looks very different, at least in part because Pratchett mocked some of the older clichés to death.

CHAPTER ELEVEN

2000–2010

*I*N 2001 the Arthur C. Clarke Award, an award understood to be for science fiction, shortlisted two novels understood by many readers to be fantasy: Mary Gentle's *Ash* (2000) and China Miéville's *Perdido Street Station* (2000). *Perdido Street Station* went on to take the award. The first Clarke Award was given in 1987; 2001 was notable not just because two novels which most readers felt were fantasy were shortlisted, but because by this date novels by British writers had come to dominate the award (in 2001 and 2002 five out of the six on the shortlist were British). We need to take a short deviation away from fantasy for a moment. In the mid-1990s British science fiction experienced a boom in both quantity and impact. The arrival on the scene of the New Space Opera – represented by writers such as Iain M. Banks, Stephen Baxter, Gwyneth Jones, Ken MacLeod and Alastair Reynolds – reconfigured the field's notion of what you could do with certain classic science fiction tropes. These writers gave a specifically post-imperialist twist to a previously embarrassing sub-genre and did so with literary panache. By 2000, US critics such as David Hartwell were having to argue forcefully for the relevance of American science fiction as the British idea of the future took hold. The authors we have mentioned have remained dominant (along with some others) for the past decade and a half. One of the great names of the New Space Opera, however, M. John Harrison (*Light*, 2002), was in most ways better known as a fantasy writer. Although he has produced no new fantasy novels in the 2000s, it is in this period that both readers and writers registered his influence on British fantasy. The influence of the New Wave of the 1960s, to which Harrison was a major contributor, could be seen vividly expressed in the New Space Opera and the newest trend in fantasy, the New Weird.

The New Weird is extremely difficult to define. Its origins are in Miéville's attempts to describe what he is writing, a Marxist subversion of classic fantasy tropes which for the most part worked well within the accepted structures of fantasy. As more writers were grouped within this category it became as much as anything a marketing label, indicated by cover art as well as by content (the cover art of the UK artist Les Edwards helped give the New Weird a visual identity). This in turn led to a certain amount of competition between those who felt their work already part of an alternative movement (as with the mostly American writers sheltered by Jeff VanderMeer's Ministry of Whimsy anthologies), and others who sought much more directly to argue for changes in genre writing, such as the Interstitialists, led by Delia Sherman and Ellen Kushner. Much of this was fought out on M. John Harrison's message board at www.ttapress.com in May, June and July 2003.

When *Perdido Street Station* came out, it caused huge excitement. China Miéville's style self-consciously harked back to the work of M. John Harrison, to Mervyn Peake and to Michael Moorcock, and melded an intense concern with style to visual inventiveness and political acuity. Miéville had already published *King Rat* (1998), a subversive and grimy version of the Pied Piper of Hamelin. *Perdido Street Station* was a very different book, set entirely in a different world, in the city of New Crobuzon. In a city where magic works, the alchemist Isaac Dan der Grimnebulin searches for the Theory of Everything, and ends by creating physics. His girlfriend, the khepri Lin, sets out to make a sculpture of a gangland leader from the spit she produces from her beetle-head. Meanwhile the city is preyed upon by slake-moths, creatures brought in from another world as part of the power politics of the city, who feed on dreams and destroy intelligence. Much of the interest is in the city itself, a polysemic hive of activity in which no one can know the whole and in which boundaries are blurred and breached. In New Crobuzon this was typified by the Remade, people punished for various crimes by being magically welded to either machinery or biological "enhancements". The Remade in *Perdido Street Station* are the unregarded. In the sequels, *The Scar* (2002) and *Iron Council* (2004), the Remade become a revolutionary proletariat. *The Scar* is the most structurally revolutionary of the books, a coruscating critique of the quest fantasy. *Iron Council*, the apparently most upbeat, is the text most concerned with the flaws in the thinking of revolutionaries.

Mary Gentle's *Ash: A Secret History* (2000, one volume in the UK, four volumes in the US) could retrospectively be regarded as part of the New Weird although it is clearly an extension of the "weird" fantasy she had been producing since *Rats and Gargoyles* in 1990. Her 1990s novels explored an alternate seventeenth century where magic had replaced science. *Ash* also looked back to a European past and imagined with painstaking detail a fifteenth-century alternate history set in the small province of Burgundy in which magic exists in the construction of the world, but in which the presence or otherwise of magic is contested and opposed. The main character, a young woman called Ash, is a child of the soldiers' camps, has survived abuse and goes on to be the person that mysterious beings in the North African desert can speak to while she is fighting against Carthage. The book is immensely complex, and has many of the hallmarks of genre fantasy (such as astonishing detail about matters such as armour), but is also a found text, and a secret history. The tale is related to us as a translation by a twentieth-century historian, who may exist in our world (although the authors of this book, both academic historians, are sceptical). If the book belongs in the New Weird, it is because of the tone and the polysemy of the structure, in which, rather than requiring the reader to seek out truth, the reader must accept that there are many truths, and all of them may be lies.

Two other writers strongly associated with the New Weird in its first years were Ian R. MacLeod and Steph Swainston. One possible way to understand the New Weird is the degree to which some aspect of the work is utterly recognizable. Thus MacLeod's *The Light Ages* (2003) is a retelling of Charles Dickens's *Great Expectations* in a magical world which is industrialized through the use of mined magical fuel, while Swainston's *The Year of Our War* (2004) reads as a typical second book in a fantasy trilogy, in which the characters are involved in fighting off the armies of darkness while the plot proceeds one inch. These descriptions are superficial, however. *The Light Ages* uses the progress of one young man to dissect the "romance" that has been imposed on Dickens's Victorian England, and is intensely concerned with the economics of cheap fuel and the consequences of industrial pollution. *The Year of Our War* uses the "middle-book syndrome" to disconcert and destabilize reader response. We are plunged into a world which has been at war for thousands of years, in which the entire economy has been twisted to serve this purpose, and in which the social structure is distorted both by the superheroes who lead the battle and the separation between the military authority under the emperor (served by the superheroes) and local authority (under absolutist kings). Although there are some wonderful battle scenes, the politics of the book (and its sequels in an ongoing series) are far more complex than in your average quest fantasy, in part because there is no end in sight. The drug to which the protagonist is addicted opens a portal to other worlds which, at the beginning of the book, he assumes to be imaginary and by the second book, *No Present Like Time* (2005), he is beginning to think is the source of his own world's insect invaders. The vicious Rabelaisian nature of the portal-world links Swainston's work back to writers such as Lewis Carroll and Edward Lear. Her presence within the category demonstrates the level of energy within this loose grouping.

The New Weird is a genre of both content and style. The Scottish writer Hal Duncan has been acclaimed as one of the great stylists in the field. *Vellum* (2005) and *Ink* (2007) (technically one book, *The Book of All Hours*) are huge sprawling stories of different manifestations of the same characters in different places, times and worlds, playing out the same Ur-story over and over again, Isis- and Osiris-like. Perhaps some of the most interesting twists of fantasy content come from K.J. Parker and Steve Cockayne. We have already discussed K.J. Parker in chapter nine. In 2001 he began the Scavenger trilogy, which might be the tale of a man who is a god but by the very terms of his godhood cannot know it, and consequently leaves chaos and disaster in his wake. The Engineers sequence began with *Devices and Desires* (2004), a tale of an epic fantasy set in motion when one factory foreman is imprisoned unjustly. In Parker's work all the destinarian expectations of quest fantasies are deployed against both protagonists and readers. Steve Cockayne began his Legends of the Land trilogy with *Wanderers and Islanders* in 2003 (the succeeding books are *The Iron Chain*, 2003, and *The Seagull Drovers*, 2004). Cockayne's texts are immensely complex and might be best described as computing-age or cyber fantasy. Someone, somewhere, has built a facsimile of the world; someone else has created a phone network. In the interstices of both, an imp gets into the network. In the outside world Rusty sets out to be a mapmaker, and becomes involved in royal politics. Elsewhere the abused and neglected illegitimate child of a court magician fails to claim a destiny. Magic leaks from the land and the Holy Isles are in danger. The three books are a lyrical exploration of memory and reality and constantly challenge us to question whose story is being told. The polysemic narrative is pushed to a point just short of breaking. In *The Good People* (2006) Steve Cockayne tells the story of four children who find a fantasy land on the other side of the hedge. The story can be read as a non-fantastical emulation of Arthur Ransome's work, as a full portal fantasy, in which some of the children simply lose access to fantasy land as they grow older, as a tale of a young boy falling victim to schizophrenia, or as something much more liminal and deeply disturbing. Cockayne has even fewer direct links to the New Weird than Swainston (he came to science fiction through his work as a TV cameraman) but his work has been celebrated by both Harrison and Miéville. Newer British writers of the New Weird include Joe Abercrombie (*The Blade Itself*, 2006) and Stephen Hunt (*The Court of the Air*, 2007).

Not all of the best British fantasy in this period can be categorized as New Weird. Neil Gaiman, already hugely popular (and by this time resident in the US), hit his stride as a novelist with *American Gods* (2001), a tale of Norse gods stranded in modern America, and in 2002 produced a very successful children's book, *Coraline*, which offered a rather "Grimmer" version of fantasy for children. In 2005 Gaiman published *Anansi Boys*, a companion to *American Gods*, but in many ways a much more interesting book. It begins in contemporary London, and tells the story of Charles Nancy, a solid stable sort who discovers he is the son of Anansi the spider god and has a very irritating brother. Nearly all the characters are black (which shouldn't be as worthy of comment as it is) and Gaiman has gone to a great deal of trouble to ensure accents match the origins of many of the characters from different islands in the Caribbean. This can be best appreciated in the audiobook version, read by the black British actor, comedian and mimic, Lenny Henry. Another writer who is not part of the New Weird but whose career benefited from the increased attention being paid to more liminal and challenging forms of fantasy is Graham Joyce. In liminal fantasy, the fantasy is often elusive, seen out of the edge of the eye (Mendlesohn, 2008). *The Facts of Life* (2002) tells of a midwife forced to accommodate the new demands of the NHS in the 1950s. *The Limits of Enchantment* (2005) created fantasy amid the ruins of bombed-out Coventry and the complex family politics of a group of sisters.

Anansi Boys is a fantasy about stories, and who owns stories. In 2001 Jasper Fforde launched what has proved to be a long-running series about a detective whose job it is to prevent books being rewritten in the past and thus preserve the original texts for a literature-obsessed fantasy world in which the Crimean War is still being fought out. In the first, *The Eyre Affair*, the detective Thursday Next has to protect the ending of *Jane Eyre* (in which Jane marries St John Rivers) but ends by changing it to what *we* know to be the "real" ending. Also busy playing with literary texts was the Welsh writer Jo Walton. Walton had previously published an Arthurian trilogy, made up of *The King's Peace* (2000), *The*

King's Name (2001) and *The Prize in the Game* (2002). In 2003 Walton published *Tooth and Claw*, in which she decided to imagine a Trollope/ Austen novel in which the rules of sociobiology and social relations that those authors took for granted were literally true. In *Tooth and Claw* almost all the characters are dragons. Dragons can grow only if they eat dragon meat, and so, in a reification of capitalism, rich dragons eat the children of poor dragons, while virgin lady dragons turn pink in the presence of gentleman dragons and are ruined forever if such proximity means that their colour turns permanently. This description does not even begin to capture the inventiveness and humour.

The big British hit of the decade was Susanna Clarke's *Jonathan Strange and Mr Norrell* (2004). Bloomsbury had been looking for another big hit to follow J.K. Rowling, and in this delicate and whimsical take on early nineteenth-century Britain they felt they had found it. The consequence was that *Jonathan Strange and Mr Norrell* was allocated a huge publicity budget, and launched at the Chicago Book Fair that year. Susanna Clarke found herself giving interviews to bemused TV and radio presenters across America and the UK. The book tells the story of an alternate Britain in which fantasy has disappeared from the land, and magicians are essentially antiquarians. Two real magicians emerge, with very different notions about who should be able to perform magic. Mr Norrell wants to hoard magic for an elite; Jonathan Strange wishes to reinvigorate the magical world. This is set against a context of Wellington's Peninsular campaigns and several tales are told: of the war, of the life of an ex-slave called Stephen, and of a Britain that is on the edge of the social upheaval of the Industrial Revolution. One notable element in the book is its northern Britain setting, something which Clarke has in common with a number of writers of the New Weird, few of whom seem to be southerners.

Released at the same time was one of the outstanding American fantasies of the period, *Mortal Love* (2004) by Elizabeth Hand. Rather overlooked in the spectacle which surrounded *Jonathan Strange*, *Mortal Love* is a fascinating companion. In *Mortal Love*, a fairy queen searches

London for her lost suitor, leaving human wreckage behind her. *Mortal Love* has a very different quality to *Jonathan Strange*: it is sewn of velvet and stitched with silk. One of the strongest characteristics of this book is the incredibly vivid picture it paints of Camden (London). As we discussed in chapter nine, Hand was helping to create a new form of indigenous fantasy, in which local landscapes were rendered fantastical. In this decade other American writers mixed this with ideas drawn from the New Weird. One of the most interesting of the new writers was Alexander C. Irvine. Where classic American urban fantasy imported its gods and fairies from Old Europe, and asked how they would cope with New America, Irvine is more interested in how the gods of Old America would cope with invading Europeans. In Irvine's *A Scattering of Jades* (2002), a human sacrifice triggers a fire in Manhattan, and a slave in Kentucky finds an Aztec mummy. Aztec gods become involved with American political gangsterism. In *The Narrows* (2005) a Detroit factory in World War II starts manufacturing golems, in response to which a local mythic figure becomes involved with a shape-shifting Native American shaman. The leading regional fantasist of the decade has been Andy Duncan, a southern American writer who began writing in the 1990s, who has written a number of exquisite, and often exquisitely funny, short stories. *Beluthahatchie and Other Stories* won the World Fantasy award in 2001. Also associated with the Weird was the work of Jeffrey Ford. *The Portrait of Mrs Charbuque* (2002) tells of a masterpiece painted in 1893, in which the artist never sees his model. This tortured text draws as much from the unseen city of New York around it as it does from the title character. Jeff VanderMeer was already an established editor, but in this decade became better known as an author. *City of Saints and Madmen: The Book of Ambergris* (1997) is a postmodern Borgesian exploration of a fabulous city and land, written as a series of short stories. In 2006, VanderMeer produced *Shriek: An Afterword*, a Rabelaisian updating of Poe's "Fall of the House of Usher". Not strictly associated with the Weird, but clearly associated with this thing we have called indigenous fantasy was Jennifer Stevenson's *Trash*

Sex Magic. Published by Small Beer Press in 2004 (itself a phenomenon), *Trash Sex Magic* is a story of tantric sex and trailer trash, vivid and rambunctious. Scott Lynch's *The Lies of Locke Lamora* (2006) is set in another world, and is very typical modern urban fantasy, with a touch of the subversion of the New Weird; it is the adventure of a trainee thief in a corrupt city. *The Lies of Locke Lamora* contains elements of the sword-and-sorcery genre that had almost disappeared by the 1990s. In the 2000s it came back heavily inflected by the New Weird. Sarah Monette's *Melusine* (2005) and the sequels *The Virtu* (2006) and *The Mirador* (2007) are the best examples: the wizard in these books is queer in a queer-hating culture. His thief sidekick is his half-brother. Many of their adventures are shaped by the macro-politics of the court, and the micro-politics of sexuality and sibling rivalry.

While the New Weird in the UK (and Australia) is predominantly showcased in novels, in the United States the New Weird is better seen in short stories, and in the products of the small presses and internet magazines. A very good collection that showcased the kinds of writers associated with the Weird in America was issue 39 of *Conjunctions*, called *The New Wave Fabulists*, guest edited by Peter Straub (2002), whose own work was becoming increasingly edgy. The collection included writers such as John Crowley, Patrick O'Leary, James Morrow and Jonathan Carroll, among others, and demonstrated the degree to which the Weird in the United States was drawing together writers who previously didn't seem to "fit" the shelving categories of fantasy with new writers conscious of the New Weird rubrics.

The best-known short-story writers of the American Weird movement are Ted Chiang and Kelly Link. Ted Chiang has published one short novel, or novella, *The Merchant and the Alchemist's Gate* (2007), but is primarily known for his short stories, many of which are collected in *Stories of Your Life: and Others* (2002). This contains the multiple-award-winning "Tower of Babylon" (1990), in which humans build a Tower of Babel, break through into Heaven, and discover themselves back on Earth, and "Hell is the Absence of God" (2001; winner of the Hugo, Nebula and Locus Awards), which explores the challenges to faith when God really exists and miracles really do happen every day. Kelly Link is also a multiple award-winner, who specializes in extremely strange short stories which are masterpieces of language and the uncanny and which are rather hard to describe. One of the simplest is "The Faery Handbag" (2004), in which a grandmother's handbag really does contain another world. Link's career is unusual, in that her first collection, *Stranger Things Happen* (2001) was self-published in her own imprint, Small Beer Press, yet despite what is normally regarded as a dubious publishing practice it was picked up as a Salon Book of the Year and a Village Voice favourite, indicating changing perceptions in the market about the nature of publishing.

Small Beer Press is now one of the best-known small presses in the field, and has published John Crowley, Carol Emshwiller and Sean Stewart among others; it also publishes a fiction magazine called *Lady Churchill's Rosebud Wristlet*, which has published such prominent authors as Karen Joy Fowler, and Ursula K. Le Guin along with up-and-coming writers such as Ellen Klages, Alex Irvine and L. Timmel Duchamp. Other small presses that have come to prominence in this decade include Nightshade, which has reprinted many well-known British authors who have otherwise found it difficult to publish certain types of science fiction and fantasy in the States (often short-story collections). In the UK, PS Publishing has specialized in the original novella, a form which otherwise has few homes. Alongside these small presses has been the growth in internet fiction publishing. Three of the best-known sites are *SciFi.Com* (now sadly closed to fiction but with its archive still available online), *Clarkesworld*, which leans towards science fiction, and *Strange Horizons*, which has been orientated towards fantasy of the New Weird type. These magazines, along with the *Internet Review of Science Fiction*, *SciFi.Com*, *The SF Site* and *The Science Fiction Review*, have also maintained active review columns which, with their instant feedback, have recreated a kind of conversation that had almost disappeared with the decline of the print fiction magazines in the 1970s and 1980s. It is impossible to make direct comparisons, because the figures are simply not available for the internet magazines, but there is a growing sense that this is where the cutting-edge short fiction is being published. Many of the new writers of the 2000s have yet to make an impact in terms of novels, but the dissemination of their short-story work has suggested that they are names to watch: names such as Paolo Bacigalupi, Theodora Goss, Michael Burstein, Ricky Ducornet and Vandana Singh. Among the novelists who came up through the short-story route in small presses and the internet magazines are L. Timmel Duchamp, Kelley Eskridge, Nisi Shawl and Jay Lake. Although only tangential to the discussion here, it is also important to note the rise in the writer's blog. Many of the best-known names of the decade are known as much for their blog writing as for their actual fiction. Writers such as Sarah Monette, Elizabeth Bear, Hal Duncan, and Sherwood Smith write elegant online prose about the matter of writing, and generate instant feedback and discussion which means that the fantasy (and sf world) today sometimes feels like a sequence of online seminars. In 2008 the (sf) novelist John Scalzi was the first person to win a Best Fanwriter Hugo with a blog, demonstrating the degree to which the electronic platform had come to matter to the community.

The success of the small presses and the internet has made it far easier for writers from continental Europe to be published in the Anglo-American market. Zoran Živković's short story "The Library" (2003) won the World Fantasy Award for Best Novella. In 2007 the Science Fiction Writers of America produced *The SFWA European Hall of Fame* anthology, edited by James Morrow and Kathryn Morrow, which included short stories by the Finnish writer Johanna Sinisalo (who had already won the American Tiptree Award in 2004), by the Polish writer Marek S. Huberath, and by the German writer Andreas Eschbach among others.

The term "New Weird" has been only one of the movements of this period. Many of the same writers have been claimed by or have identified themselves with a group called the Interstitialists. Where the Weird was understood to be about subverting recognized forms, the Interstitialists (see the website of the Interstitial Arts Foundation) understand themselves as blending genres, mixing horror with science fiction, or fantasy with history. The authors of this book have problems with seeing this as new, but it has been a very popular label and can be accessed through the recent publication *Interfictions* (Small Beer Press, 2007), which is unusual in bringing together not only Anglo-American traditions but also stories from French, Hungarian, and Spanish writers. New writers who have been associated with this movement are Christopher Barzak, whose *One For Sorrow* (2007), a ghost story, won the Locus and Crawford Awards, and Jay Lake, whose *Mainspring* (2007) is a science fiction novel set in a clockwork fantasy world in which the Archangel Gabriel takes a hand. More established writers who have also been drawn in include Greer Gilman, who produced a number of short stories in this period, which have been assembled as *Cloud and Ashes* (2009). Jonathan Carroll's *The Wooden Sea* (2001), *White Apples* (2002) and *Glass Soup* (2005) have been embraced enthusiastically by fantasy critics, although they are often described as magical realism or slipstream; these frequently contain elements of posthumous fantasy (adventures after death). The two best-known figures of this movement are Delia Sherman and Ellen Kushner. In 2002 they wrote *The Fall of the Kings*, in which a young historian sets out to find the truth about magic. In 2006 Ellen Kushner produced *The Privilege of the Sword*, a historical picaresque which was a sequel to *Swordspoint* (1987).

Loosely associated with both the Interstitialists and the New Weird is the long-established tradition of the historical picaresque fantasy. This type of fantasy in the 2000s became entwined with the New Weird theme of introducing the study of science as a subject for fantasy (see also China Miéville's *The Scar* and K.J. Parker's Engineer sequence.) In 2003–4 Neal Stephenson produced his trilogy known as the Baroque Cycle: *Quicksilver*, *The Confusion* and *The System of the World*. These begin in the years of the English Restoration (1660) and travel over Europe, the Mediterranean and Asia, concluding in London in the

1710s. The principal characters move through a world very slightly different from our own, in which alchemy is giving way to science. It is part family-saga and part a tale of the Immortal Wanderer. A much more plot-driven picaresque is James Morrow's *The Last Witchfinder* (2006), in which Jennet Stearne sets out on a journey to prove the non-existence of witchcraft and absolve her learned aunt, who had been burned at the stake by Jennet's father. Jennet's adventures take her to America and into a love affair with Benjamin Franklin, but the book is told by the voice of Newton's *Principia Mathematica*, which offers an alternate history of the world in which history is a series of great events in the battle between books and ideas. (Franklin was also a hero of Greg Keyes's *Newton's Cannon*, 1998, which began a four-volume sequence known as The Age of Unreason.) It is worth mentioning here a third superb picaresque produced by the British author Frances Hardinge. *Fly By Night* (2005) was Frances Hardinge's first novel and tells of Mosca Mye, the daughter of a scrivener in a world where writing has become taboo. In Mosca's country there has been a civil war, but attempts to restore the monarchy have foundered, and the guilds have occupied the power vacuum. Mosca wanders this world with a goose under her arms, falling in and out of other people's political schemes.

American writers who continued to work in an older historical tradition included Marie Brennan, whose most recent book *Midnight Never Come* (2008) is set in Elizabethan England, as is Sarah A. Hoyt's *Ill Met by Moonlight* (2001), in her Shakespearean fantasy series. Megan Whalen Turner continued her Byzantine fantasy novel *The Thief* (1996) and its sequels. The most successful historical fantasy writer of this decade has been Naomi Novik, whose Temeraire sequence began with *His Majesty's Dragon* (2006). These books are probably best described as Patrick O'Brian with dragons: Napoleonic naval battles are rather different when flying flame-throwers are involved. There are currently five books in the series and a movie is on the way.

There are a number of other notable American fantasy writers publishing in this period. Kate Elliott (previously writing under her real name, Alis A. Rasmussen) has achieved success with a seven-book sequence *Crown of Stars* (*King's Dragon*, 1997). Gregory Frost has continued the tradition of reworking fairytales (*Fitcher's Brides*, 2002), but also created a fantasy world in which one of the main characters is a storyteller (*Shadowbridge*, 2008). Jacqueline Carey, whose Kushiel's Legacy series began with *Kushiel's Dart* (2001) is about a medieval alternate Earth, heavily influenced by Jewish folklore, and the tales are set in Terre d'Ange, where a range of sexual practices and relationship structures influence the politics. Cecelia Holland began her five-book Viking series with *The Soul Thief* in 2002, an accurate portrayal of the period, but with sorcery thrown into the mix; Guy Gavriel Kay did something similar with his *The Last Light of the Sun* (2004). Kij Johnson's *The Fox Woman* (1999) and *Fudoki* (2001) tackle territory previously almost entirely untouched by American fantasy authors, the folk-tales of ancient Japan; also working with Japanese tradition is *The Grass-Cutting Sword* (2006) by Catherynne M. Valente. Ekaterina Sedia, an emigré to the USA from Moscow is an excellent new writer, whose books, *The Secret History of Moscow* (2007) and *The Alchemy of Stone* (2008) combine urban fantasy with magic realism.

Paranormal romance, already popular in the 1990s, developed in the 2000s into a publishing category of its own. According to the figures compiled by *Locus*, in addition to 460 fantasy titles published in 2007, there were 243 paranormal romances. We obviously cannot cover them all here, but note the series Charlaine Harris began with *Dead Until Dark* (2001); Mary Janice Davidson's *Undead and Unwed* (2002), the first of the Betsy the Vampire Queen series; Ilona Andrews, *Magic Bites* (2007), and the immensely popular Stephenie Meyer, whose *Twilight* began with the book of that name in 2005. The first book debuted at number five on the *New York Times* bestseller list of "young adult chapter books", however, the books continue to have a very wide readership among adults.

Notable amongst new American fantasy writers who have just begun to make their mark are M. Rickert, Christopher Barzak and Joe Hill, all

three of who have won the Crawford Award for best first fantasy book.
All excelled in short stories, again pointing to the revival in the short-
story form. Today, it is becoming common for an anthology of short
stories to mark the break into the market rather than, as has been the
case for the past thirty years, an indication of having achieved success
as a novelist.

Up until now we have, for better or worse and certainly with an
overtone of colonialism, treated Canadian and Australian writers as
part of the Anglo-American nexus. In practical terms this arises because
these writers have not been able to flourish without publication in either
the US or the UK. (It is worth noting that while the children's market
was structured by the Commonwealth, in the adult sf and fantasy
market both countries had stronger links to the USA.) However, by the
beginning of the second millennium – partially due to the growing ease
of making submissions overseas (easily printed manuscripts no longer
had to be sent with return post) – it was clear that in both science fiction
and fantasy Canada and Australia, and to a lesser extent New Zealand,
had developed significant communities of writers. What marked out
this wave was less the numbers than the appearance of a distinctive
voice, where before writers from these countries had felt obliged to meet
the demands of the US market.

We have already mentioned a number of Canadian writers whose
careers began in the 1990s or earlier, such as Steven Erikson, Guy
Gavriel Kay, Tanya Huff, and Charles de Lint. We do not intend to
discuss them in detail here, but as their fellow Canadians came to the
front of the stage, these writers were re-examined for their Canadian-
ness and increasingly seen as the herald of the Canadian boom. Among
the major names of Canadian fantasy are R. Scott Bakker (an epic
fantasy writer), Joël Charpentier (representing the growing number of
Francophone writers being translated into English), and S.M. Stirling
who has specialized in time-travel alternate pasts which at least begin
as sf, but tend to drift towards fantasy as the worlds deviate from the
original time-lines.

One reason that the Canadians made such an impact in the 2000s was that they produced a number of rather subversive writers. The first writer we want to mention is Candas Jane Dorsey, who published her first novel in 1976. However, her breakthrough novel was *Black Wine* (1997), which won the Tiptree Award and the Aurora Award, and was also listed in the *Locus* poll in third place. The book is part science fiction and part quest fantasy, with openly queer and non-monogamous characters, and demonstrated the degree to which fantasy could be as subversive of social structures as science fiction. *Black Wine* was one of the very first books to challenge conservative heteronormativity in a way which takes for granted the Other rather than making an argument for acceptance. Dorsey is an outstanding lyrical writer, but she has not been prolific. In many ways her major impact on Canadian fantasy and science fiction has been as an editor. She edited a number of *Tesseracts* collections and other anthologies, and for several years she ran a small press as part of the Books Collective, formed in 1992, which eventually bought out Tesseracts Books in 1994.

One phenomenon of the Canadian boom is the presence of expatriates in both directions. Two writers who live in other countries but who continue to be identified as Canadian are Geoff Ryman and Sean Stewart. Geoff Ryman now lives in London, and we discussed his 1992 novel *"Was…"* in chapter nine. In the 2000s he produced two novels, both of which could be understood as either science fiction or fantasy. In *Lust* (2001) a young man discovers that he can bring to life any real or fictional character from the past. His first choice is Tarzan (as played by Johnny Weissmuller). Eventually he moves on to Picasso, thus giving Picasso a chance to create the most astonishing digital art. As with *"Was …"*, this is also a novel about coming to terms with surviving the AIDS crisis, and the new and unexpected complexities of uncloseted gay relationships. *Air* (2005) was shortlisted for the Nebula Award, and won the Clarke and Tiptree Awards. On one level this is a science fiction novel about what happens to a small and isolated community used as an experiment for in-the-head information exchange. However, the novel's protagonist acquires the soul of a dead person and undergoes a very strange pregnancy; the rhetoric of the novel by the end is far more like that of magic realism. Sean Stewart was born in Texas, but moved to Canada in 1968 at the age of three; he now lives in California. The worlds he creates are not precisely magic realist, because the protagonists are aware of a wrongness. Instead these tales are stories of how one copes with invasions and invaders. His career began in the early 1990s, but one of his most significant novels is *Galveston* (2000), in which an island attempts to hold back the floodwaters of magic while its young people increasingly wonder why. *Perfect Circle* (2004) is an ostensibly rather simple novel about a man who sees ghosts, and has received much critical acclaim. Sean Stewart has also worked in the YA genre, producing *Cathy's Book* in 2006, and has written a very effective tie-in for the *Star Wars* universe called *Yoda: Dark Rendezvous* (2002).

Two incomers who have become identified with Canadian fantasy and who have contributed immensely to the nature of Canadian-ness in modern fantasy are Hiromi Goto and Nalo Hopkinson. Hiromi Goto and her family emigrated from Japan when she was three. Her third novel *The Kappa Child* (2001) won the Tiptree Award. Goto's previous novel, *The Water of Possibility* (2001) was a portal fantasy for children, in which a Japanese-Canadian child moves from the city to the prairies and finds a door to another world, but this portal fantasy avoids the classic colonialist tropes of the genre, while mixing Japanese and Canadian myth figures. In *The Kappa Child* Goto reverses the structure to create an intrusion fantasy, in which the Kappa, a trickster character from Japanese tradition, is transported to the Canadian prairie and trapped by obligations to her family, her pregnancy and her community.

The most important of the new Canadian writers is probably Nalo Hopkinson, a Jamaican-born writer who went to live in Canada in her teens. Hopkinson won the Warner Aspect Award in 1997, the prize for which was publication of her first novel. *Brown Girl in the Ring* (1998) is a magical realist novel set in a post-apocalyptic Canada. Her second novel, *Midnight Robber* (2000), is science fiction; but in 2003 she published *The Salt Roads*, a complex tale set partially in nineteenth-century France and partially in the Caribbean. It tells of fertility gods, of tricksters, of survival and of revolution against white slavers. Hopkinson is also an astonishing short-story writer. Many of her tales are reworkings of classic folk- and fairytale. She has written two versions of Little Red Riding Hood, "Riding the Red", told in a Somerset accent, and a revisioning of it, "Red Rider", told in a Jamaican accent. Both of these turn this into a bloody and lustful tale of menarche. Like Candas Jane Dorsey, Nalo Hopkinson has also edited a number of collections, drawing attention to the Caribbean voices that make up the "North American" tradition of the fantastic. The most recent of these is *So Long Been Dreaming: Postcolonial Science Fiction and Fantasy*, co-edited with the Indian-Canadian academic Uppinder Mehan.

The contribution of Australian writers of fantasy has been more prominent than that of Canada, at least as far as the book-shelves are concerned, since most of the two dozen or so active writers of fantasy in Australia have written multiple trilogies. Indeed, some of the most popular writers of quest fantasy today, such as Sara Douglass and Trudi Canavan, whose work has recently been repackaged for the lucrative Young Adult (teenage) segment of the market, are writing in Australia. These works are indistinguishable from American fantasies. However, some of these writers distinguish themselves clearly from the American quest fantasy tradition: Cecilia Dart-Thornton for instance very effectively uses her considerable knowledge of English folklore in the Bitterbynde trilogy that began with *The Ill-Made Mute* (2001) in ways that we recognize from American writers similarly expert in folklore, but her work stands out for its bitterness and cynicism. Ian Irvine has published sixteen novels since 1998, making him one of the most prolific of the Australians. These are set in the Three Worlds series which is technically science fiction in that it involves alien invasion, but is treated very much as fantasy. Glenda Larke's first trilogy, The Isles of Glory, which began with *The Aware* (2003) stands out because of the very original culture which she creates perhaps through her own residence in Malaysia, but also because of the way in which the series deals with the *necessary* destruction of magic since the magic-using elite is inevitably exploitative. K.J. Bishop's work is unclassifiable although it was linked with the New Weird: *The Etched City* (2003), an urban fantasy in which magic permeates the environment and magic users are endangered by their practice, was published by a small press (Prime Books, Ohio), then by Tor UK in association with Pan Macmillan, and then by Spectra, USA. Bishop has only produced the one book so far, but the book's impact demonstrated both its quality *and* some of the shifts in the market and the routes to publication we have discussed above.

Other Australian fantasy writers include Tom Arden (now resident in the UK), Isobelle Carmody, Kate Constable, Marianne Curley, Stephen Dedman, Jennifer Fallon, Kate Forsyth, Fiona McIntosh, Caisel Mór, Karen Miller, and Shaun Tan. Skipping over the immensely successful Garth Nix whom we will discuss later as part of the renaissance in children's fantasy, the best-known Australian writers are possibly Sean McMullen and Margo Lanagan. Sean McMullen is part of the equally successful sf renaissance in Australia. After his sf debut, McMullen began writing a sequence of fantasy books known as the Moonworlds saga which began with *Voyage of the Shadowmoon* (2002, first published in New York). One reason why McMullen's work stands out is that he makes no attempt to replicate either the American landscape or the pseudo-European landscapes which make much fantasy seem ersatz; instead, McMullen (who has a PhD in medieval history) uses his experience of the Australia around him to indulge in what we might call "method writing". In his article "The Profession of Science Fiction: Forced Marches and Desert Quests" in *Foundation* 96, McMullen describes his experiments with a suit of armour in the Australian desert. And his conclusion is that, after a long route march:

> **Pillage:** if it weighs more than a few small gold coins, then the losers can keep it.

Sex: if the women/girls/boys/sheep are unwilling – and capable of running faster than an arthritic tortoise – then they are a poor alternative to a good night's sleep for anyone who has been on a forced march.

Vandalism: only if it smashes really easily. Even throwing rocks is quite an effort after 9 hours of backpack straps and chainmail pressing on the shoulders.

Arson: very attractive prospect. You just start a few fires, then sit back, put your feet up, relax, and watch the show.

Now is an appropriate moment to mention Russell Kirkpatrick, one of the very few fantasy writers (along with the quest fantasy writer Juliet Marillier) from New Zealand. Like McMullen, Kirkpatrick – a professional geographer – gives us a thorough understanding of a fantasy landscape in the Fire of Heaven series, beginning with *Across the Face of the World* (2005).

The most interesting Australian writer to come to the attention of the Anglo-American fantasy world recently is Margo Lanagan. As she has been publishing novels in Australia since 1990 this is rather embarrassing but is probably as much because she writes for the (until recently) rather despised YA market as because her residence is in Australia. Lanagan's breakthrough publication was *Black Juice* (2004), a collection of very disturbing short stories. The collection won the World Fantasy Award in 2005, and also, separately, its opening story "Singing My Sister Down". The collection was widely considered one of the most varied and expert collections of short stories in the field. What has surprised many American reviewers is the degree to which Lanagan feels able to write about sex, sexual abuse, and death in very bold terms for a YA audience (see the later short story "The Goosle", a spin-off from Hansel and Gretel, and the online controversy this aroused) demonstrating a difference in cultures which has affected many children's and YA authors. Lanagan's reputation in the field was sealed by the reprint of the short-story collection *White Time* (2000) in the

US and the release of *Red Spikes* (2006). Her most recent book, a novel, *Tender Morsels* (2008), uses the rather unstructured paradigm of the German fairytale "Snow White and Rose Red", but to describe it as a retelling rather loses its majesty.

Lanagan's rise has run alongside a general increase in, and market for, children's and YA and fantasy. It is not too much of a stretch to suggest that the the first decade of the twenty-first century has seen an upsurge in both quantity and quality as publishers have realised that children *do* want fantastic fiction and that many adults are perfectly happy to read books written for a young audience. Of the 460 fantasy books *Locus* received in 2007, 185 were YA. There is no question that there were more opportunities for writers of fantasy for children and teens in the 2000s than in any previous decade, and that much of this opportunity came from the huge success of J.K. Rowling. Publishers were quite consciously looking for another hit. This naturally resulted in a great deal of dross, which we will overlook here, but also in the emergence of a large number of excellent new writers, so many that we must apologise to those we cannot fit in (but see our list of important fiction at the end), and also note that, in this burst of creativity, we will only mention one book even where writers have been extremely prolific. First, however, it is worth noting the degree to which a number of older writers received a boost from this trend. While it is very unclear what effect Rowling has had on reading among children (it is not clear that readers of Harry Potter go on to read other books), she and Pullman had an immense effect on the way in which children's and teen fiction was viewed. Specifically, the mainstream gaze turned towards writers such as Diana Wynne Jones, Jane Yolen, Eva Ibbotson, Joan Aiken and Peter Dickinson and realized that many outstanding texts had passed them by. All of these writers were able to publish new novels in the 2000s and many of their older works were brought back into print.

Among the new fantasy writers one trend that was taken up very quickly was for series books. Series books are a much-disparaged form in which a novel of around 1,000 pages is broken up into segments of around

150. Two fantasy authors who showed that powerful fiction could be written in this form were Lemony Snicket and K.A. Applegate. Lemony Snicket is actually the name of the narrator of the series by Daniel Handler, which begins with *A Series of Unfortunate Events: The Bad Beginning* (1999) and ends thirteen books later with *The End* (2006). The series is technically not fantasy, but rather Gothic romance that becomes transcendentalist and flat-out weird. The Snicket books show the clear influence of Edith Nesbit, and this knowingness of genre could be seen as the hallmark of this decade's new fantasy writing for younger readers. K.A. Applegate is unusual in being the writer of a number of series in several different genres, including romance. In 1999 she began a series called *Everworld*, with *Search for Senna*, ending with *Entertaining the End: Book Twelve* (2001). These books, which take five high-school teenagers into a pocket universe, are extremely dark and disturbing.

Both Handler and Applegate demonstrated that it was possible to publish extremely frightening fiction for both younger children and teens, which may have assisted writers such as N.M. Browne (*Hunted*, 2002, a tale of a young girl who takes refuge from vicious bullies as a ghost-fox in another world), Neil Gaiman (*Coraline*, 2002, and *The Graveyard Book*, 2008), Martine Leavitt (*Katura and Lord Death*, 2006, in which a young woman is courted by Death), and Kathleen Duey (*Skin Hunger*, 2007, which portrays a wizard's school in which access to food is absolutely dependent on one's ability to perform magic, and cooperation is forbidden).

The rise of dark fantasy for children was another notable element in the mix. Much of this form of fantasy looks just like its adult progenitors, but with younger protagonists, more lurve and less sex. Stephenie Meyer's Twilight series (first book, *Twilight*, 2005) in which an innocent young thing falls in love with a vampire and struggles to preserve her purity was a great hit with young female readers, although the most recent book in the series left many disillusioned. Robin McKinley, already a well-known writer, produced a book with a similar theme, *Sunshine* (2003).

Meanwhile Darren Shan's *Cirque du Freak* (1999) began a long-running sequence about a young boy turned vampire. Dark urban fantasy also became popular. Holly Black's *Tithe* (2003) places the protagonist in danger in the warfare between two faerie powers. Chris Wooding's *The Haunting of Alaizabel Cray* (2001) tells of a seventeen-year-old witch hunter in Victorian London.

One characteristic of children's books and books for teens is how often they can be described as apprentice/education books, in which a character is either sent on a quest or is associated with a mentor and learns to be an adult in the process. The Australian Garth Nix, already highly respected for his portal fantasies (*Sabriel*, 1995 and its sequels), in 2003 began a sequence called The Keys to the Kingdom. In the first book, *Mr Monday* (2003), Arthur Penhaligan finds himself with a mission to find the keys that keep the mechanism of the world turning. Terry Pratchett began a young-adult annex to Discworld, with *The Wee Free Men* (2003), featuring Tiffany Aching on her route to witchcraft. Jonathan Stroud's Bartimaeus trilogy (*The Amulet of Samarkand*, 2003), tells of Nathaniel, a magician's apprentice, and seeks to examine much of the taken-for-granted hierarchies of wizard-worlds. Justine Larbalestier's *Magic or Madness* (2005) and its sequels is much more about rejecting magic, but uses the mentor–apprentice structure, as does N.M. Browne's *The Spellgrinder's Apprentice* (2007) and Joseph Delaney's *The Spook's Apprentice* (2004).

Not all children's fantasy has been so deathly serious. More light-hearted are works from writers such as Eva Ibbotson, whose *Island of the Aunts* (2000) is a whimsical eco-fantasy, and Jane Yolen's *Boots and the Seven Leaguers* (2000), in which a teen troll goes to work as a roadie for a rock-and-roll band. One of the funniest new writers of the decade was Eoin Colfer, who produced a series beginning with *Artemis Fowl* (2001), in which a boy supervillain concocts audacious plans to raid fairyland. Derek Landy has produced a series beginning with *Skulduggery Pleasant* (2007), in which a walking talking skeleton is the ace detective. Debi Gliori's *Pure Dead Magic* (2001, the first in the Pure

Dead series) combines humorous YA family problems with the kind of magical mistakes that Edith Nesbit used in many of her books. In Herbie Brennan's *The Faerie Wars* Henry thinks he is saving a butterfly who is about to be eaten by a neighbour's cat, but in fact is rescuing a fairy prince and rapidly gets involved in faerie politics. In 2007 Ysabeau Wilce published *Flora Segunda: Being the Magickal Mishaps of a Girl of Spirit, Her Glass-Gazing Sidekick, Two Ominous Butlers (One Blue), a House with Eleven-Thousand Rooms, and a Red Dog*, a screwball take on an edifice fantasy, continued in a sequel.

Although this was a period in which bad-joke fantasy was being seen as particularly attractive to the under-11s, there was a great deal of very sophisticated humour available for the older age group. Diana Wynne Jones followed up *Dark Lord of Derkholm* with *Year of the Griffin* (2000), a rather cutting analysis of the British higher-education system (and incidentally containing one of the best descriptions of creative research ever written). Patrice Kindl published *Goose Chase* (2001), in which a goose-girl finds the gift of pearls and rubies and the wondrous beauty granted by the fairy godmother to be a pain in the neck. One of the most successful series to begin in this period is Holly Black and Tony DiTerlizzi's *Spiderwick Chronicles: The Field Guide* (2003). This combined a belief in the existence of the fairy with a scientific analysis of the fairy kingdom, and a great sense of threat coming from those who would attempt to exploit it. Intruders other than fairies were also popular. Scott Westerfield, one of the best-selling writers of science fiction and fantasy in the USA, produced a series of books called *Midnighters* (from 2004), in which teenagers find themselves patrolling their suburb to keep out sinister dark shadows. Ghost stories had always been popular amongst younger readers, and Perry Nodelman and Carol Matas began *Ghosthunters (The Proof that Ghosts Exist)* (2007), in which a family sets out to discover why they have a family ghost.

Retellings of fairytales remained popular. As well as Kindl, above, Shannon Hale also wrote a version of the goose-girl (called *Goose Girl*, 2003). Frannie Billingsley's *The Folk Keeper* (2000) is a very dark retelling of the selkie story. If Peter Pan can be regarded as an "original" tale, then Geraldine McCaughrean's *Peter Pan in Scarlet* (2006) can be added in here. Janet McNaughton, in *An Unearthly Night* (2004), tells the story of Tam Lin. Anthologizing such reworkings specifically for the younger market (some for children and some for YA) are Ellen Datlow and Terri Windling, who begin their series with *The Green Man: Tales of the Mythic Forest* (2002). There are also some writers creating "original" folk- and fairytales. Geraldine McCaughrean's *The Stones Are Hatching* (2000) creates folktale from the raw materials of a deserted countryside during the First World War. In 2006 Delia Sherman published *Changeling*, an urban fantasy about a human baby brought up in "New York Between", until she breaks the law of fairy and has to face the challenge of the Lady of Central Park. Working from Irish tradition, Kate Thompson published *The New Policeman* (2007), in which the relationship between a town and the *sidhe* has been the source of great distress in the past.

Quest fantasies continued to be highly popular. Tamora Pierce remains widely read amongst younger teenage girls. Her most recent book is *Terrier* (2006), set 2000 years before *Alanna: The First Adventure*. One of the most highly recommended from teachers and children is Erin Hunter, a working alias for the writers Kate Carey, Cherith Baldry, Tui Sutherland and Victoria Holmes. The series follows the adventures of groups of wild cats, trying to survive in their forest home; the first book was *Into the Wild* (2003). Unusual takes on the quest fantasy came from Lian Hearn (aka Gillian Rubinstein), with The Tales of the Otori, set in a fictional feudal Japan and beginning with *Across the Nightingale Floor* (2002); Peter Dickinson, with *The Rope Maker* (2004), in which the protagonist sets out to find a magician to save her valley, only to discover that she is the powerful one; Stuart Hill's *The Cry of the Icemark* (2005), the story of a small village holding out against a great empire; and Michael Chabon, in *Summerland* (2002), about children who save the world from destruction by playing baseball. Michael Chabon chose to set much of his fantasy in contemporary America; Charlie Fletcher set his fantasy trilogy beginning with *Stoneheart* (2006) on the streets of

London. As in Neil Gaiman's *Neverwhere* (1996), the two protagonists (a boy and a girl) find themselves invisible to Londoners, while they themselves become sensitive to the animist spirit of the city, and in particular to its statues. China Miéville moved into the YA market with *Un Lun Dun* (2007), an attempt to remove the destinarian and colonial aspects from this form. A similar idea can be found in Tom Becker's *Darkside* (2007). The most successful attempt in this direction, however, is Rhiannon Lassiter's Rites of Passage sequence, which began with *Borderland* (2003). In this, a number of teenagers find out what really happens when people with high ideals attempt to interfere with the politics of another country.

The best-known quest fantasy of the decade was Christopher Paolini's *Eragon* (2001). Written by a fifteen-year-old with lots of help from his family (see his acknowledgements), this was originally self-published and distributed by hand. Picked up by a mainstream publisher, this book aroused adoration from younger readers and loathing from experienced fantasy readers (go to amazon.com and see the readers' responses from the five-star down to the one-star). As Diana Wynne Jones observed, the book meets every criteria set for the high fantasy; it could in fact have been written with Jones's *Tough Guide to Fantasyland* by the side of the author's computer but reading it as How-To manual rather than as devastating critique.

The two other highly commercial children's fantasies were G.P. Taylor's *Shadowmancer* (2002) and Sally Gardner's *I, Coriander* (2005). *Shadowmancer* was also self-published, before being picked up by a major publisher. It depicts an eighteenth century very much like our own, in which a traveller arrives from overseas to spread the Good News. All the names are changed, but this is transparently a Christian fantasy in which magic performed by the traveller are miracles from God, though magic performed by anyone else is the work of the Devil. The moral hierarchies of the book suggest that hating your father who beats you, or playing cards on a Sunday, is infinitely worse than exploiting your workers and building slums. On the other hand, at least Taylor gets his basic history right. In *I, Coriander*, set during the English Commonwealth (1649–60) Sally Gardner produces a potentially delightful fantasy, in which a young girl seeks refuge from a wicked stepmother in fairyland, and falls in love with a fairy prince, who might be an analogue for the uncrowned Charles II. However, Gardner's merchant father is a secret royalist and the Puritans of the novel (who in reality thought everybody should be able to read their own Bible) think girls shouldn't be taught to read. Throughout the book the English Revolution is made out to be a wicked and retrograde event. This is not simply a question of pro-royalist bias, but of wilful ignorance.

Despite the success of *Eragon*, *I, Coriander* and *Shadowmancer*, our faith in child readers (and also publishers) is supported by the extremely good original fantasy that was published in this period, of which the following is just a selection. Sherwood Smith's *A Posse of Princesses* (2008) sends princesses on a quest in search of a kidnapped princess. Charles Butler's *The Death of a Ghost* (2006) and Nancy Farmer's *The Sea of Trolls* (2005) are both set in very early periods of British history. Butler's book alternates between a country house setting in modern England with a pre-Roman goddess-temple, and explores the sacrifice of spring mythos. Farmer's is set in Anglo-Saxon England, where the protagonist Jack trains as a bard and becomes involved with the trolls. Elizabeth Knox published *Dreamhunter* (2005) and *Dreamquake* (2007), set in a faux nineteenth-century, with a very Antipodean feel, in which the talented can cross a portal into a world in which dreams can be mined, and in which the origin of dreams is tied up with the politics of the world. Mary Hoffman, better known as an historical novelist, began her Stravaganza series with *City of Masks* (2002), in which a sick child crosses into an alternate Italy and becomes involved in city politics. Marcus Sedgwick, writing throughout this decade, produced a range of books so varied that they are impossible to summarize, but *My Sword Hand is Singing* (2006) reworks and intensifies the traditional vampire story, emphasizing the terror of the victimized. We have already mentioned Frances Hardinge's *Fly By Night*; her other book in this period is *Verdigris Deep* (2007), which begins with three children missing a bus and raiding a wishing-well to get more busfare, only to find that they have become servants of the well-spirit. *Zahrah the Windseeker* (2005) by Nnedi Okorafor-Mbachu, can be read as science fiction, but is about a protagonist with the type of hair that identifies her as a magic-user, and she explores the fantastical wild woods around her. Also possibly science fiction is Oisín McGann's *Ancient Appetites* (2007), set in an alternative nineteenth-century Ireland in which one of the characters is fascinated by the animated machines which can be found in the unexplored parts of the world, and which hint at a theory of evolution. For older readers Steve Cockayne's *The Good People*, discussed earlier, forces fantasy readers to question what they understand as the fantastic, as does Rhiannon Lassiter's *Bad Blood* (2007), a riff on haunted houses and family rivalries. Roderick Townley's *The Great Good Thing* (2001), and its sequels, takes a slightly different tack. Told from the point of view of the protagonists *in* a book, *The Great Good Thing* is very much about the narrative causality of fantasy, as is Chris Wooding's *Poison* (2003). Cornelia Funke, in *Inkheart* (2003), does it the other way round, and has book characters coming to life. The most original anthologist of the period has been Sharyn November, of Viking Books (Penguin). In 2003 she produced *Firebirds* and in 2006 *Firebirds Rising*, both of which are excellent samplings of writers of fantasy who are not usually marketed to teen readers.

After *Buffy the Vampire Slayer* it was clear to a number of companies that good fantasy would attract audiences. The dissolution of the broadcasting monopolies in most countries meant that a 6-million-viewer show which would have been considered a failure in the 1970s, in the 2000s was understood as a highly successful niche product. A direct *Buffy* spin off was the detective series, *Angel* (1999–2004) in which the vampire went on to live a life of an undercover detective in LA along with several other members of the original show. Other successful fantasy shows of the decade include the mini-series *The 10th Kingdom* (2000), which was not initially very successful on TV but has had an extensive afterlife in DVD form (a medium which has extended the niche market of many sf and fantasy sequences). In *The 10ᵗʰ Kingdom* a young woman and her father find themselves in a fairy world a hundred years on from the time of the "classic" fairytales, in a land ruled by the princesses of those stories. The show is witty, amusing and knowledgeable, clearly aimed at a "core" fantasy audience. Aiming for a wider viewing were *Six Feet Under* (2001–5) and *Lost* (2004–10). Neither of these series is unequivocally fantasy. Their success is that how you understand them depends on your own reading codes. *Six Feet Under* is a posthumous fantasy set in a mortuary in which there are continual conversations with the dead, often about the matter of death, and with a question mark about whether the dead are there to continue their part of the conversation. Other posthumous fantasies included *Dead Like Me* (a Canadian series about two young women who are – jointly – the grim reaper), and *Wonderfalls* in which a shop assistant holds conversations with animal figurines. Both aired in 2004, both with creative input from Bryan Fuller who later produced *Pushing Daisies* (2007), in which murders are solved by reanimating the dead.

Lost (2004–10) is set on an island after a plane crash and is heavily influenced by the game *Myst*, one of the most successful computer fantasy games ever (an area that is simply too large for us to cover here). Various mysterious things happen and by the end of the 2008 season, there was some suggestion that the characters were trapped in a pocket universe. To a degree, however, *Lost* is fantasy *because* it excites fantasy fans, a kind of retrofitting which seems to be becoming more common (see *Nip and Tuck*, 2003–07, a programme about plastic surgery which makes heavy use of Gothic symbolism). *Heroes* (2006–ongoing) was extremely popular, taking the fairly standard premise of people who discover that they have unusual abilities, but placing their struggles to come to terms with this as the centre of the emotional dynamic.

On the big screen, among the blockbuster movies of the 2000s were the three *Lord of the Rings* movies (2001–3), five Harry Potter movies (2001–7), getting progressively darker, and a new attempt to translate

The Chronicles of Narnia beginning with *The Lion, the Witch and the Wardrobe* (2005) and continuing with *Prince Caspian* (2008). All of these movies were considered some of the first really successful big screen adaptations of classic fantasy thanks in large part to technological developments in computer graphics but also because there was a real sense that the directors involved actually liked the texts they were working with (as opposed to David Cunningham's *The Seeker* (2007, UK: *The Dark is Rising*), which was generally felt to have taken a brilliant children's book – by Susan Cooper – and beaten, flogged and shredded it until nothing was left).

Other notable movies included adaptations of major children's books including *Eragon* (adapt. 2006), and *The Golden Compass* (adapt. 2007) and some very nice but less faithful adaptations such as *Ella Enchanted* (2004) based on the superb "Cinderella" retelling by Gail Carson Levine (1997) and the excellent *Stardust* (dir. Mathew Vaughn, 2007) based on the illustrated novel by Neil Gaiman and Charles Vess (1998). Of original movies, several stand out. *Shrek* was an animated movie directed by Andrew Adamson and Vicky Jenson (2001) and an adaptation of William Steig's 1990 picture book, *Shrek!*, The movie's appeal lay with its direct attack on many Disney conventions (this had faded by the third movie) and to children in particular because of its vulgar humour (reminiscent of Raymond Briggs's graphic novel, *Fungus the Bogeyman*, 1977). Hayao Miyazaki's *Spirited Away* (2002) was only one of his many important fantasy movies in the 2000s (including the adaptation of Diana Wynne Jones's *Howl's Moving Castle*), but the most interesting, with its dreamy portal fantasy and an Alice-like heroine using the expectations of Japanese rather than Western fantasy traditions making a very real impact on the Western audience. *Donnie Darko* (dir. Richard Kelly, 2001) was a hallucinatory dream of a possible false death, and apocalypse wrapped up in possible alternate worlds and shaped by a rather scary man in a rabbit costume. Equally complex and in the same vein was *Eternal Sunshine of the Spotless Mind* (dir. Michelle Gondry, 2004) which is a taut tale of memory and romance which can be viewed as science fiction, as fantasy, or as horror and, like *Donnie Darko*, is highly demanding of its audience. *Pan's Labyrinth* (dir. Guillermo del Toro, 2006), was a fairytale woven around the years after the Spanish Civil War and owing much to Grimm. As with *Donnie Darko* and *Eternal Sunshine of the Spotless Mind* there is a porousness to the narrative voice which means that the "reality" of the fantasy is continually questioned without being ruptured. At the more frivolous end was *Pirates of the Caribbean* (dir. Gore Verbinski) and its sequels, which originated as a theme park ride, and in 2003 the utterly delightful Disney confection, *Enchanted* (dir. Kevin Lima, 2007) in which a fairytale bride is thrust into New York by her potential stepmother.

The graphic novel industry had, by the 2000s, become such a genre in itself, with its own fans and its own conventions (Comic-Con, the major comics convention, was attracting over 120,000 attendees) and was producing so many titles that it is not possible to list all the fantasy titles here. Some of the outstanding graphic novels and novelists of the decade include P. Craig Russell's adaptation of Wagner's Ring Cycle, *The Ring* (2001); *The Tale of One Bad Rat* (1995), Bryan Talbot's complex tale of overcoming parental rape, making use of the work of Beatrix Potter to underscore the story; and Linda Medley's *Castle Waiting* (2006), which tells of what happens to the inhabitants of the castle after the prince and princess have gone off to their happily ever after. Among the series, Mike Mignola produced the superb "The Right Hand of Doom" (2002) for his *Hellboy* sequence, and Jeff Smith continued his epic Bone series with *Rose* (with Charles Vess, 2001) and *Bone* (2004). Alan Moore's *The League of Extraordinary Gentlemen*, written by Alan Moore and drawn by Kevin O'Neill, continued into the decade, surviving the film version (2003) to see *The Black Dossier* published in 2008. The final graphic novel we want to draw your attention to is Bryan Talbot's extraordinary *Alice in Sunderland* (2007), a complex collage of meta-text which explores the links between Lewis Carroll, the northern town of Sunderland and the career of the well-known British actor Sid James.

By the 2000s, the form in which most young children and teens encountered fantasy was computer games. Many, many games were simply adaptations of already popular books, TV programmes and movies, as well as graphic novels, but several original games and gaming environments became hugely popular in the decade as the virtual realities created by the programmers began to match the expectations of players, and also as young players grew up with a stronger sense of their connection to the virtual worlds. Most of these games have some connection to quest or epic fantasy: *Myst*, launched in 1993, was a hit well into 2002 (being surpassed at the time only by *The Sims*, a soap opera reality, launched in that year). *Final Fantasy*, a media franchise that appears in a number of platforms (games, graphic novels etc), released several immensely popular game episodes in the 2000s. The biggest shift, however, may have been to online shared world gaming, in which millions of people interacted over huge virtual areas: the two best known are *Second Life* (2003) which is a "reality" game much like *The Sims* but in which you are the character rather than somebody who moves characters around, more like virtual facebook than a game as such, and *World of Warcraft* (launched 2004 but an outgrowth of earlier games), a massive epic fantasy game of sword-and-sorcery, quests and battles.

This short history ends in 2008. Lovers of the field can probably be optimistic about the future health and diversity of fantasy. It is likely that the field will continue to grow and to diversify as it has done for the last three decades. Changes in marketing, the growing opportunities for readers to buy the books they want rather than the books which book shops sell, the possibilities for internet book sellers to hold far more books, and hence in some cases to support small presses, coupled with the popularity of internet magazines, have changed the dynamic of the field, but also make it difficult to predict its future.

It is possible that fantasy will continue to dominate in the area of children's books, comics, computer games and blockbuster movies, without the adult readership of fantasy literature actually increasing. At the beginning of the twenty-first century, fantasy was moving from the margins into the cultural mainstream. Popular culture is increasingly permeated with images and ideas drawn from fantasy (and from science fiction). Writers of self-consciously "literary books", such as Yann Martel, Michael Chabon and David Mitchell, the books which win Booker Prizes, are introducing elements drawn from fantasy literature, and often in ways that show their engagement with the field.

Writers and critics in the post-modern world are sympathetic to the playfulness and willingness to experiment that has characterized much of the best fantasy. Some have begun to realize that fantasy does not necessarily equate with escapism, but offers alternative ways of explaining and coping with reality. Fantasy has the potential to bring huge changes to our understanding of literature in the twenty-first century, therefore, but to imagine that we can predict the long-term future of literature is, of course, sheer fantasy.

Chronology of Important Works and People

Important Fiction

c.1300 BC?	Anon.	*Epic of Gilgamesh*
c.750 BC?	Homer	*The Odyssey*
c.250 BC?	Anon.	*The Alexander Romance*
29–19 BC	Virgil	*Aeneid*
8 AD	Ovid	*Metamorphoses*
c.170 AD	Apuleius	*The Golden Ass*
800 AD?	Anon.	*Beowulf*
1100?	Anon.	*The Mabinogion*
1136	Geoffrey of Monmouth	*History of the Kings of Britain*
1190	Chrétien de Troyes	*Perceval*
c.1200	Anon.	*Nibelungenlied*
1200	Snorri Sturluson	*Prose Edda*
1469	Sir Thomas Malory	*Le Morte D'Arthur*
16th C?	Anon.	"Tam Lin" and "Thomas the Rhymer"
1532	François Rabelais	*The Horrible and Most Astonishing Deeds of Pantagruel*
1590	Edmund Spenser	*The Faerie Queen*
1594	William Shakespeare	*A Midsummer Night's Dream*
1603	William Shakespeare	*Macbeth*
1610	William Shakespeare	*The Winter's Tale*
1678	John Bunyan	*Pilgrim's Progress*
1696	Madame D'Aulnoy	*Tales of the Fairys* (trans. 1699)
1697	Charles Perrault	*Histories, or Tales of Past Times* (trans. 1729)
1704	Antoine Galland (trans.)	*The Thousand and One Nights*
1726	Jonathan Swift	*Gulliver's Travels*
1764	Horace Walpole	*The Castle of Otranto*
1784	Marquis de Sade	*The One Hundred and Twenty Days of Sodom*

1786	William Beckford	*Vathek: An Arabian Tale*
1794	Ann Radcliffe	*The Mysteries of Udolpho*
1796	Matthew Lewis	*The Monk: A Romance*
1811	Baron de la Motte Fouqué	*Undine*
1816	Charles Brockden Brown	*Wieland*
1817	E.T.A. Hoffmann	"The Sandman"
1817	Samuel Taylor Coleridge	"Kubla Khan"
1818	Mary Shelley	*Frankenstein*
1818	Percy Bysshe Shelley	"Ozymandias"
1819	Washington Irving	"Rip Van Winkle"
1820	Charles Maturin	*Melmoth the Wanderer*
1820	John Keats	"La Belle Dame Sans Merci"
1820	Washington Irving	"The Legend of Sleepy Hollow"
1821	John Polidori	*The Vampyre: A Tale*
1837	Hans Christian Andersen	"The Little Mermaid"
1839	Edgar Allan Poe	"The Fall of the House of Usher"
1839	Sara Coleridge	*Phantasmion: A Fairy Tale*
1843	Charles Dickens	"A Christmas Carol"
1843	Edgar Allan Poe	"The Pit and the Pendulum"
1844	Nathaniel Hawthorne	"Rappacini's Daughter"
1844	Hans Christian Andersen	"The Ugly Duckling"
1845	Hans Christian Andersen	"The Snow Queen"
1845	Hans Christian Andersen	"The Red Shoes"
1845	Hans Christian Andersen	"The Little Match Girl"
1850	Mark Lemon	*The Enchanted Doll*
1851	John Ruskin	*King of the Golden River*
1855	Nathaniel Hawthorne	"Feathertop"
1855	Robert Browning	"Childe Roland to the Dark Tower Came"
1855	William Makepeace Thackeray	*The Rose and the Ring*
1858	Frances Brown	*Granny's Wonderful Chair*
1858	George MacDonald	*Phantastes*
1859	Edward Bulwer-Lytton	*The Haunted and the Haunters*, or *The House and the Brain*
1862	Christina Rossetti	*Goblin Market and Other Poems*
1862	Jane Austin	*Fairy Dreams: or Wanderings in Elfland*
1863	Charles Kingsley	*The Water Babies*
1865	Lewis Carroll	*Alice's Adventures in Wonderland*
1871	George MacDonald	*At the Back of the North Wind*
1871	Jean Ingelow	*Mopsa the Fairy*
1871	Lewis Carroll	*Through the Looking-Glass*

1872	George MacDonald	*The Princess and the Goblin*
1872	Sheridan Le Fanu	*In a Glass Darkly* (collection)
1881	Guy de Maupassant	"The Withered Hand"
1881	Joel Chandler Harris	*Uncle Remus: His Songs and His Stories*
1881	Walter Crane	*A Fairy Masque*
1882	F. Anstey	*Vice Versâ: or A Lesson to Fathers*
1883	George MacDonald	*The Princess and Curdie*
1886	Marie Corelli	*A Romance of Two Worlds*
1886	Robert Louis Stevenson	*Strange Case of Dr. Jekyll and Mr. Hyde*
1888	H. Rider Haggard	*She*
1888	Oscar Wilde	*The Happy Prince and Other Stories*
1888	Richard Garnett	*The Twilight of the Gods*
1889	Andrew Lang	*The Blue Fairy Book*
1889	E. Nesbit	*The Story of the Treasure Seekers*
1890	Mark Twain	*A Connecticut Yankee in King Arthur's Court*
1891	Mary Elizabeth Braddon	*The World, the Flesh and the Devil*
1891	Oscar Wilde	*The Picture of Dorian Gray*
1894	Lewis Carroll	*Sylvie and Bruno*
1894	Rudyard Kipling	*The Jungle Book*
1894	William Morris	*The Wood Beyond the World*
1895	Arthur Machen	*The Great God Pan*
1895	Edwin Lester Arnold	*The Story of Ulla and Other Tales*
1896	George MacDonald	*Lilith*
1896	William Morris	*The Well at the World's End*
1897	Bram Stoker	*Dracula*
1897	William Morris	*The Water of the Wondrous Isles*
1900	Frank L. Baum	*The Wonderful Wizard of Oz*
1900	Lucy Lane Clifford	"The New Mother"
1902	Beatrix Potter	*The Tale of Peter Rabbit*
1902	E. Nesbit	*Five Children and It*
1902	E.F. Benson	*Luck of the Vails*
1902	Rudyard Kipling	*Just So Stories*
1903	Beatrix Potter	*The Tale of Squirrel Nutkin*
1903	George Warwick Deeping	*Uther and Igraine*
1904	E. Nesbit	*The Phoenix and the Carpet*
1904	M.R. James	*Ghost Stories of an Antiquary*
1906	E. Nesbit	*The Story of the Amulet*
1906	J.M. Barrie	*Peter Pan in Kensington Gardens*
1906	Rudyard Kipling	*Puck of Pook's Hill*
1907	M.P. Sheil	*The Last Miracle*
1907	William Hope Hodgson	*The Boats of the "Glen Carrig"*

1908	Algernon Blackwood	*John Silence, Physician Extraordinary*
1908	Beatrix Potter	*The Tale of Jemima Puddle-Duck*
1908	Kenneth Grahame	*The Wind in the Willows*
1908	Maurice Maeterlinck	*The Blue Bird*
1908	William Hope Hodgson	*The House on the Borderland*
1910	Andrew Lang	*The Lilac Fairy Book*
1910	E. Nesbit	*The Magic City*
1910	William Hope Hodgson	*Carnacki the Ghost Finder*
1911	Ford Madox Ford	*Ladies Whose Bright Eyes*
1911	J.M. Barrie	*Peter Pan and Wendy*
1911	Rudyard Kipling	*Rewards and Fairies*
1911	Saki [H.H. Munro]	*The Chronicles of Clovis* (collection)
1912	M.P. Sheil	*The Pale Ape and Other Pulses*
1912	William Hope Hodgson	*The Night Land: A Love Tale*
1913	Beatrix Potter	*The Tale of Pigling Bland*
1915	Franz Kafka	*The Metamorphosis*
1915	Gustav Meyrink	*The Golem*
1918	Norman Lindsay	*The Magic Pudding: Being the Adventures of Bunyip Bluegum and his Friends Bill Barnacle and Sam Sawnoff*
1919	Abraham Merritt	*The Moon Pool*
1919	James Branch Cabell	*Jurgen: A Comedy of Justice*
1920	David Lindsay	*A Voyage to Arcturus*
1921	Eleanor Farjeon	*Martin Pippin in the Apple-Orchard*
1921	Hugh Lofting	*The Story of Dr. Dolittle*
1922	David Garnett	*Lady into Fox*
1922	E.R. Eddison	*The Worm Ouroboros*
1922	Margery Williams	*The Velveteen Rabbit*
1924	Gerald Bullet	*Mr. Godly Beside Himself*
1924	H.P. Lovecraft	"The Rats in the Walls"
1924	Lord Dunsany	*The King of Elfland's Daughter*
1925	Christine Campbell Thompson (ed.)	*Not at Night*
1925	John Erskine	*The Private Life of Helen of Troy*
1925	Walter de la Mare	*Broomsticks and Other Tales*
1926	A.A. Milne	*Winnie-the-Pooh*
1926	Abraham Merritt	*The Ship of Ishtar*
1926	August Derleth	"Bat's Belfry"
1926	Helen Beauclerk	*The Green Lacquer Pavilion*
1926	Hope Mirrlees	*Lud-In-the-Mist*
1926	Lady Cynthia Asquith (ed.)	*The Ghost Book*
1926	M.R. James	*A Warning to the Curious*

1926	Thorne Smith	*Topper: An Improbable Adventure*
1927	H.P. Lovecraft	"The Color Out of Space"
1927	John Masefield	*The Midnight Folk*
1927	Leslie Barringer	*Gerfalcon*
1928	H.P. Lovecraft	"The Call of Cthulhu"
1928	M.P. Sheil	*Here Comes the Lady*
1928	Robert Nathan	*The Bishop's Wife*
1928	Walter Brooks	*Freddy Goes to Florida*
1929	Carl Grabo	*The Cat in Grandfather's House*
1929	Lady Cynthia Asquith (ed.)	*Shudders*
1929	Rachel Field	*Hetty, Her First Hundred Years*
1929	Robert Nathan	*There is Another Heaven*
1929	Virginia Woolf	*Orlando*
1930	Charles Williams	*War in Heaven*
1930	Edward Fenton	*The Nine Questions*
1931	John Collier	*His Monkey Wife*
1931	Lady Cynthia Asquith (ed.)	*When Churchyards Yawn*
1931	Thorne Smith	*The Night Life of the Gods*
1932	Abraham Merritt	*Dwellers in the Mirage*
1932–1936	Robert E. Howard	Conan stories in *Weird Tales*
1933	C.L. Moore	"Shambleau"
1934	C.L. Moore	"The Black God's Kiss"
1934	P.L. Travers	*Mary Poppins*
1935	Charles G. Finney	*The Circus of Dr. Lao*
1935	Dennis Wheatley	*The Devil Rides Out*
1935	E.R. Eddison	*Mistress of Mistresses*
1935	Herbert E. Read	*The Green Child: A Romance*
1935	John Masefield	*The Box of Delights*
1936	Enid Blyton	*The Adventures of the Wishing-Chair*
1936	Evangeline Walton	*The Virgin and the Swine (aka The Island of the Mighty)*
1936	Hilda Lewis	*The Ship that Flew*
1937	Christine Campbell Thompson (ed.)	*The Not at Night Omnibus*
1937	H.P. Lovecraft	"The Shadow Over Innsmouth"
1937	J.R.R. Tolkien	*The Hobbit*
1938	T.H. White	*The Sword in the Stone*
1939	C.S. Lewis	*Out of the Silent Planet*
1939	Enid Blyton	*The Enchanted Wood*
1939	Fritz Leiber	"Two Sought Adventure"
1939	Horace L. Gold	"Trouble with Water"
1939	T.H. White	*The Witch in the Wood*
1940	Elizabeth Goudge	*The Little White Horse*

1940	L. Ron Hubbard	"Typewriter in the Sky"
1940	L. Sprague de Camp	"The Incomplete Enchanter"
1940	Robert A. Heinlein	"The Devil Makes the Law!" (reprinted as *Magic, Inc.*)
1940	Robert Nathan	*Portrait of Jenny*
1940	T.H. White	*The Ill-Made Knight*
1941	E.R. Eddison	*A Fish Dinner in Memison*
1942	C.S. Lewis	*The Screwtape Letters*
1942	Jorge Luis Borges	"Tlön, Uqbar, Orbis Tertius"
1942	Robert A. Heinlein	"The Unpleasant Profession of Jonathan Hoag"
1943	C.S. Lewis	*Perelandra* (aka *Voyage to Venus*)
1943	Enid Blyton	*The Magic Faraway Tree*
1943	Mary Norton	*The Magic Bedknob*
1945	C.S. Lewis	*That Hideous Strength*
1945	E.B. White	*Stuart Little*
1945	James Thurber	*The White Deer*
1945	Tove Jansson	*Comet in Moominland*
1946	Carolyn Sherwin Bailey	*Miss Hickory*
1946	Mervyn Peake	*Titus Groan*
1946	T.H. White	*Mistress Masham's Repose*
1947	Ray Bradbury	*Dark Carnival* (collection)
1948	Fletcher Pratt	*The Well of the Unicorn*
1948	George Orwell	*Animal Farm: A Fairy Story*
1948	Ruth Gannett	*My Father's Dragon*
1948	Shirley Jackson	"The Lottery"
1949	James Thurber	*The Thirteen Clocks*
1949	John Myers Myers	*Silverlock*
1949–1951	Leigh Brackett	stories about Eric John Stark
1950	Archie Binns	*The Radio Imp*
1950	C.S. Lewis	*The Lion, the Witch and the Wardrobe*
1950	Jack Vance	*The Dying Earth* (collection)
1950	Mervyn Peake	*Gormenghast*
1950	Paul Gallico	*Jennie*
1950	Ray Bradbury	*The Martian Chronicles*
1951	Andre Norton	*Huon of the Horn*
1951	C.S. Lewis	*Prince Caspian: the Return to Narnia*
1951	Lucy M. Boston	*The Children of Green Knowe*
1951	Robert Aickman	"The Trains"
1951	Ray Bradbury	*The Illustrated Man*
1952	C.S. Lewis	*The Voyage of the Dawn Treader*
1952	E.B. White	*Charlotte's Web*

1952	Fletcher Pratt	*The Blue Star*
1952	Jack Vance	*Big Planet*
1952	Jerome Bixby	*"It's a Good Life"*
1952	Mary Norton	*The Borrowers*
1952	P.L. Travers	*Mary Poppins in the Park*
1952	Shirley Jackson	*The Sundial*
1953	C.S. Lewis	*The Silver Chair*
1953	Dennis Wheatley	*To the Devil – A Daughter*
1953	Fritz Leiber	*Conjure Wife*
1953	Poul Anderson	*Three Hearts and Three Lions*
1953	Ray Bradbury	*Fahrenheit 451*
1953	Ray Bradbury	*The Golden Apples of the Sun*
1953	Theodore Sturgeon	*E. Pluribus Unicorn*
1954	C.S. Lewis	*The Horse and His Boy*
1954	Edward Eager	*Half Magic*
1954	Eleanor Cameron	*Voyage to the Mushroom Planet*
1954	Eleanor Farjeon	*The Glass Slipper*
1954	Fredric Brown	*Angels and Spaceships*
1954–1955	J.R.R. Tolkien	*The Lord of the Rings* (3 vols)
1954	Richard Matheson	*I Am Legend*
1955	Barbara Sleigh	*Carbonel*
1955	C.S. Lewis	*The Magician's Nephew*
1955	James Thurber	*The Wonderful O*
1955	John Wyndham	*The Chrysalids*
1955	L. Sprague de Camp	*Tales of Conan*
1955	Poul Anderson	*The Broken Sword*
1955	Ray Bradbury	*Dandelion Wine*
1956	C.S. Lewis	*The Last Battle*
1956	Dodie Smith	*The Hundred and One Dalmatians*
1957	Dr. Seuss	*The Cat in the Hat*
1957	Jane Gaskell	*Strange Evil*
1957	L. Sprague de Camp	*The Return of Conan*
1957	Richard Brautigan	*A Confederate General from Big Sur*
1958	Elizabeth Marie Pope	*The Sherwood Ring*
1958	Marion Zimmer Bradley	*"The Planet Savers"*
1958	Philippa Pearce	*Tom's Midnight Garden*
1958	T.H. White	*The Once and Future King*
1959	Carol Kendall	*The Minnipins*
1959	Mervyn Peake	*Titus Alone*
1959	Shirley Jackson	*The Haunting of Hill House*
1960	Alan Garner	*The Weirdstone of Brisingamen*
1960	George Selden	*The Cricket in Times Square*

1960	Isaac Bashevis Singer	*The Magician of Lublin*
1960	Walter J. Miller Jr.	*A Canticle for Leibowitz*
1960	Wilson Harris	*Palace of the Peacock*
1961	Michael Moorcock	"The Dreaming City"
1961	Norton Juster	*The Phantom Tollbooth*
1961	Peter S. Beagle	*A Fine and Private Place*
1961	Roald Dahl	*James and the Giant Peach*
1962	Alison Uttley	*A Traveller in Time*
1962	Clarke, Pauline	*The Twelve and the Genii*
1962	Madeleine L'Engle	*A Wrinkle in Time*
1962	Shirley Jackson	*We Have Always Lived in the Castle*
1963	Alan Garner	*The Moon of Gomrath*
1963	Andre Norton	*Witch World*
1963	Joan Aiken	*The Wolves of Willoughby Chase*
1963	Maurice Sendak	*Where the Wild Things Are*
1964	Catherine Storr	*Marianne Dreams*
1964	J.P. Martin	*Uncle*
1964	Joan Aiken	*Black Hearts in Battersea*
1964	Lloyd Alexander	*The Book of Three*
1964	Roald Dahl	*Charlie and the Chocolate Factory*
1964	Robert Aickman	*Dark Entries*
1964	Roger Corman (dir.)	*Masque of the Red Death*
1965	Alan Garner	*Elidor*
1965	Lloyd Alexander	*The Black Cauldron*
1965	Philip Jose Farmer	*To Your Scattered Bodies Go*
1965	Susan Cooper	*Under Sea, Under Stone*
1966	John Bellairs	*The Face in the Frost*
1966	John Norman	*Tarnsman of Gor*
1966	Lloyd Alexander	*The Castle of Llyr*
1966	Randall Garrett	*Too Many Magicians*
1966	Thomas Pynchon	*The Crying of Lot 49*
1966	William Mayne	*Earthfasts*
1966	Zilpha Keatley Snyder	*Black and Blue Magic*
1967	Alan Garner	*The Owl Service*
1967	Dodie Smith	*The Starlight Barking*
1967	Lloyd Alexander	*Taran Wanderer*
1967	Richard Brautigan	*Troutfishing in America*
1967	Russell Hoban	*The Mouse and His Child*
1968	Anne McCaffrey	*Dragonflight*
1968	Elisabeth Beresford	*The Wombles*
1968	Harlan Ellison (ed.)	*Dangerous Visions*
1968	Keith Roberts	*Pavane*

1968	Lloyd Alexander	*The High King*
1968	Peter S. Beagle	*The Last Unicorn*
1968	Richard Brautigan	*In Water Melon Sugar*
1968	Rosemary Harris	*The Moon in the Cloud*
1968	Ursula K. Le Guin	*A Wizard of Earthsea*
1969	Antony Boucher	*The Compleat Werewolf*
1969	Christopher Stasheff	*The Warlock in Spite of Himself*
1969	Jane Langton	*The Diamond in the Window*
1969	Kingsley Amis	*The Green Man*
1969	Natalie Babbit	*The Search for Delicious*
1969	Penelope Farmer	*Charlotte Sometimes*
1969	Robert Bloch	*Dragons and Nightmares*
1970	Fritz Leiber	"Ill Met in Lankhmar"
1970	Joy Chant	*Red Moon and Black Mountain*
1970	Katherine Kurtz	*Deryni Rising*
1970	Mary Stewart	*The Crystal Cave*
1970	Maurice Sendak	*In the Night Kitchen*
1970	Richard Bach	*Jonathan Livingston Seagull*
1970	Roger Zelazny	*Nine Princes in Amber*
1971	Anne McCaffrey	*Dragonquest*
1971	Evangeline Walton	*The Children of Llyr*
1971	John Brunner	*The Traveller in Black* (collection)
1971	M. John Harrison	*The Pastel City*
1971	Michael Moorcock	*The Warlord of the Air*
1971	Penelope Farmer	*A Castle of Bone*
1971	Penelope Lively	*The Wild Hunt of Hagworthy*
1971	Phyllis Eisenstein	*Born to Exile*
1971	Robert C. O'Brien	*Mrs Frisby and the Rats of NIMH*
1971	Thomas Burnett Swan	*The Forest of Forever*
1971	Ursula K. Le Guin	*The Tombs of Atuan*
1971	William Mayne	*A Game of Dark*
1972	Elisabeth Beresford	*Dangerous Magic*
1972	Evangeline Walton	*The Song of Rhiannon*
1972	Joan Aiken	"The Rose of Puddlefratrum"
1972	Joan Aiken	"Humblepuppy"
1972	John Gardner	*Grendel*
1972	K.M. Briggs	*Hobberdy Dick*
1972	Leon Garfield	*The Ghost Downstairs*
1972	Marion Zimmer Bradley	*Darkover Landfall*
1972	Richard Adams	*Watership Down*
1972	Ursula K. Le Guin	*The Farthest Shore*
1973	Alan Garner	*Red Shift*

1973	Anne McCaffrey	*To Ride Pegasus*
1973	Astrid Lindgren	*The Brothers Lionheart*
1973	Diana Wynne Jones	*Wilkin's Tooth* (US: *Witch's Business*)
1973	Gabriel García Márquez	*One Hundred Years of Solitude* (trans.)
1973	Mary Stewart	*The Hollow Hills*
1973	Roald Dahl	*Charlie and the Great Glass Elevator*
1973	Susan Cooper	*The Dark is Rising*
1973	William Goldman	*The Princess Bride*
1974	Diana Wynne Jones	*The Ogre Downstairs*
1974	Elizabeth Marie Pope	*The Perilous Gard*
1974	Evangeline Walton	*The Prince of Annwn*
1974	H. Warner Munn	*Merlin's Ring*
1974	Jill Murphy	*The Worst Witch*
1974	Joan Aiken	*Midnight is a Place*
1974	Keith Roberts	*The Chalk Giants*
1974	Madeleine L'Engle	*A Wind in the Door*
1974	Marion Zimmer Bradley	*The Spell Sword*
1974	Marion Zimmer Bradley	*The Jewel of Arwen*
1974	Marion Zimmer Bradley	*The Parting of Arwen*
1974	Poul Anderson	*A Midsummer Tempest*
1974	Stephen King	*Carrie*
1975	Clifford Simak	*Enchanted Pilgrimage*
1975	Diana Wynne Jones	*Eight Days of Luke*
1975	Diana Wynne Jones	*Dogsbody*
1975	Marion Zimmer Bradley	*The Heritage of Hastur*
1975	Patricia McKillip	*The Forgotten Beasts of Eld*
1975	Penelope Lively	*The Ghost of Thomas Kempe*
1975	Penelope Lively	*A Stitch in Time*
1975	Stephen King	*Salem's Lot*
1976	Anne McCaffrey	*Dragonsong*
1976	Anne Rice	*Interview with the Vampire*
1976	C.J. Cherryh	*Gate of Ivrel*
1976	Gene Wolfe	*The Devil in a Forest*
1976	Gordon R. Dickson	*The Dragon and the George*
1976	Joan Aiken	*Castle Barebane*
1976	Joanna Russ	*The Adventures of Alyx*
1976	John Steinbeck	*The Acts of King Arthur and His Noble Knights*
1976	Marion Zimmer Bradley	*The Shattered Chain*
1976	Marion Zimmer Bradley	*The Forbidden Tower*
1976	Michael de Larrabeiti	*The Borribles*
1976	Natalie Babbit	*Tuck Everlasting*

1976	Patricia McKillip	*The Riddle Master of Hed*
1976	Piers Anthony	*A Spell for Chameleon*
1976	Ramsey Campbell	*The Doll Who Ate His Mother*
1976	Richard Matheson	*Bid Time Return*
1976	Robert Aickman	*Compulsory Games*
1977	Angela Carter	*The Infernal Desire Machines of Doctor Hoffman*
1977	Anne McCaffrey	*Dragonsinger: Harper of Pern*
1977	Charles L. Grant	*The Hour of the Oxrun Dead*
1977	Diana Wynne Jones	*Charmed Life*
1977	Italo Calvino	*The Castle of Crossed Destinies*
1977	J.R.R. Tolkien	*The Silmarillion*
1977	John Norman	*Slave Girl of Gor*
1977	Nancy Bond	*A String in the Harp*
1977	Patricia McKillip	*Heir of Sea and Fire*
1977	Peter Straub	*If You Could See Me Now*
1977	Raymond Briggs	*Fungus the Bogeyman*
1977	Stephen R. Donaldson	*Lord Foul's Bane*
1977	Sylvia Townsend Warner	*Kingdoms of Elfin*
1977	Tanith Lee	*East of Midnight*
1977	Terry Brooks	*The Sword of Shannara*
1977	Thomas Burnett Swann	*Cry Silver Bells*
1977	William Kotzwinkle	*Doctor Rat*
1978	Chelsea Quinn Yarbro	*Hotel Transylvania*
1978	Joan Aiken	*Go Saddle the Sea*
1978	Les Daniels	*The Black Castle*
1978	Madeleine L'Engle	*A Swiftly Tilting Planet*
1978	Marion Zimmer Bradley	*Stormqueen!*
1978	Michael Moorcock	*Gloriana*
1978	Patricia McKillip	*Harpist in the Wind*
1978	Raymond Briggs	*The Snowman*
1978	Robert Asprin	*Another Fine Myth*
1978	Robin McKinley	*Beauty: The Retelling of the Story of Beauty and the Beast*
1978	Virginia Hamilton	*Justice and Her Brothers*
1979	Angela Carter	*The Bloody Chamber and Other Stories*
1979	Anne McCaffrey	*Dragondrums*
1979	Chelsea Quinn Yarbro	*The Palace*
1979	Colin Dann	*The Animals of Farthing Wood*
1979	Elizabeth Anne Lynn	*The Dancers of Arun*
1979	Elizabeth Anne Lynn	*Watchtower*
1979	Randall Garrett	*Murder and Magic*

1979	Samuel R. Delany	*Tales of Nevèrÿon*
1979	Tim Powers	*The Drawing of the Dark*
1979	William Horwood	*Duncton Wood*
1980	Chelsea Quinn Yarbro	*Blood Games*
1980	Diana Wynne Jones	*The Magicians of Caprona*
1980	Elizabeth Anne Lynn	*The Northern Girl*
1980	Harlan Ellison	*Shatterday*
1980	James Herbert	*The Dark*
1980	Jonathan Carroll	*The Land of Laughs*
1980	Lynne Reid Banks	*The Indian in the Cupboard*
1980	Marion Zimmer Bradley	*Two to Conquer*
1980	Patricia Wrightson	*The Dark Bright Water*
1980	Peter Straub	*Shadowland*
1980	Phyllis Gotlieb	*A Judgement of Dragons*
1980	Ramsey Campbell	*To Wake the Dead*
1980	Robert Asprin	*Myth Conceptions*
1980	Robert Silverberg	*Lord Valentine's Castle*
1980	Suzy McKee Charnas	*The Vampire Tapestry*
1980	Vivien Alcock	*The Haunting of Cassie Palmer*
1981	Charles R. Saunders	*Imaro*
1981	Chelsea Quinn Yarbro	*Tempting Fate*
1981	Christopher Priest	*The Affirmation*
1981	D.M. Thomas	*The White Hotel*
1981	Gene Wolfe	*The Shadow of the Torturer* (The Book of the New Sun)
1981	Joan Aiken	*The Haunting of Lamb House*
1981	John Crowley	*Little, Big*
1981	Joyce Carol Oates	*A Bloodsmoor Romance*
1981	Mildred Downey Broxon	*Too Long a Sacrifice*
1981	Nancy Kress	*The Prince of the Morning Bells*
1981	P.C. Hodgell	*God Stalk*
1981	Ramsey Campbell	*The Nameless*
1981	Randall Garrett	*Lord Darcy Investigates*
1981	Robin McKinley	*The Door in the Hedge*
1982	David Eddings	*Pawn of Prophecy*
1982	Diana Paxson	*Lady of Light*
1982	George R.R. Martin	*Fevre Dream*
1982	Geraldine Harris	*Prince of the Godborn*
1982	James Blaylock	*The Elfin Ship*
1982	Jane Yolen	*Dragon's Blood*
1982	Julian May	*The Many-Colored Land* (The Saga of Pliocene Exile)

1984	David Gemmell	*Legend*
1984	Glen Cook	*The Black Company*
1984	Guy Gavriel Kay	*The Summer Tree (The Fionavar Tapestry)*
1984	Jennifer Roberson	*Shapechangers (Chronicles of the Cheysuli)*
1984	Joyce Carol Oates	*Bellefleur*
1984	Lloyd Arthur Eshbach	*The Land Beyond the Gate*
1984	Lucius Shepard	*"The Man Who Painted the Dragon Griaule"*
1984	Margaret Mahy	*The Changeover: A Supernatural Romance*
1984	Peter Straub and Stephen King	*The Talisman*
1984	Robert Holdstock	*Mythago Wood*
1984	Robin McKinley	*The Hero and the Crown*
1984	T.E.D. Klein	*The Ceremonies*
1984	Tamora Pierce	*In the Hand of the Goddess*
1984	Tracy Hickman and Margaret Weiss	*Dragonlance: Dragons of Autumn Twilight*
1985	Anne Rice	*The Vampire Lestat*
1985	Barbara Hambly	*Dragonsbane*
1985	Charles R. Saunders	*The Trial of Bobu*
1985	Craig Shaw Gardner	*A Malady of Magicks*
1985	Dan Simmons	*Song of Kali*
1985	Diana Wynne Jones	*Fire and Hemlock*
1985	Geoff Ryman	*The Warrior Who Carried Life*
1985	Isabelle Allende	*The House of the Spirits*
1985	Jack Vance	*The Green Pearl (Lyonesse)*
1985	Jeanette Winterson	*Oranges are Not the Only Fruit*
1985	Jessica Salmonson	*Ou Lu Khen and the Beautiful Madwoman*
1985	Lisa Goldstein	*The Dream Years*
1985	Pat O'Shea	*The Hounds of the Morrigan*
1985	Paul Hazel	*Winterking*
1985	Peter Carey	*Illywhacker*
1985	Sheri S. Tepper	*Marianne, the Magus and the Manticore*
1985	Sheri S. Tepper	*The Song of Mavin Manyshaped*
1985	Stephen Bowkett	*Spellbinder*
1985	Suniti Namjoshi	*Conversations With a Cow*
1985	Tad Williams	*Tailchaser's Song*
1986	Avram Davidson	*Virgil in Averno*

1988	Anne Rice	*The Queen of the Damned*
1988	Carol Emshwiller	*Carmen Dog*
1988	Caroline Stevermer and	
	Patricia Wrede	*Sorcery and Cecilia*
1988	Constance Ash	*The Horsegirl*
1988	David Gemmell	*The Ghost King*
1988	David Gemmell	*Last Sword of Power*
1988	Elizabeth Hand	*Winterlong*
1988	Melanie Rawn	*Dragon Prince*
1988	Michael Moorcock	*Mother London*
1988	Roald Dahl	*Matilda*
1988	Robert Cormier	*Fade*
1988	Scott Bradfield	*The Secret Lives of Houses* (collection)
1988	Stephen Lawhead	*Merlin*
1988	Tad Williams	*The Dragonbone Chair*
		(Memory, Sorrow and Thorn)
1988	Tamora Pierce	*Lioness Rampant*
1988	Terry Pratchett	*Wyrd Sisters*
1988	Umberto Eco	*Foucault's Pendulum*
1989	Francesca Lia Bloch	*Weetzie Bat*
1989	Gary Kilworth	*Hunter's Moon*
1989	Jack Vance	*Madouc* (Lyonesse)
1989	Joan Aiken	"A Foot in the Grave"
1989	Nancy A. Collins	*Sunglasses After Dark*
1989–1996	Neil Gaiman and others	*The Sandman*
1989	Robin Jarvis	*The Dark Portal*
1989	Stephen Lawhead	*Arthur*
1989	Steven Erickson	*Terrors of the Black Clock*
1989	Terry Pratchett	*Guards! Guards!*
1989	Ursula K. Le Guin	*Tehanu*
1990	Brian Stableford	*The Werewolves of London*
1990	David Hartwell (ed.)	*The Color of Evil* (anthology)
1990	Debra Doyle and	
	James MacDonald	*School of Wizardry*
1990	Ellen Galford	*Queendom Come*
1990	Ellen Kushner	*Thomas the Rhymer*
1990	Geraldine McCaughrean	*Fire's Astonishment*
1990	Guy Gavriel Kay	*Tigana*
1990	James Morrow	*Only Begotten Daughter*
1990	Jenny Jones	*Fly by Night*
1990	Mary Gentle	*Rats and Gargoyles*

1990	Neil Gaiman and Terry Pratchett	*Good Omens: The Nice and Accurate Prophecies of Agnes Nutter, Witch*
1990	Robert Jordan	*The Eye of the World* (The Wheel of Time)
1990	Salman Rushdie	*Haroun and the Sea of Stories*
1990	Ted Chiang	"Tower of Babylon"
1990	Terry Pratchett	~~*Faust*~~ *Eric*
1990	William Gibson and Bruce Sterling	*The Difference Engine*
1991	Anne McCaffrey	*All the Weyrs of Pern*
1991	Barbara Hambly	*The Rainbow Abyss*
1991	Ben Okri	*The Famished Road*
1991	Brian Stableford	*The Angel of Pain*
1991	Diana Gabaldon	*Outland*
1991	Emma Bull	*Bone Dance*
1991	Greer Gilman	*Moonwise*
1991	Ian McDonald	*King of Morning, Queen of Day*
1991	Jane Yolen	*Briar Rose*
1991	Jane Yolen	*Wizard's Hall*
1991	Jim Crace	*Arcadia*
1991	Jonathan Carroll	*Outside the Dog Museum*
1991	Louise Cooper	*The Deceiver*
1991	Monica Furlong	*Juniper*
1991	Patricia McKillip	*The Sorceress and the Cygnet*
1991	S.P. Somtow	*Riverrun*
1991	Tanith Lee	*Black Unicorn* (Unicorn)
1991	Tanya Huff	*Blood Price*
1992	Barbara Hambly	*The Magicians of Night*
1992	Ben Okri	*Songs of Enchantment*
1992	Diana Wynne Jones	*A Sudden Wild Magic*
1992	Elizabeth Hand	*Aestival Tide*
1992	Freda Warrington	*A Taste of Blood Wine*
1992	Geoff Ryman	"*Was …*"
1992	Guy Gavriel Kay	*A Song for Arbonne*
1992	John Whitbourn	*A Dangerous Energy*
1992	Jonathan Carroll	*After Silence*
1992	Kim Newman	*Anno Dracula*
1992	M. John Harrison	*The Course of the Heart*
1992	Sean Stewart	*Passion Play*
1992	Tanith Lee	*Dark Dance* (Blood Opera)

1992	Terry Bisson	*Bears Discover Fire* (collection)
1992	Terry Pratchett	*Small Gods*
1992	Terry Pratchett, Jack Cohen	
	and Ian Stewart	*The Science of Discworld*
1992	Vivian Van Velde	*Dragon's Bait*
1993	C.J. Cherryh	*Faery in Shadow*
1993	Colin Greenland	*Harm's Way*
1993	Datlow and Windling	*Snow White, Blood Red*
1993	Delia Sherman	*The Porcelain Dove*
1993	Elizabeth E. Wein	*The Winter Prince*
1993	Elizabeth Hand	*Icarus Descending*
1993	Ellen Galford	*The Dyke and the Dybbuk*
1993	Holly Lisle	*Bones of the Past*
1993	Kathe Koja	*Skin*
1993	Laurell K. Hamilton	*Guilty Pleasures*
1993	Lucius Shepherd	*The Golden*
1993	Michael Moorcock	*A Nomad in the Time Streams*
1993	Michael Swanwick	*The Iron Dragon's Daughter*
1993	Nina Kiriki Hoffman	*The Thread That Binds the Bones*
1993	Patrice Kindl	*Owl in Love*
1993	Patricia McKillip	*The Cygnet and the Firebird*
1993	Peter Ackroyd	*The House of Doctor Dee*
1993	Robert Holdstock	*The Hollowing*
1993	Robin McKinley	*Deerskin*
1993	Terry Pratchett	*Johnny and the Dead*
1994	Brian Stableford	*The Carnival of Destruction*
1994	Caroline Stevermer	*A College of Magics*
1994	Elizabeth Ann Scarborough	*The Godmother*
1994	Elizabeth Hand	*Waking the Moon*
1994	Eva Ibbotson	*The Secret of Platform 13*
1994	James Morrow	*Towing Jehovah*
1994	Jonathan Carroll	*From the Teeth of Angels*
1994	Jonathan Lethem	*Gun, with Occasional Music*
1994	Melanie Rawn	*Exiles 1: The Ruins of Ambrai*
1994	Nancy Springer	*Larque on the Wing*
1994	Rachel Pollack	*Temporary Agency*
1994	Raymond E. Feist	*Shadow of a Dark Queen*
1994	Rebecca Ore	*Slow Funeral*
1994	Robert Holdstock	*Merlin's Wood*
1994	Stephan Grundy	*Rhinegold*
1994	Stephen Lawhead	*Pendragon*
1994	Steven Brust	*Five Hundred Years After*

1994	Tanya Huff	*Sing The Four Quarters*
1994	Terry Goodkind	*Wizard's First Rule* (The Sword of Truth)
1994	Thomas M. Disch	*The Priest: A Gothic Romance*
1995	Bryan Talbot	*The Tale of One Bad Rat*
1995	C.S. Friedmann	*Crown of Shadows*
1995	Christopher Priest	*The Prestige*
1995	Garth Nix	*Sabriel*
1995	George R.R. Martin	*A Game of Thrones* (The Song of Fire and Ice)
1995	Gregory Maguire	*Wicked: The Life and Times of the Wicked Witch of the West*
1995	Guy Gavriel Kay	*The Lions of Al-Rassan*
1995	Holly Lisle	*Sympathy for the Devil*
1995	John Whitbourn	*To Build Jerusalem*
1995	Kim Newman	*The Bloody Red Baron*
1995	Maggie Furey	*Harp of Winds*
1995	Martha Wells	*City of Bones*
1995	Nina Kiriki Hoffman	*The Silent Strength of Bones*
1995	Patrick O'Leary	*Door Number Three*
1995	Philip Pullman	*Northern Lights* (US: *The Golden Compass*)
1995	Robin Hobb	*Assassin's Apprentice*
1995	Sara Douglass	*Battleaxe*
1995	Sharon Shinn	*The Shape-Changer's Wife*
1995	Vikram Chandra	*Red Earth and Pouring Rain*
1996	Diana Wynne Jones	*The Tough Guide to Fantasyland*
1996	James Morrow	*Bible Stories for Adults*
1996	John Barnes	*One for the Morning Glory*
1996–2001	K.A. Applegate	*Animorphs* (54 books)
1996	Mark Laidlaw	*The 37th Mandala*
1996	Megan Whalen Turner	*The Thief*
1996	Neil Gaiman	*Neverwhere*
1996	Neil Gaiman and Charles Vess	*Stardust*
1996	Patricia McKillip	*Winter Rose*
1996	Rachel Pollack	*Godmother Night*
1996	Terri Windling	*The Wood Wife*
1996	Terry Pratchett	*Johnny and the Bomb*
1997	Candas Jane Dorsey	*Black Wine*
1997	Eric S. Nylund	*Dry Water*
1997	Gail Carson Levine	*Ella Enchanted*

1997	J.K. Rowling	*Harry Potter and the Philosopher's Stone*
1997	Jeff VanderMeer	*City of Saints and Madmen: The Book of Ambergris*
1997	Kate Elliott	*King's Dragon* (Crown of Stars 1)
1997	Michael Swanwick	*Jack Faust*
1997	Patrick O'Leary	*The Gift*
1997	Paul Witcover	*Waking Beauty*
1997	Philip Pullman	*The Subtle Knife* (His Dark Materials 2)
1997	Robin McKinley	*Rose's Daughter*
1997	Stephen Lawhead	*Grail*
1997	Tananarive Due	*My Soul to Keep*
1997	Tom Arden	*The Harlequin's Dance*
1998	Diana Wynne Jones	*The Dark Lord of Derkholm*
1998	Elizabeth Hand	*Last Summer at Mars Hill*
1998	Elizabeth Knox	*The Vintner's Luck*
1998	Graham Joyce	*The Tooth Fairy*
1998	Greg Keyes	*Newton's Cannon*
1998	Guy Gavriel Kay	*Sailing to Sarantium*
1998	Jane Yolen	*The One-Armed Queen*
1998	John Whitbourn	*The Royal Changeling*
1998	Midori Snyder	*The Innamorati*
1998	Nalo Hopkinson	*Brown Girl in the Ring*
1998	Neil Gaiman	*Stardust*
1998	Robin Hobb	*Ship of Magic* (Live Traders)
1998	Sean Stewart	*Mockingbird*
1998	Tanith Lee	*Faces Under Water* (Venus)
1999	Barbara Hambly	*Dragonshadow*
1999	China Miéville	*King Rat*
1999	Darren Shan	*Cirque du Freak*
1999	Elizabeth Hand	*Black Light*
1999	Gabriel King	*Tailchaser's Song*
1999	Gregory Maguire	*Confessions of an Ugly Stepsister*
1999	J.K. Rowling	*Harry Potter and the Prisoner of Azkaban*
1999–2001	K.A. Applegate	*Search for Senna* (1st of 12 Everworld books)
1999	Lemony Snicket (Daniel Handler)	*A Series of Unfortunate Events: The Bad Beginning*
1999	Lisa Goldstein	*Dark Cities Underground*
1999	Louise Erdrich	*The Antelope Wife*

1999	Philip Pullman	*I Was a Rat! or The Scarlet Slippers*
1999	Ricardo Pinto	*The Chosen*
1999	Stephen Lawhead	*Avalon*
1999	Steven Erickson	*Gardens of the Moon*
1999	Terry Pratchett	*The Fifth Elephant*
1999	Thomas M. Disch	*The Sub: A Study in Witchcraft*
2000	Barbara Hambly	*Knight of the Demon Queen*
2000	China Miéville	*Perdido Street Station*
2000	Datlow and Windling	*Black Heart, Ivory Bones*
2000	Diana Wynne Jones	*Year of the Griffin*
2000	Eva Ibbotson	*Island of the Aunts*
2000	Franny Billingsley	*The Folk Keeper*
2000	Geraldine McCaughrean	*The Stones Are Hatching*
2000	Guy Gavriel Kay	*Lord of Emperors*
2000	J.K. Rowling	*Harry Potter and the Goblet of Fire*
2000	Jane Yolen	*Boots and the Seven Leaguers*
2000	Jo Walton	*The King's Peace*
2000	K.J. Parker	*Colours in the Steel* (The Fencer Trilogy)
2000	Kevin Brockmaier	"The Brief History of the Dead"
2000	Kij Johnson	*The Fox Woman*
2000	Margo Lanagan	*White Time*
2000	Martin Scott	*Thraxas*
2000	Mary Gentle	*Ash*
2000	Pat Murphy	*Adventures in Time and Space with Max Merriwell*
2000	Paula Volsky	*The Grand Ellipse*
2000	Philip Pullman	*The Amber Spyglass* (His Dark Materials 3)
2000	Sean Stewart	*Galveston*
2001	Andy Duncan	*Beluthahatchie and Other Stories*
2001	Cecilia Dart-Thornton	*The Ill-Made Mute* (Bitterbynde)
2001	Charlaine Harris	*Dead Until Dark* (The Southern Vampire Mysteries)
2001	Chris Wooding	*The Haunting of Alaizabel Cray*
2001	Christopher Paolini	*Eragon*
2001	Debi Gliori	*Pure Dead Magic*
2001	Eoin Colfer	*Artemis Fowl*
2001	G.P. Taylor	*Shadowmancer*
2001	Geoff Ryman	*Lust*
2001	Hiromi Goto	*The Kappa Child*
2001	Hiromi Goto	*The Water of Possibility*

2001	Jacqueline Carey	Kushiel's Dart
2001	Jasper Fforde	The Eyre Affair
2001	Jeff Smith and Charles Vess	Bone
2001	Jo Walton	The King's Name
2001	Jonathan Carroll	The Wooden Sea
2001	K.J. Parker	Shadow (Scavengers trilogy)
2001	Kelly Link	Stranger Things Happen
2001	Lois McMaster Bujold	The Curse of Chalion
2001	Michael Scott	The Alchemist: The Secrets of the Immortal Nicholas Flamel
2001	Neil Gaiman	American Gods
2001	P. Craig Russell	The Ring
2001	Patrice Kindl	Goose Chase
2001	Paul Di Filippo	"Karuna, Inc."
2001	Peter Dickinson	The Ropemaker
2001	Peter Straub and Stephen King	The Black House
2001	Roderick Townley	The Great Good Thing
2001	Sarah A. Hoyt	Ill Met by Moonlight
2001	Ted Chiang	"Hell is the Absence of God"
2001	Terry Pratchett	The Amazing Maurice and His Educated Rodents
2001	Trudi Canavan	The Magician's Guild
2002	Alexander C. Irvine	A Scattering of Jades
2002	Barbara Hambly	Dragonstar
2002	Catherine Fisher	Corbenic
2002	Cecelia Holland	The Soul Thief
2002	China Miéville	The Scar
2002	Ellen Datlow and Terri Windling (eds)	The Green Man: Tales from the Mythic Forest
2002	Ellen Kushner and Delia Sherman	The Fall of the Kings
2002	Graham Joyce	The Facts of Life
2002	Gregory Frost	Fitcher's Brides
2002	Jasper Fforde	Lost in a Good Book
2002	Jeffrey Ford	The Portrait of Mrs Charbuque
2002	Jo Walton	The Prize in the Game
2002	Jonathan Carroll	White Apples
2002	M. John Harrison	Light
2002	Mary Hoffman	City of Masks
2002	Mary Janice Davidson	Undead and Unwed (Betsy the Vampire Queen]
2002	Michael Chabon	Summerland

2002	Mike Mignola	*The Right Hand of Doom* (Hellboy)
2002	N.M. Browne	*Hunted*
2002	Neil Gaiman	*Coraline*
2002	Paul Di Filippo	"A Year in the Linear City"
2002	Peter Straub (ed.)	*Conjunctions: 39*
2002	Sean McMullen	*Voyage of the Shadowmoon*
2002	Ted Chiang	*Stories of Your Life: And Others*
2002	Terry Pratchett	*Night Watch*
2002	Zoran Živković	"The Library"
2003	Cameron Dokey	*The Storyteller's Daughter*
2003	Chris Wooding	*Poison*
2003	Cornelia Funke	*Inkheart*
2003	Erin Hunter (Victoria Holmes, Kate Cary, Cherith Baldry)	*Into the Wild*
2003	Garth Nix	*Mr Monday* (The Keys to the Kingdom)
2003	Glenda Larke	*The Aware*
2003	Greer Gilman	"A Crowd of Bone"
2003	Gregory Maguire	*Mirror, Mirror*
2003	Herbie Brennan	*The Faerie Wars*
2003	Holly Black	*Tithe*
2003	Holly Black and Tony DiTerlizzi	*Spiderwick Chronicles: The Field Guide*
2003	Ian R. MacLeod	*The Light Ages*
2003	Jeff VanderMeer	*Veniss Undergound*
2003	Jo Walton	*Tooth and Claw*
2003	Jonathan Stroud	*The Amulet of Samarkand*
2003	K.J. Bishop	*The Etched City*
2003	Kij Johnson	*Fudoki*
2003	Lian Hearn	*Across the Nightingale Floor*
2003	Lisa Goldstein	*The Alchemist's Door*
2003	Liz Williams	*The Poison Master*
2003	Lois McMaster Bujold	*Paladin of Souls*
2003	Nalo Hopkinson	*The Salt Roads*
2003	Neal Stephenson	*Quicksilver*
2003	Neal Stephenson	*The Confusion*
2003	Peter Straub	*lost boy lost girl*
2003	Rhiannon Lassiter	*Borderland*
2003	Shannon Hale	*Goose Girl*
2003	Sharyn November (ed.)	*Firebirds: An Original Anthology of Science Fiction and Fantasy*
2003	Steve Cockayne	*Wanderers and Islanders*

2003	Steve Cockayne	*The Iron Chain*
2003	Tad Williams	*The War of the Flowers*
2003	Terry Pratchett	*The Wee Free Men*
2003	Terry Pratchett	*Monstrous Regiment*
2004	Charles Butler	*The Fetch of Mardy Watt*
2004	Charles de Lint	*The Blue Girl*
2004	China Miéville	*Iron Council*
2004	David Mitchell	*Cloud Atlas*
2004	Elizabeth Hand	*Mortal Love*
2004	Gene Wolfe	*The Wizard Knight*
2004	Guy Gavriel Kay	*The Last Light of the Sun*
2004	Janet McNaughton	*An Unearthly Knight*
2004	Jennifer Stevenson	*Trash Sex Magic*
2004	Joseph Delaney	*The Spook's Apprentice*
2004	Lisa Tuttle	"My Death"
2004	Margo Lanagan	"Singing My Sister Down"
2004	Mette Ivie Harrison	*Mira Mirror*
2004	Mike Resnick	"Travels with My Cats"
2004	Nalo Hopkinson and Uppinder Mehan	*So Long Been Dreaming*
2004	Neal Stephenson	*The System of the World*
2004	Patrick Nielsen Hayden	*New Magics*
2004	Peter Straub	*In the Night Room*
2004	Russell Kirkpatrick	*Across the Face of the World*
2004	Sarah Micklem	*Firethorn*
2004	Scott Westerfield	*Midnighters 1: The Secret Hour*
2004	Sean McMullen	*Glass Dragons*
2004	Sean Stewart	*Perfect Circle*
2004	Steph Swainston	*The Year of Our War*
2004	Steve Cockayne	*The Seagull Drovers*
2004	Susanna Clarke	*Jonathan Strange and Mr Norrell*
2004	Theodora Goss	"The Wings of Meister Wilhelm"
2005	Alexander C. Irvine	*The Narrows*
2005	Caitlin R. Kiernan	"La Peau Verte"
2005	Elizabeth Knox	*Dreamhunter*
2005	Frances Hardinge	*Fly By Night*
2005	Geoff Ryman	*Air*
2005	Graham Joyce	*The Limits of Enchantment*
2005	Hal Duncan	*Vellum*
2005	Helen Dunmore	*Ingo*
2005	Ian R. MacLeod	*The House of Storms*
2005	Isabel Hoving	*The Dream Merchant*

2005	James Morrow	*The Last Witchfinder*
2005	Jane Johnson	*The Secret Country*
2005	Joe Hill	*Twentieth-Century Ghosts* (collection)
2005	Jonathan Carroll	*Glass Soup*
2005	Jonathan Stroud	*Ptolemy's Gate*
2005	Kelly Link	"The Faery Handbag"
2005	K.J. Parker	*Devices and Desires* (The Engineers)
2005	Laird Barron	"The Imago Sequence"
2005	Liz Williams	*Snake Agent*
2005	Margo Lanagan	*Black Juice*
2005	Nancy Farmer	*Sea of Trolls*
2005	Neil Gaiman	*Anansi Boys*
2005	Nnedi Okorafor-Mbachu	*Zahrah the Windseeker*
2005	Obert Skye	*Leven Thumps and the Gateway to Foo*
2005	Octavia E. Butler	*Fledgling*
2005	Paul Park	*A Princess of Roumania*
2005	Rick Riordan	*Percy Jackson and the Lightning Thief*
2005	Sally Gardner	*I, Coriander*
2005	Sarah Monette	*Melusine*
2005	Steph Swainston	*No Present Like Time*
2005	Stephanie Meyer	*Twilight*
2005	Stuart Hill	*The Cry of the Icemark*
2005	Theodora Goss	"Pip and the Fairies"
2006	Andy Duncan	"Unique Chicken goes in Reverse"
2006	Benjamin Rosenbaum	"A Siege of Cranes"
2006	Brandon Mull	*Fablehaven*
2006	Catherynne M. Valente	*The Grass-Cutting Sword*
2006	Charles Butler	*The Death of A Ghost*
2006	Charlie Fletcher	*Stoneheart*
2006	Christopher Rowe	"Another Word for Map is Faith"
2006	Daniel Abraham	*A Shadow in Summer*
2006	Delia Sherman	*Changeling*
2006	Ellen Kushner	*The Privilege of the Sword*
2006	Geraldine McCaughrean	*Peter Pan in Scarlet*
2006	Haruki Murakami	*Kafka on the Shore*
2006	Jeff Smith	*Rose*
2006	Jeff VanderMeer	*Shriek: An Afterword*
2006	Jessica Day George	*Dragon Slippers*
2006	Joe Abercrombie	*The Blade Itself*
2006	Julie E. Czerneda	*A Thousand Words for Stranger*
2006	Linda Medley	*Castle Waiting*
2006	Lois Lowry	*Gossamer*

2006	M. Rickert	*Map of Dreams* (collection)
2006	M. Rickert	"Journey into the Kingdom"
2006	Marcus Sedgwick	*My Sword Hand is Singing*
2006	Martine Leavitt	*Keturah and Lord Death*
2006	Michael Swanwick	*The Dragons of Babel*
2006	Naomi Novik	*Temeraire/His Majesty's Dragon*
2006	Norman Partridge	"Dark Harvest"
2006	Philip Reeve	*Larklight*
2006	Sarah Monette	*The Virtu*
2006	Scott Lynch	*The Lies of Locke Lamora*
2006	Sean Stewart	*Cathy's Book*
2006	Sharyn November (ed.)	*Firebirds Rising: An Original Anthology of Science Fiction and Fantasy*
2006	Steve Cockayne	*The Good People*
2006	Tamora Pierce	*Terrier*
2007	Brandon Sanderson	*Alcatraz Versus the Evil Librarians*
2007	Bryan Talbot	*Alice in Sunderland*
2007	Caitlin R. Kiernan	*Daughter of Hounds*
2007	Carol Matas and Perry Nodelman	*Ghosthunters 1: the Proof that Ghosts Exist*
2007	Cassandra Clare	*City of Bones*
2007	Charles de Lint	*Little (Grrl) Lost*
2007	China Miéville	*Un Lun Dun*
2007	Christopher Barzak	*One for Sorrow*
2007	Delia Sherman and Theodora Goss (eds)	*Interfictions* (anthology)
2007	Derek Landy	*Skulduggery Pleasant*
2007	Ekaterina Sedia	*The Secret History of Moscow*
2007	Elizabeth Bear	*Whiskey and Water*
2007	Elizabeth Knox	*Dreamquake*
2007	Frances Hardinge	*Verdigris Deep*
2007	George R.R. Martin	*A Dance with Dragons* (The Song of Fire and Ice)
2007	Hal Duncan	*Ink*
2007	Ilona Andrews	*Magic Bites*
2007	J.K. Rowling	*Harry Potter and the Deathly Hallows*
2007	James Morrow and Kathryn Morrow (eds)	*The SFWA European Hall of Fame Anthology*
2007	Janet Lee	*Dragon's Keep*
2007	Jay Lake	*Mainspring*
2007	Joe Hill	*Heart-Shaped Box*
2007	John C. Wright	*Titans of Chaos*

2008	Marie Brennan	*Midnight Never Come*
2008	Neil Gaiman	*The Graveyard Book*
2008	Nnedi Okorafor-Mbachu	*The Shadow Speaker*
2008	Paul Auster	*Man in the Dark*
2008	Richard Morgan	*The Steel Remains*
2008	Robert V.S. Redick	*The Red Wolf Conspiracy*
2008	Sarah Prineas	*The Magic Thief*
2008	Scott Westerfield	*"Ass Hat Magic Spider"*
2008	Sherwood Smith	*A Posse of Princesses*
2008	Suzanne McLeod	*The Sweet Scent of Blood*
2008	T.A. Pratt	*Poison Sleep*
2008	Ysabeau Wilce	*Flora's Dare*
2009	Greer Gilman	*Cloud and Ashes*
2009	James Anderson and Mark Seabanc	*Stoneholding*
2009	Kari Sperring	*Living with Ghosts*
2009	Ken Scholes	*Lamentation*
2009	Lisa Mantchev	*Eyes Life Stars*
2009	Mark Newton	*Nights of Villjamur*
2009	Seanan McGuire	*Rosemary and Rue*
2009	Sharon Lee and Steve Miller	*Duainfey*
2009	Stephen Deas	*The Adamantine Palace*
2010	Beth Bernobich	*Passion Play*

Important Movies, TV Series, and Other Media

1919	Wilhelm Murnau (dir.)	*Nosferatu*
1920	Robert Weine (dir.)	*The Cabinet of Doctor Caligari*
1924	Raoul Walsh (dir.)	*The Thief of Baghdad*
1926	D.W. Griffith (dir.)	*The Sorrows of Satan*
1926	Wilhelm Murnau (dir.)	*Faust*
1927	Fritz Lang (dir.)	*Metropolis*
1931	David Butler (dir.)	*A Connecticut Yankee*
1931	Fritz Lang (dir.)	*M*
1933	Merian C. Cooper (dir.)	*King Kong*
1933	Norman Z. McLeod (dir.)	*Alice in Wonderland*
1937	Walt Disney (prod.)	*Snow White and the Seven Dwarfs*
1939	Victor Fleming (dir.)	*The Wizard of Oz*
1940	Walt Disney (prod.)	*Fantasia*
1944	Jules Dassin and Norman Z. McLeod (dir.)	*A Canterville Ghost*

1945	David Lean (dir.)	*Blithe Spirit*
1946	Frank Capra (dir.)	*It's a Wonderful Life*
1946	Walt Disney (prod.)	*Song of the South*
1949	Tay Garnett (dir.)	*A Connecticut Yankee in King Arthur's Court*
1951–1957	Desi Arnaz (creator)	*I Love Lucy* (TV)
1954	Vincente Minelli (dir.)	*Brigadoon*
1958	Terence Fisher (dir.)	*Dracula* (Hammer)
1959,		
1975–1977	Oliver Postgate (creator)	*Ivor the Engine* (TV)
1959–1964	Rod Serling (creator)	*The Twilight Zone* (TV)
1959–1965	Oliver Postgate (creator)	*The Saga of Noggin the Nog* (TV)
1963	George Pal (dir.)	*7 Faces of Dr. Lao*
1964–1972	Sol Saks (creator)	*Bewitched* (TV)
1965–1977	Eric Thompson (creator of English version)	*The Magic Roundabout*
1966	Gerald Thomas (dir.)	*Carry On Screaming*
1968	Ken Hughes (dir.)	*Chitty-Chitty-Bang-Bang*
1969–1974	Oliver Postgate (creator)	*The Clangers* (TV)
1971	Mel Stuart (dir.)	*Willy Wonka and the Chocolate Factory*
1971–1973	John Badham, Leonard Nimoy, Steven Spielberg et al.	*Rod Serling's Night Gallery* (TV)
1973	Robin Hardy (dir.)	*The Wicker Man*
1974	Bryan Forbes (dir.)	*The Stepford Wives*
1974	Gary Gygax and Dave Arneson	*Dungeons and Dragons* (RPG)
1974	Oliver Postgate (creator)	*Bagpuss* (TV)
1974–1975	Ivor Wood (dir.)	*The Wombles* (TV)
1975	Jim Sharman (dir.)	*The Rocky Horror Picture Show*
1976	Brian De Palma (dir.)	*Carrie*
1976	Richard Donner (dir.)	*The Omen*
1977	George Lucas (dir.)	*Star Wars*
1977	Steven Spielberg (dir.)	*Close Encounters of the Third Kind*
1978	Irvin Keshner (dir.)	*The Eyes of Laura Mars*
1978	John Hubley (dir.)	*Watership Down*
1978	Ralph Bakshi (dir.)	*J.R.R. Tolkien's Lord of the Rings*
1980	John Landis (dir.)	*An American Werewolf in London*
1980	Stanley Kubrick (dir.)	*The Shining*
1981	Terry Gilliam (dir.)	*Time Bandits*
1981	Sandy Petersen (and Chaosium)	*The Call of Cthulhu* (RPG)
1982	Jim Henson, Frank Oz (dir.)	*The Dark Crystal*
1982	John Milius (dir.)	*Conan the Barbarian*

1983	Terry Jones (dir.)	*The Saga of Erik the Viking*
1984	Ivan Reitman (dir.)	*Ghostbusters*
1984	Neil Jordan (dir.)	*The Company of Wolves*
1984	Richard Fliescher (dir.)	*Conan the Destroyer*
1984	Terry Gilliam (dir.)	*Brazil*
1984	Wes Craven (dir.)	*A Nightmare on Elm Street*
1984	Wolfgang Petersen (dir.)	*The Neverending Story*
1984	Woody Allen (dir.)	*The Purple Rose of Cairo*
1984–1986	Richard Carpenter (creator)	*Robin of Sherwood* (TV)
1985	Richard Donner (dir.)	*Ladyhawke*
1986	Jim Henson (dir.)	*Labyrinth*
1986	Roman Polanski (dir.)	*Rosemary's Baby*
1987	Joel Schumacher (dir.)	*The Lost Boys*
1987–1989	Ron Koslow (creator)	*Beauty and the Beast* (TV)
1988	Terry Gilliam (dir.)	*The Adventures of Baron Munchausen*
1988	Tim Burton (dir.)	*Beetlejuice*
1989	Tim Burton (dir.)	*Batman*
1989	Tim Burton (dir.)	*Edward Scissorhands*
1990	Pete Hewitt (dir.)	*Bill and Ted's Bogus Journey*
1991	Terry Gilliam (dir.)	*The Fisher King*
1992	Anthony Minghella (dir.)	*Truly Madly Deeply*
1992	Fran Rubel Kuzui (dir.)	*Buffy the Vampire Slayer* (movie)
1992	Sally Potter (dir.)	*Orlando*
1993	Charles Russell (dir.)	*The Mask*
1993	Harold Ramis (dir.)	*Groundhog Day*
1993	Robin and Rand Miller	*Myst* (computer game)
1993	Tim Burton (dir.)	*The Nightmare Before Christmas*
1995–1999	Christian Williams (creator)	*Hercules: The Legendary Journeys*
1995–2001	Robert Tapert (creator)	*Xena: Warrior Princess*
1996	Tim Burton (dir.)	*James and the Giant Peach*
1996	Tim Burton (dir.)	*Mars Attacks!*
1997	Hayao Miyazaki (dir.)	*Princess Mononoke*
1997–2003	Joss Whedon (dir.)	*Buffy the Vampire Slayer* (TV)
1998	Peter Howitt (dir.)	*Sliding Doors*
1999	Tim Burton (dir.)	*Sleepy Hollow*
1999–2004	Joss Whedon and David Greenwalt (creators)	*Angel* (TV)
2000	David Carson and Herbert Wise (dir.)	*The 10th Kingdom* (TV)
2001	Andrew Adamson and Vicky Jenson (dir.)	*Shrek*

2001	Ang Lee (dir.)	*Crouching Tiger Hidden Dragon*
2001	Chris Columbus (dir.)	*Harry Potter and the Philosopher's Stone*
2001–2003	Peter Jackson (dir).	*Lord of the Rings* Trilogy
2001–2005	Alan Ball (creator)	*Six Feet Under* (TV)
2001	Richard Kelly (dir.)	*Donnie Darko*
2002	Hayao Miyazaki (dir.)	*Spirited Away*
2002	Will Wright (creator)	*The Sims* (computer game)
2003	Gore Vernbinski (dir.)	*Pirates of the Caribbean*
2003	Linden Research Inc.	*Second Life* (computer)
2003	Tim Burton (dir.)	*Big Fish*
2003–2007	Ryan Murphy (creator)	*Nip and Tuck* (TV)
2004	Blizzard Entertainment	*World of Warcraft*
2004	Bryan Fuller (creator)	*Dead Like Me* (TV)
2004	Bryan Fuller and Todd Holland (creators)	*Wonderfalls* (TV)
2004	Hayao Miyazaki (dir.)	*Howl's Moving Castle*
2004	Michel Gondry (dir.)	*Eternal Sunshine of the Spotless Mind*
2004	Tommy O'Haver (dir.)	*Ella Enchanted*
2004–2010	Jeffrey Lieber, J.J. Abrams, David Lindelof (creators)	*Lost* (TV)
2005	Andrew Adamson (dir.)	*The Chronicles of Narnia: The Lion, the Witch and the Wardrobe*
2005	Rob Thomas (creator)	*Veronica Mars* (TV)
2005	Terry Gilliam (dir.)	*The Brothers Grimm*
2005	Tim Burton (dir.)	*Charlie and the Chocolate Factory*
2006	Christopher Nolan (dir.)	*The Prestige*
2006	Guillermo del Toro (dir.)	*Pan's Labyrinth*
2006	Stefen Fangmeier (dir.)	*Eragon*
2007	Bryan Fuller (creator)	*Pushing Daisies* (TV)
2007	Chris Weitz (dir.)	*The Golden Compass*
2007	Kevin Lima (dir.)	*Enchanted*
2007	Matthew Vaughn (dir.)	*Stardust*
2008	Andrew Adamson (dir.)	*The Chronicles of Narnia: Prince Caspian*

Important Artists

Addams, Charles	1912–1988	cartoonist of the macabre, "The Addams Family"
Alma-Tadema, Sir Laurence	1836–1912	Eroticised fantasy painter of the ancient world

Baynes, Pauline	1922–2008	Children's book artist (Narnia books)
Beardsley, Aubrey	1872–1898	Art Nouveau cartoonist and illustrator
Burne-Jones, Edward	1833–1898	Pre-Raphaelite painter
Dadd, Richard	1817–1886	Fairy painter; *The Fairy Feller's Masterstroke*
Dalí, Salvador	1904–1989	Catalan surrealist artist; *The Persistence of Memory*
Doré, Gustave	1832–1883	French illustrator of Dante and fairytales
Dulac, Edmund	1882–1953	French illustrator of fairytales
Eggleton, Bob	1960–	American fantasy and horror artist
Escher, M.C.	1898–1972	Dutch graphic artist, painter of paradoxes
Finlay, Virgil	1914–1971	Fantasy illustrator for *Weird Tales* and others
Ford, H.J.	1860–1941	Illustrator (Andrew Lang's Fairy Books)
Frazetta, Frank	1928–	Illustrator for sword-and-sorcery and others
Friedrich, Caspar David	1774–1840	German Romantic landscape painter; *Chalk Cliffs on Rügen*
Froud, Brian	1947–	English fairy painter
Fuseli, Henry	1741–1825	Swiss artist of the Gothic, living in England; *The Nightmare*
Gorey, Edward St John	1925–2000	American artist and cartoonist of the macabre
Harryhausen, Ray	1920–	American master of stop motion animation
Hunt, William Holman	1827–1910	Pre-Raphaelite painter
Keeping, Charles	1924–1988	British illustrator of children's books
Kirby, Josh	1928–2001	British poster and cover artist (Pratchett books)
Lee, Alan	1947–	English book illustrator (Tolkien)
Martin, John	1789–1854	English Romantic artist of apocalypse and catastrophe
McKean, Dave	1963–	British comic book artist (*Hellblazer*, *Sandman*)
Morrill, Rowena A.	1944–	American fantasy and science fiction illustrator
Nielsen, Kay	1886–1957	Danish illustrator of fairytales
Pyle, Howard	1853–1911	American illustrator of Arthurian tales
Rackham, Arthur	1867–1939	English illustrator of fairytales
Robinson, W. Heath	1872–1944	English cartoonist; inventor of curious devices
Sime, Sidney	1867–1941	English artist and illustrator (Lord Dunsany)

Vallejo, Boris	1941–	Peruvian-American painter of fantasy and sword-and-sorcery
Vess, Charles	1951–	American comic book artist and illustrator
Wilson, Gahan	1930–	American cartoonist of the macabre

Important Editors and Series

Aickman, Robert   1964–1984
editor, *Fontana Book of Great Ghost Stories* (followed by R. Chetwynd-Hayes)
Argosy   1882–1978
Ballantine Adult Fantasy   1966–1971
Blackwood's Magazine   1817–1960
Boucher, Anthony   1949–1957
editor of *The Magazine of Fantasy and Science Fiction*
Campbell, John W. Jr.   1939–1943
editor of *Unknown*
Campbell, John W. Jr.   1937–1971
editor of *Astounding Science-Fiction* (from 1960 *Analog*)
Carnell, John   1949–1964
editor of *New Worlds*
Carnell, John   1950–1967
editor of *Science Fantasy*
Carter, Lin   1969–1971
editor of Ballantine Adult Fantasy
The Clack Book   1896–1897
Clarkesworld   2004–
Fantastic   1952–1980
Grant, Gavin and Kelly Link   1996
editors of *Lady Churchill's Rosebud Wristlet*
The Idler   1892–1911
Internet Review of Science Fiction   2004–
Jones, Stephen   1990–2005
editor, *Best New Horror*
The Magazine of Fantasy and Science Fiction   1949–
Marion Zimmer Bradley's Fantasy Magazine   1988–2000
Martin, George R.R.   1987–2006
editor, *Wild Cards*, 17 volumes
Misty   1978–1984
Moorcock, Michael   1964–1971
editor of *New Worlds*
Pall Mall Magazine   1893–1937

Realms of Fantasy	1994–
The Thrill Book	1919
SciFi.com	1995
Strand Magazine	1891–1950
Strange Horizons	2000
Weird Tales	1923–1954, 1988–
Windling, Terri and Datlow, Ellen	1986–2003
editors of *The Year's Best Fantasy and Horror*	

Glossary

A name in brackets indicates the creator or popularizer of the term

Creator copyright universe: a fantasy world created by an author to set his or her stories in, as opposed to setting stories in a shared world or a licensed world.

Dark fantasy: a fantasy story which borrows elements from horror, and which typically does not end in eucatastrophe.

Eucatastrophe: the uplifting and joyful moment when the story resolves into its happy ending (J.R.R. Tolkien).

Fairytale: a story involving the fantastic, usually involving familiar traditional formulas and often ending in eucatastrophe (after which people live happily ever after).

Gothic: a form of fantasy combining horror, melodrama and romance, and frequently invoking medieval trappings (including castles, dungeons, monks).

Heroic fantasy: fantasy set in a world which often resembles the ancient or medieval past, drawing on their epic traditions of heroes; barely distinguishable from high fantasy or sword-and-sorcery.

High fantasy: fantasy that deals with the activities of heroes, drawing on the literary tradition of epic; immersive fantasy, and not set in our world (as low fantasy is).

Immersive fantasy: a story set entirely within an imagined world, without any overt reference to the world of the reader (Farah Mendlesohn).

Indigenous fantasy: a story "that is, like an indigenous species, adapted to and reflective of its native environment" (Brian Attebery); also called "low fantasy", and may overlap with "urban fantasy".

Interstitial fantasy: stories which draw on other genres than fantasy, and which cannot easily be categorized in genre terms (Ellen Kushner and Delia Sherman).

Intrusion fantasy: a story in which the fantastic intrudes into the mundane world; commonly found in dark fantasy and in horror (Farah Mendlesohn).

Liminal fantasy: a story set usually in our world in which the fantastic element is glimpsed or suspected by the reader but never fully realized or explained (Farah Mendlesohn).

Low fantasy: a story in which the fantastic appears in the ordinary world (as indigenous fantasy), as opposed to the epic other worlds of high fantasy.

Magic realism: a story in which the fantastic appears within an otherwise "normal" world, and is generally accepted as normal. In practice, a term used of literary fiction rather than of genre fantasy (cf. indigenous fantasy).

Matter of Britain: stories dealing with the mythical world of King Arthur and his knights, whether written in the Middle Ages or subsequently; usually called "Arthurian fantasy".

Medievalist fantasy: a story set in a world based in some loose way on the world of the European Middle Ages, often drawing its inspiration from medieval romance and the Matter of Britain, and frequently in the form of a quest fantasy.

New Weird: a marketing category (or perhaps a movement) around the turn of the millennium, which explored new and often disturbing ways of looking at fantasy motifs and at the borderlands between science fiction and fantasy (China Miéville).

Paranormal romance: a subgenre halfway between dark fantasy and romance, usually featuring romantic relationships between humans and fantasy beings such as vampires or werewolves.

Portal fantasy: a story in which the fantasy world is reached through a gateway (such as one might find in a wardrobe). Frequently these stories involve exploring the new world and solving its problems or fulfilling some quest, so these have also been designated portal-quest stories (Farah Mendlesohn).

Posthumous fantasy: a story concerning, and frequently told from the point of view of, a dead person; sometimes set in the land of the dead.

Quest fantasy: a story (frequently in multiple volumes) involving one or more people travelling through a landscape, learning about the world, and fulfilling some quest or destiny; cf. "portal-quest".

Rationalized fantasy: a story in which the magic or other fantastic element is explained in scientific or pseudo-scientific ways.

Science fiction: a story distinguishable from fantasy (except at the margins) by being entirely set within a universe that can be explained rationally in scientific terms.

Slick fantasy: a story in which, often, a wise-cracking modern urbanite gets involved with one of the standard scenarios of fantasy: the granting of three wishes, a pact with the devil, and so on.

Slipstream: a literary story that slips across the boundaries between the mundane and the fantastic (Bruce Sterling); mainstream fiction with fantastic elements. Cf. interstitial fantasy and magic realism.

Steampunk: fantasy (or science fiction) set in a real or fantasized nineteenth century.

Sword-and-sorcery: fantasy set in a pre-industrial world, involving warriors in conflict with magical or supernatural forces; largely indistinguishable from heroic fantasy or high fantasy, although perhaps better seen as a subset of them (Fritz Leiber).

Taproot text: significant texts from before the emergence of the genre of fantasy, which have fed into the genre (e.g. *The Odyssey, The Faerie Queen*) (John Clute).

Theatre fantasy: stories which take place in a fantasy world devised to serve as a stage for a series of such stories (Farah Mendlesohn).

Urban fantasy: stories which involve the intersection of the fantastic and the "real world", and in which the city itself is frequently a focus of attention.

Weird fantasy: stories involving supernatural and horror, and often the occult; the staple of the US magazine *Weird Tales*.

YA (young adult fiction): fiction written for, published for, or marketed to adolescents, roughly between the ages of 12 and 18.

Critical Works:
Further Reading

Armitt, Lucie. *Fantasy Fiction: An Introduction*. London: Continuum, 2005.

Attebery, Brian. *The Fantasy Tradition in American Literature: from Irving to Le Guin*. Bloomington: Indiana University Press, 1980.

———. *Strategies of Fantasy*. Bloomington and Indianapolis: Indiana University Press, 1992.

Barron, Neil, ed. *Fantasy and Horror: A Critical and Historical Guide to Literature, Illustration, Film, TV, Radio, and the Internet*. Lanham MD: Scarecrow Press, 1999.

Bleiler, E.F. *A Guide to Supernatural Fiction*. Kent OH: Kent State University Press, 1983.

———, ed. *Supernatural Fiction Writers: Fantasy and Horror*. 2 vols. New York: Scribner, 1985.

Bould, Mark, and Reid, Michelle, eds. *Parietal Games: Critical Writings By and On M. John Harrison*. Foundation Studies in Science Fiction 4. London: Science Fiction Foundation, 2005.

Butler, Andrew M. *The Pocket Essentials Terry Pratchett*. Harpenden: Pocket Essentials, 2001.

———, ed. *An Unofficial Companion to the Novels of Terry Pratchett*. Oxford: Greenwood World, 2007.

Butler, Andrew M., James, Edward, and Mendlesohn, Farah, eds. *Terry Pratchett: Guilty of Literature*. 2nd ed. Baltimore MD: Old Earth Books, 2004.

Butler, Charles. *Four British Fantasists: Place and Culture in the Children's Fantasies of Penelope Lively, Alan Garner, Diana Wynne Jones, and Susan Cooper*. Lanham MD and Oxford: Children's Literature Association and Scarecrow Press, 2006.

Campbell, Joseph. *The Hero with a Thousand Faces*. New York: Pantheon, 1949.

Clark, Beverly Lyon. *Kiddie Lit: The Cultural Construction of Children's Literature in America*. Baltimore and London: Johns Hopkins University Press, 2003.

Clute, John, and Grant, John, eds. *The Encyclopedia of Fantasy*. London: Orbit, 1997.

Clute, John, and Nicholls, Peter, eds. *The Encyclopedia of Science Fiction*. London: Orbit, 1993.

de Camp, L. Sprague. *Literary Swordsmen and Sorcerers: The Makers of Heroic Fantasy*. Sauk City WI: Arkham House, 1976.

Doody, Margaret Anne. *The True Story of the Novel*. London: Fontana, 1998.

Frazer, James George. *The Golden Bough: A Study in Comparative Religion*. London: Macmillan, 1890.

Garner, Alan. *The Voice that Thunders: Essay and Lectures*. London: Harvill, 1997.

Garth, John. *Tolkien and the Great War: The Threshold of Middle Earth*. London: HarperCollins, 2004.

Glyer, Diana Pavlac. *C.S. Lewis and J.R.R. Tolkien as Writers in Community*. Kent OH: Kent State University Press, 2007.

Heilman, Elizabeth E., ed. *Critical Perspectives on Harry Potter*. 2nd ed. London and New York: Routledge, 2008.

Hume, Kathryn. *Fantasy and Mimesis: Responses to Reality in Western Literature*. London: Methuen, 1984.

Irwin, W.R. *The Game of the Impossible: A Rhetoric of Fantasy*. Urbana, Chicago, London: University of Illinois Press, 1976.

Jackson, Rosemary. *Fantasy: The Literature of Subversion*. London: Methuen, 1981.

James, Edward. *Science Fiction in the Twentieth Century*. Oxford: Oxford University Press, 1994.

James, Edward, and Mendlesohn, Farah, eds. *The Cambridge Companion to Science Fiction*. Cambridge: Cambridge University Press, 2003.

Jones, Diana Wynne. "The Shape of the Narrative in *Lord of the Rings*", in *J.R.R. Tolkien: This Far Land*, edited by Robert Giddings. London: Vista, 1983, 87–107.

———. *The Tough Guide to Fantasyland*. London: Vista, 1996.

———. "The Profession of Science Fiction, 51: Answers to Some Questions", *Foundation: The International Review of Science Fiction* 70 (Summer 1997), 5–14.

Joshi, S.T. *The Weird Tale: Arthur Machen, Lord Dunsany, Algernon Blackwood, M.R. James, Ambrose Bierce, H.P. Lovecraft*. Austin TX: University of Texas Press, 1990.

Lenz, Millicent, and Scott, Carole, eds. *His Dark Materials Illuminated: Critical Essays on Philip Pullman's Trilogy*. Detroit MI: Wayne State University Press, 2005.

Lewis, C.S. *Of This and Other Worlds*. London: Collins, 1982.

Luckhurst, Roger. *Science Fiction*, Cultural History of Literature. London: Polity Press, 2005.

Magill, Frank N., ed. *Survey of Modern Fantasy Literature*. 5 vols. Englewood Cliffs NJ: Salem Press, 1983.

Manlove, C.N. *The Impulse of Fantasy Literature*. London and Basingstoke: Macmillan, 1983.

Manlove, C.N. *The Fantasy Literature of England*. Basingstoke: Macmillan, 1999.

Mendlesohn, Farah. "Crowning the King: Harry Potter and the Construction of Authority", in *The Ivory Tower and Harry Potter: Perspectives on a Literary Phenomenon*, edited by Lana A. Whited. Columbia and London: University of Missouri Press, 2002, 159–81.

———. *Diana Wynne Jones: Children's Literature and the Fantastic Tradition*. New York: Routledge, 2005.

———. *Rhetorics of Fantasy*. Middletown CT: Wesleyan University Press, 2008.

Moorcock, Michael. *Wizardry and Wild Romance*. London: Gollancz, 1987.

Moretti, Franco. *Graphs, Maps and Trees: Abstract Models for a Literary History*. London, New York: Verso, 2005.

Pringle, David, ed. *St James Guide to Fantasy Writers*. New York: St James Press, 1996.

Punter, David. *The Literature of Terror: A History of Gothic Fictions from 1765 to the Present Day*. London: Longman, 1980.

Roberts, Adam. *The History of Science Fiction*. Basingstoke: Palgrave Macmillan, 2006.

Schlobin, Roger C. *The Aesthetics of Fantasy Literature and art*. Notre Dame IN: University of Notre Dame Press, 1982.

Senior, William A. *Stephen R. Donaldson's Chronicles of Thomas Covenant: Variations on the Fantasy Tradition*. Kent OH: Kent State University Press, 1995.

Shippey, T.A. *The Road to Middle Earth*. 3rd ed. London: HarperCollins, 1998.

———. *J.R.R. Tolkien: Author of the Century*. London: HarperCollins, 2000.

———. *Roots and Branches: Selected Papers on Tolkien*. Zurich and Berne: Walking Tree Press, 2007.

Stableford, Brian. "Science Fiction Before the Genre", in *The Cambridge Companion to Science Fiction*, edited by Edward James and Farah Mendlesohn. Cambridge: Cambridge University Press, 2003, 15–31.

———. *Historical Dictionary of Fantasy Literature*, Historical Dictionaries of Literature and the Arts 5. Lanham MD, Toronto, Oxford: Scarecrow Press, 2005.

Suvin, Darko. "Considering the Sense of 'Fantasy' or 'Fantastic Fiction': an Effusion", *Extrapolation* 41 (2000), 209–48.

Thompson, Kristin. *The Frodo Franchise: The Lord of the Rings and Modern Hollywood*. Berkeley CA: University of California Press, 2007.

Todorov, Tzvetan. *The Fantastic: A Structural Approach to a Literary Genre*. Translated by Richard Howard. Ithaca NY: Cornell University Press, 1973.

Tolkien, J.R.R. *The Monsters and the Critics: and Other Essays*. London: HarperCollins, 1997.

———. *Tolkien on Fairy-Stories*, edited by Verlyn Flieger and Douglas A. Anderson. London: HarperCollins, 2008.

Tymn, Marshall B., and Ashley, Mike. *Science Fiction, Fantasy and Weird Fiction Magazines*. Westport CT: Greenwood Press, 1985.

Waggoner, Diana. *The Hills of Faraway: A Guide to Fantasy*. New York: Atheneum, 1978.

Ward, Michael. *Planet Narnia: The Seven Heavens in the Imagination of C.S. Lewis*. New York: Oxford University Press, 2008.

Wolfe, Gary K. "Symbolic Fantasy", *Genre* 8, no. 3 (1975), 194–209.

———. *Critical Terms for Science Fiction and Fantasy: A Glossary and Guide to Scholarship*. New York and Westport CT: Greenwood Press, 1986.

Index of Titles

Index of Authors and Topics

CPSIA information can be obtained
at www.ICGtesting.com
Printed in the USA
BVOW11s1100280316
441997BV00032B/403/P